Art PSYCHOTHERAPY & Narrative THERAPY:

An account of practitioner research

BOOK SERIES:

RETHINKING RESEARCH AND PROFESSIONAL PRACTICES IN TERMS OF RELATIONALITY, SUBJECTIVITY AND POWER

BOOK SERIES EDITOR:

BRONWYN DAVIES, UNIVERSITY OF MELBOURNE

ART PSYCHOTHERAPY AND NARRATIVE THERAPY: AN ACCOUNT OF PRACTITIONER RESEARCH

SHERIDAN LINNELL
UNIVERSITY OF WESTERN SYDNEY

for Galiindurra, the sisters and all their mob

&

'Leticia', 'Groovy Gran', Emma and their family

We go toward the best known unknown thing, where knowing and not knowing touch, where we hope we will know what is unknown. Where we hope we will not be afraid of understanding the incomprehensible, facing the invisible, hearing the inaudible, thinking the unthinkable... Painting is trying to paint what you cannot paint and writing is writing what you cannot know...

Hélène Cixous

COVER ARTWORK: 'RED HAT', COURTESY OF THE ARTIST, ANITA SWANSON

TABLE OF CONTENTS

TABLE OF MALCONTENTS

Hang on there! says an imaginary Voice of Reason. *There might be some very good reasons for not inviting these poststructural ideas to the art therapy table.*

I heard that these ideas gatecrashed a much bigger party than ours, organised by the whole area of the human sciences, and behaved themselves appallingly. They poked their grubby fingers into every philosophical and political pie that was served: neoliberalism, neo-Marxism, post-Marxism, positivism, post-positivism, you name it.

They refused to partake of the main course, humanism, which as we all know everybody loves. Then, they began de-constructing the psycho-dynamic dessert before it even reached the table—as the chef was passing it across the counter to the waiter. Now, there's an example of counter transference for you!

When one of the ideas was asked if she wasn't deeply ashamed of herself, she replied that she didn't believe in an essential and autonomous self to be ashamed of.

As for the idea of 'deeply' ashamed, she claimed that metaphors of depth are related to the hermeneutic of the self that developed out of the expansion and secularisation of the Christian practice of confession, and that 'shame', in this instance, was an effect of modern normalising power. Boy, did she have a mouth on her!

Then, to top it all off, the bloody lot of them got raving drunk on that late-picked French wine, what was it called? The 1984 Chateau de Foucault…

FOREWORD

In this compelling, engaging and lovingly crafted book, Sheridan Linnell presents us with a very vivid account of practitioner research in the form of a 'discursive hall of mirrors'. She portrays moments of intersection between the author's life lived as a therapist, activist, feminist and 'person', and her contact with a rich reservoir of poststructuralist ideas and practices, illustrated with textually and visually poignant and politically purposeful accounts from therapeutic practice. Linnell uses a non-linear narrative form of 'writing as inquiry' to weave/embroider/wander nomadically across the landscapes of poststructuralist/therapeutic/arts-based research and practice. She has an excellent visual and textual story-telling ability, and I found myself reading late into the night in order to finish each chapter and get on to the next.

Sheridan Linnell has found a way of engaging readers with complex ideas that is clearly and even brilliantly articulated, yet without the suggestions of certainty or fixity that can often accompany such endeavours. The early chapters that offer the creative fiction of the department store (storeys) of poststructural/feminist/postcolonial theory are a delicious vehicle for interrogating these ideas. In later chapters we glance into a studio, a kitchen, an ethics of living, entering into spaces and relationships that are, by implication, highly nuanced exemplars of myriad other spaces and relationships and encounters. We are moved, touched by these stories and made uncomfortable.

This book stands as an original, indeed a unique contribution to the literatures on expressive therapies/art therapy, not the least because it situates these endeavours within a discursively constructed world of social engagement and political action. The effect of reading this book is different for each of us, and we are left with traces that may take seed, rather than findings or conclusions.

JANE SPEEDY
UNIVERSITY OF BRISTOL

Book series: *Rethinking research and professional practices in terms of relationality, subjectivity and power*

Book series editor: *Bronwyn Davies, University of Melbourne*

PREFACE

Bronwyn Davies

This wonderful book by Sheridan Linnell, *Art psychotherapy and narrative therapy: an account of practitioner research*, is the first volume in this new e-book series. Each book in the series develops an approach to research and practice that takes up the radical potential of philosophers such as Foucault, Deleuze, Butler and Nancy. Each book provides a radical model for re-thinking research and professional practices in light of poststructuralist reflections on subjectivity, relationality, ethics, spatiality, and power. This series will have an ongoing focus on the relations between individual subjects and the social, discursive and spatial relations within which they are produced, and produce themselves, as subjects.

Poststructuralist theory made a significant break with Hegel's structuralism, with its "model of history's unbroken intelligibility" (Foucault, 2000, p. 248). In poststructuralist theory the familiar, repetitive, and habituated practices through which the creation of individual selves is done is interesting so far as it reveals the changing practices that produce, over time, different kinds of subjects. Seeing history as discontinuous opens up the possibility that modernity's subject too can change. Rather than being locked into present crises and patterns, such as neoliberalism and its devastating production of global economic crisis and of global warming, poststructuralist theory seeks the ways in which we might break loose from the already known, habitual practices, and in which we might produce difference in ourselves rather than sameness.

In the modern world we have placed the sovereign individual of humanism, the agent in command of and creating his/her own life, on centre stage. Poststructuralist theory decentres that individual, examining instead the repeated citations through which "individuals" are produced. It thus cuts loose from phenomenology and existentialism with their maintenance of "the primacy of the subject and its fundamental value" (Foucault, 2000, p. 248). This is not to deny the existence of the subject, but to open up questions about its origin, its beginning point. From a poststructuralist perspective our individual agency is an *effect* of the ways in which we are constituted; it was not through our own agency that we were made what we are, but through our location within particular histories and cultural practices. We are generally unaware of the way discourse works through us to create us in predictable, historically specific ways. Poststructuralist theory suggests it is the very conceptualisation of the individual as primary, and as originary, that blocks this awareness.

Phenomenology is a philosophy that makes the individual subject its foundation, and sets out to "recapture the meaning of everyday experience in order to rediscover the sense in which the subject that I am is indeed responsible, in its transcendental functions, for founding that experience together with its meanings" (Foucault, 2000, p. 241). In contrast, Foucault sees his own work, following Bataille and Blanchot, as using experience to wrench "the subject from itself", to find ways to make the subject "no longer itself" (2000, p. 241). He wants to annihilate the subject of phenomenology, the subject that endlessly repeats its self, that understands itself as its own origin – to dissolve it, through what he calls a "project of desubjectification" (2000, p. 241).

Writing against the grain of the already-known is central to this radical project of opening up the not-yet-known. The already known for Foucault, in his early years in particular, was the subject capable of permitting Nazism, or the bourgeois intellectual choosing between Truman's America or Stalin's USSR. Whereas other post-war scholars sought to realize an ethical and responsible subject no longer capable of mindless obedience, Foucault's project was more radical. He wanted to write his way into new understandings of how we become, in one historical period or another, subjects. His books are, he says, "experiences aimed at pulling myself free of myself, at preventing me from being the same" (2000, p. 242). It is the possibility of this kind of difference that is the driving force of his work. He seeks to open up an experience of modernity that generates a transformative effect.

The work that has grown out of Foucault's programme of writing, and the writing of other poststructuralist scholars, has also had a second and more recent driving force. That is the advent of the intensified individualism of neoliberal governmentality. Capitalism, according to Deleuze and Guattari (1987), is schizophrenic. It needs to control its labour force in order to extract maximum productivity from it, while at the same time enhancing the production of new and creative ideas. It convinces individuals they are free at the same time as it shapes them to be whatever capital thinks it wants. This madness of the modern capitalist state has had devastating effects on individuals and on the professions. The program of desubjectification is thus also aimed at the hyper-individualism of modern capitalism, that produces sameness and repetition under the banner of freedom.

Foucault also had an abiding interest in madness. He worked to re-think the ways in which madness is produced. Talking in an interview about his writing on madness Foucault says that his aim was: "that at the end of a book we would establish new relationships with the subject at issue: the I who wrote the book and those who have read it would have a different relationship with madness, with its contemporary status, and its history in the modern world" (2000: 242). Such thought does not *discover* subjects but *changes* them in relation to others. Poststructuralist researchers are not interested in representing a pre-existing order of things, but in changing how they are thought and thus how they are produced. Foucault's book, *Madness and Civilization* is, Foucault says:

> a book that functions as an experience, for its writer and reader alike, much more than as the establishment of a historical truth... For one to be able to have that experience through the book, what it says and does need to be true in terms of academic, historically verifiable truth. It can't exactly be a novel. Yet the essential thing ... [lies] in the experience that the book makes possible. ... [This] book makes use of true documents, but in such a way that through them it is possible not only to arrive at an establishment of truth but also to experience something that permits a change, a transformation of the relationship we have with ourselves and with the world ... in short, a transformation of the relationship we have with knowledge. ... [That transformation] is not just mine but can have a certain value, a certain accessibility for others, so that the experience is available for others to have. (Foucault, 2000, p. 243-4)

Through coming to know differently, as writer, and as reader, Foucault shows how we might detach ourselves from the habitual repetitions of thought and practice through which we previously accomplished ourselves as predictable maintainers of the status quo. The individual is thus for Foucault, not the *end-point* of a process of subjectification, but the potential sticking point, the place where thought gets stuck. Writing is the medium through which both thought and the writer/reader can be changed.

Foucault was delighted when correctional officers and social workers said of *Madness and Civilization:* "The book is paralysing. It may contain some correct observations, but even so it has clear limits, because it impedes us; it prevents us from going on with our activity" (2000, p. 245). He said in response:

> My reply is that this very reaction proves that the work was successful, that it functioned just as I intended. It shows that people read it as an experience that changed them, that prevented them from always being the same or from having the same relations with things, with others, that they had before reading it. This shows that an experience is expressed in the book that is wider than mine alone. The readers have simply found themselves involved in a process that was underway—we could say, in the transformation of contemporary man with respect to the idea that he has of himself. And the book worked toward that transformation. To a small degree it was even an agent in it. This is what I mean by an experience book, as opposed to a truth book or a demonstration book. (Foucault, 2000, p. 246)

This book by Sheridan Linnell, *Art psychotherapy and narrative therapy: an account of practitioner research,* is just such an experience book. It draws on her own experiences as practitioner and teacher, to write a transformative book, a book through which she transforms both thought and herself, and potentially her readers. She has engaged in an experience/experiment in writing that taps into a change already underway, taking it further, participating, in doing so, in a transformation of the fields that she writes about. She does not set out to produce the truth about art and narrative therapies, as if they were objects capable of being studied. Rather she shows how truths function within these discourses to produce the practitioners and clients, and the Deleuzian flows between them that are called "therapy".

The theoretical net she casts over the complex waters of poststructuralist theory brings together the challenges of Foucault with other important poststructuralist thinkers. She begins with Foucault's call for us to practice an aesthetics of existence, and an art of self rather than a hermeneutic of self. To this she adds Derrida's notion of writing 'under erasure', Couze Venn's metaphor of apprenticeship to the Other, along with his elaboration of the choreography of early relationships, and his call for a poetics as well as a politics of transformation. To these she adds Judith Butler's exploration of the citational and performative dimensions of subjectivity, and of the limits of anyone's ability to give an account of themselves.

This book sets out to disrupt narrative and subjective coherence, creating and unravelling theoretical, clinical and personal accounts, in order to critique dominant theories and practices while at the same time unsettling the assumption of a decisive critical agency. In this way, the book constructs an aesthetics of self together with an ethics of uncertainty and of obligation to the Other, producing a new kind of knowledge of narrative and art therapies.

Foucault (2000) makes an important distinction between two kinds of knowledge: *savoir* and *connaissance*. *Savoir* involves doing work in order to know differently, and in the process, being modified through what one comes to know. *Connaissance* makes possible the knowledge of objects, that is, it makes those objects intelligible, while leaving the subject, the determinate knower, untouched. Linnell's book generates *savoir*—a knowledge of art therapy and of narrative therapy, not as objects that leave the writer and reader untouched, but as knowledge that has implicated the writer in changing herself in the process of thinking and writing, and that will invite the reader to be similarly changed. In order to facilitate this shift in self and subject matter, Linnell occasionally stands aside from herself, or beside herself, and tells us stories from her experience of self as writer, self as researcher, self as therapist, that cast her differently from the familiar, repeated patterns of "I-I-I". This is not experience drawn on to tell us the true story of this particular author/subject, but stories that set the subject loose from its moorings in this process of coming to know differently.

Linnell has been a counsellor since 1984, a narrative therapist for more than two decades, and an art therapist for 15 years. She has been a teacher of art therapy at the University of Western Sydney since 1995. She has written an important handbook for practitioners (Linnell and Cora, 1993), and has been publishing her re-thinking of therapies since 2003. She is also a talented poet (Linnell, 2001) and artist, and this is important for understanding her writing in this book, which is often playfully poetic, and artfully conceived. She does not present herself as the author with authoritative knowledge, but as a multiple and contradictory figure, setting out a complicated and yet playful work in which she comes to think differently—to be made different in that process. *Savoir* rather than *connaissance.* She offers her readers a transformative experience if they go with her, shifting the ground of what might be thought and done.

References

Deleuze, G. and Guattari, F. (1987). *A Thousand Plateaus: Capitalism and Schizophrenia.* London: Athlone Press.

Foucault, M. (2000). 'An interview with Michel Foucault'. In Faubion, J. (Ed.). *Essential works of Foucault 1954—1984, Volume 3, Michel Foucault: Power* (pp. 239—297). London: Penguin Books. Original interview conducted 1980.

Linnell, S. (2001). *Cutting room.* New Poets Series 8. Wollongong: Five Islands Press.

Linnell, S. & Cora, D. (1993). *Discoveries: a group resource guide for women who were sexually abused in childhood.* Sydney: Dympna House.

CHAPTER 1

INTRODUCTIONS: SKETCHING THE TERRAIN OF A POST-STRUCTURALIST, CREATIVE ENQUIRY INTO NARRATIVE AND ARTS-BASED THERAPEUTIC PRACTICE

> *The ethical question of politics, or of responsibility has always haunted me, as I imagine it haunts all the fireflies irresistibly attracted by the flame of the art-candle.*
>
> (Cixous, in Cixous and Calle-Gruber, 1997, p. 6)

> *[T]he unknown remains with us to haunt us from its horizon even after we have consciously begun.*
>
> (Said, 1975, p. 78)

Abstract: In the introductory chapter, I offer a sketch of the terrain of this book, which is a poststructural enquiry into (my) practices of art psychotherapy and narrative therapy. Through academic discourse and the more intimate practices of memoir, I introduce my understandings of and relationships to poststructural theory, art therapy, narrative therapy and the expressive therapies. I introduce the dominant theoretical frameworks, disciplinary regimes and professional areas, together with memories of pedagogies, politics and practices, that frame my concern with working towards therapy as an ethical 'art of existence'. I also introduce some of my-selves, as I/we traverse the domains of therapy and research, theory and practice, truth and fiction, in the hope that these initial meetings will be sufficient enticement for you, the reader, to come with us on what is at times a challenging journey.

For many years I have practiced and taught both art psychotherapy and narrative therapy. These two therapies are both informed by aesthetic metaphors and practices. Both art therapy and narrative therapy suggest that relationships, biographies and creative processes are central to the work of therapy. However, art therapy and narrative therapy differ radically in the emphases they respectively place upon the domains of the psychic and the social. This book explores what opens up, for the theory and practice of therapy, when these two therapeutic practices are brought (and thought) together. I explore the obvious differences and subtle compatibilities of the apparently diverse approaches of art psychotherapies and narrative therapies, the differences and commonalities in their historical and theoretical antecedents, and the possibilities and limitations of each.

My work is inspired by and irreducibly indebted to therapeutic meetings with many people over many years, especially with the children and families whose stories inform the later chapters of the book. I also draw inspiration from the intellectual work of Michel Foucault, Judith Butler and

Sheridan Linnell

other poststructural theorists, particularly those working at the intersections of poststructuralism with feminist and postcolonial theory.

Having worked extensively in the areas of family and domestic violence, sexual assault and child protection, my work as a therapist has, from the beginning, been inseparable from issues of social justice, and has led to a heightened awareness of relations of gender and power. I have been concerned to explore how the domain of therapy can mediate its tendency to reconstitute, and even produce, the problems it seeks to redress. I have also questioned what it means to practice therapy in a (post)colonial context, where the first people of the land are radically over-represented in almost all of the categories of distress that bring people to therapy. I have been drawn to approaches that foreground these concerns, and therefore to narrative therapy. Thus, while I am professionally trained and registered as an art therapist, it is undoubtedly the extensive project of narrative therapy (White and Epston, 1990) that has been, and continues to be, most powerfully constitutive of my 'identity' and practice as a therapist.

As a professional art therapist and therapy educator with an extensive engagement and strong political identification with narrative therapies, I have been interested in the emergence of narrative approaches to arts therapy (Freeman, Epston and Lobovits, 1997; Riley, 1999; Riley and Malchiodi, 2003; Hoshino and Cameron, 2008). However, I have come to question whether it is sufficient to practice arts-based therapy from a 'narrative perspective'. This book has inevitably involved taking myself up within "a tradition of immanent critique" (Butler, 1999, p. vii) in relation to narrative therapy, art psychotherapy and the expressive therapies more broadly. In relation to narrative therapy in particular, this form of critique has involved a close questioning of my current ethics and ethicalisation as a therapist, and of the limits and possibilities of the narrative metaphor in accounting for my-self, as well as for my work.

Alongside practicing and teaching therapies, I have also written poetry and collaborated with colleagues in joint art exhibitions. As I move between the different domains of creative writing, contemporary art, social action, intellectual work and clinical practice, I find that all these areas inform each other and shape my subjectivity, in ways that I cannot easily predict. My teaching and theorisation of therapy is shaped by my clinical experience and my clinical practice is shaped by academic theories and pedagogies. My writing and art are mutually constitutive with my understandings and practices of therapy. All of these creative, clinical and pedagogical practices are conditioned by and open into social actions, and they also profoundly shape my sense of self and my relationships within and beyond the professional sphere.

I seek to enquire further into what shapes and emerges from my understanding and practice of art psychotherapy and narrative therapy, in a manner that opens a space for critique and creativity, rather than closes it down. I have approached this complex task by writing a 'book of experience' (Foucault, 2000a). Foucault describes how he takes up each piece of work in connection with the processes unfolding around him, in response to the cracks, the "silent tremors", in the institutional contexts within which he finds himself and in the specificities of his relations with others, so that "each time is always the fragment of an autobiography" (Foucault, 2000a, p. 458). Foucault's suggestion of a book of experience has enabled me to engage in research that exceeds an apparent contradiction—between critiquing how I am governed and shaped by modern discourses and practices, and embracing the task of creating myself and my relationships as a work of art. In writing this book I have found that, through art, therapy and writing, I can pull "myself free of myself" (Foucault, 2000a, p. 242), even though "all demystification sends you back to your own self" (Clément, 1987, p. 69).

Beside myself

Butler (2004a) claims that her books are addressed to those of us who are 'beside ourselves' with rage, grief and passion. Butler's phrase captures, for my project, the infinite relation of social, interpersonal and psychic pain—and how an ethical response to violence and injustice not only 'moves' us to action, but also profoundly decentres the 'self'.

At times I take up a position 'beside myself' in this book, by writing about my self, or selves, in a third person narrative form. This opens up a ficto-critical space for reflecting upon subjectivity and self-hood, through close attention to a particular self's biography. I write in this way as a form of enquiry, thereby provoking the question: who or what is this embodied being taking up authorship, and being changed by what she writes? Movements between different genres of writing are often signified, in this text, by changes in font, so that more informal passages have, for instance, the texture of handwriting. In the remainder of this chapter, I will playfully and disruptively insert my-self, and sometimes 'real' or fictionalised others, into the text, while tracing some of the concerns and debates that inform my research.

"Why don't you tell them something about why this is so important to you?" she says to herself.

"Why are you passionate about it? What would make you agonise over this for so many years? Why don't you tell them about the almost unbearable ethical discomfort of sitting in endless clinical supervisions where interpretations through the lens of clinical theory erase the voices of 'patients', trainee therapists and dissenting clinicians? How, as an art therapy trainee, your political resistance to internalising discourses was recast as intrapsychic resistance? How you were required and came to require yourself to 'recognise' your protest as intrapsychic resistance in order to be the proper therapeutic/pedagogical subject? Why don't you tell them about the marginalisation of dissenting voices, of your voice(s), even within therapies that apparently promote dissent? What exactly are you composing when you, or at any rate your text, appears to be so 'composed'?

"Have a bit of patience," she replies from some other location. "You have a whole book ahead of you. You don't have to do it all in the very first paragraph. Anyway, is naming a research problem so very different from the externalisation of a problem in narrative therapy—a practice that you are somewhat committed to? Might it be a way of 'pulling yourself free' of certain discursive constitutions of yourself, your professional and disciplinary areas, and so forth?"

This book addresses the problem of how arts-based therapy could be conceptualised and practiced in relation to the mobile, unstable constellations of thought that constitute 'a poststructural framework' (Davies, 2000). This question involves a close engagement with theory, but it is not an attempt to propose a new theoretical basis for art therapy. Intellectual work in a poststructural vein unseats both dominant power and the modern subject, and more often undermines than underwrites its own assumptions. This fits with my desire to destabilise the power relations of therapy and to unsettle those pedagogies that transmit the mystique of therapeutic knowledge through practices of subjectification and ethicalisation. As Sally Swartz has pointed out, "[t]o unlearn clinical privilege is not simply to replace one theory with another, but to move into the realm of negotiating subjectivity itself" (2005, p. 508).

Accordingly, I engage in this book with theories and methodologies that are inconclusive, that trade in complexities, uncertainties and contradictions, and yet offer the intellectual and performative force of a commitment to critique as the work of transformation (Foucault, 2000b). Such a commitment necessarily entails an ongoing questioning of my own practices, subject position and subjectivity as a therapist. In particular, I respond to the possible implications for my practice of therapy and my positioning and constitution as a therapist—and for writing about this practice—of Foucault's suggestion that our contemporary task might be to practice an art of self and an aesthetics of existence, as an alternative to a hermeneutics of self and a truth of existence (Foucault, 1992, 2000c). I critically extend this suggestion by engaging with the work of other poststructural theorists. I attend to Couze Venn's question, when he asks, from beyond the space of Occidentalism, what we might become 'after modernity' (Venn, 2000, 2002). Butler's work has been particularly crucial for my book, given her projects of writing with and against Foucault, questioning the limits of narrativity and revisioning psychoanalysis beyond the Oedipalisation of culture (Butler, 1997a, 2000, 2004b, 2005). The writing of Hélène Cixous, too, in excess of my initial intentions, has threaded itself delicately and insistently throughout this project (Cixous, 1993, 2008; Cixous and Calle-Gruber, 1997).

I take up the ideas and writing practices that flow from this engagement with theory in relation to specific accounts of my work as a therapist. Such an engagement with poststructural theory opens a philosophical and methodological space, within a specific practice of arts-based and narrative therapy, for the reconceptualisation of problematics and the problematisation of truth claims. As well as locating and discussing the effects of certain dominant discourses and discursive practices within art therapy, I hope to 'make visible' some marginalised possibilities for theorising and practicing an arts-based therapy.

In giving context to this enquiry, I note how the broader field of the expressive therapies both includes and separates itself from art psychotherapy. I consider how psychoanalysis, as the theoretical antecedent of the psychotherapies, including art psychotherapy, shapes their assumptions, effects and potentialities. I position myself alongside other art therapists who engage art practice and aesthetic theory to challenge and exceed the normative and dominating tendencies of psychoanalysis while also questioning the binary this positioning may produce.

In accordance with the poststructuralist view that writing does not simply represent but actively constitutes knowledge, my (re)search attempts to *produce* the (im)possibility of a 'poststructural' arts-based therapy—or at least one among many such (im)possibilities. As an integral part of a poststructural approach to this research, I trace the effects of the research process on my own subjectivity and multiple positionings as an art therapist and narrative therapist, and as a poet and researcher. I chart my interrelations with like-minded and challenging 'others' to whom I am indebted and with whom I am at times intertwined. I juxtapose diverse genres of textual production (poetry, narrative, drama, ekphrasis [1], exposition, drawing, painting, photography), moving between the broad strokes of historical and theoretical speculation, the microworlds of therapeutic practice and memoir, and even the virtual/imagined subjects and socialities of fiction.

Following Foucault, I take up the suggestion that therapy is constituted, through forms of modern power, as a crucial contemporary site of both governance and resistance. I consider how the historical and theoretical antecedents of art psychotherapy and of narrative therapy shape the respective possibilities and limits of each of these therapeutic practices, including their predominantly oppositional relation to each other. I propose that in different ways art psychotherapy and narrative therapy bring into question the rational, autonomous subject and disrupt the dominance of humanist and positivist regimes. Through thinking/writing art psychotherapy and narrative therapy together, I seek to destabilise the normative tendencies of each, bringing the binary of the social and the psychic into question.

I suggest how therapy might be thought and performed beyond the discursive categories of 'self-knowledge' and 'expert knowledge'. Moving beyond binaries of process-oriented and outcome-oriented therapy, it becomes possible to acknowledge the subtle and powerful transformations in relationships and subjectivities that are paradoxically enabled by stepping away from expectations of specific behavioural outcomes (Linnell, Hanslow and Rummery, 2006).

Rather than 'applying' a poststructural theoretical framework and poststructural research methodology to practice examples from the field of therapy, this book problematises the production of the subjects and objects of therapy and research. Rather than synthesising new possibilities for the domains of theory and practice through a dialectic of academic theory and clinical practice, I engage in this work with the simultaneous possibility and impossibility—the (im)possibility—of deconstructing the theory/practice divide. Within a poststructural analytic of power, the theory/practice divide itself can be considered as a binary that is continually reconstituted through relations of power and knowledge, and is thus vulnerable to resistance. My work inevitably re-cites/reconstitutes the binary of theory and practice in relation to researching and writing (about) therapy, even as it questions and moves at least momentarily beyond that binary.

I hope this research will make it a little more difficult for me, and for other interested therapy practitioners and researchers, to think as we may have habitually come to think and to do as we may have habitually come to do. I hope to generate textual/aesthetic practices that make visible and reach beyond what we may otherwise take (and make) for granted. Given the material force of discourses in (re)constituting the normal, the natural and the true, it follows that the textual practices composing the book itself, the 'performativity' (Butler, 1997b) of its writing and making, are crucial to my endeavour.

My subjectivities as therapy practitioner and beginning researcher come under erasure in this book through writing methodologies that disrupt narrative and subjective coherence. My work is that of creating and unravelling, of shaping a productive critique while unsettling the possibility of a decisive critical agency. Thus my research is necessarily an experiment in constituting and deconstructing the 'I' embodied in the text of the book. 'I' want to catch how 'I' am spoken and made visible by discourse; how 'I' am implicated in producing the very discourses that 'I' resist. I want to write and draw into being, at least momentarily, a poststructural subject whose possibility challenges the inscription within therapy of the normative tendencies of the 'psy' disciplines (Rose, 1998). This writing calls my autonomy, rationality and subjectivity as a therapist, and as researcher/writer, radically into question.

This text enacts how practices of poststructural thought are interwoven with therapeutic and artistic thinking and practice; how reading and writing practices, socialities and (inter)subjectivities, are variously intertwined. I offer passionate and partial narratives of my relationships with poststructuralisms, with therapeutic practice and identity, with those who come to meet with me in therapy, and with Other possibilities that disrupt the narrative trajectory of my attempts to 'give an account' of my-self (Butler, 2001, 2005) and my work. Through messy stories and glittering fragments, I perform the opacity and vulnerability of the subject and the infinite indebtedness of each to the other. Such writing attempts to illuminate the multiplicity and indeterminacy of narratives even while it is shadowed by the limits of narrativity itself. In these ways, I shape an aesthetics of self together with an ethics of uncertainty and obligation to the Other, working towards a politics and poetics of transformation.

Introducing poststructuralisms

When I notice, as never before, how 'empire' nestles within the word 'empirical', positivism appears less innocent. The 'advancement of knowledge' is exposed as the colonisation of the other in the guise of progress.

How did she meet poststructuralism? She had written a psychoanalytic account of some Harold Pinter plays for her undergraduate Honours thesis, but was troubled by some of the conservative implications of this work for women. An academic in the English

Literature department suggested she should read Lacan. She found the reading so difficult that she began 'sitting in' on Elizabeth Grosz's lecture series on Lacan in the School of General Philosophy, where she had studied for a while before specialising in literature. She became taken with French theory, began going to Liz's lectures on Foucault as well. At the same time, her marriage was breaking up. She left her husband, moved into a flat with her daughter, then into a communal house. Went out for a while with a man who read Deleuze in French. She experimented with hallucinogenic drugs while struggling with translations of the *AntiOedipus*. The man dumped her. She remembers the giddy, sick feeling of embracing the idea that there is no essential self. She had affairs, simultaneously, with her best female friend/companion/lover, and a man they had both fallen in love with. At first she had withdrawn, leaving the field to her friend. Later, through an invitation she remembers for its generosity, loving wryness and sense of inevitability, she had become 'involved'. This initially ecstatic experience became riven with rivalries and misunderstandings, went horribly wrong. She had rationally argued for non-possessiveness while being all the time in the grip of monstrous insecurities, jealousies and obsessions. She had tried to manipulate the situation to meet her own needs but had failed miserably. She was shocked at herself. In the wake of this torture of humiliation and loss, she became angry for a while with all the men in her life—friends, lovers, family, and French theorists. She read Cixous, Wittig, Irigaray, Clément, Duras, Spivak. She took female lovers and moved into a women's household, flirting with but soon abandoning separatism, although, come to think of it, she has been with women ever since.

She remembers attending a meeting around this time with women academics and postgraduate students who were hoping to set up a study group at the University of Sydney for women interested in feminism and poststructural theory. Some women from the Sparticist Club, an ultra left organisation that insisted women's oppression was a consequence of and secondary to class oppression, had also come along to stir things up. The 'Sparts' had hijacked the meeting, arguing that unless childcare was provided they would be excluding marginalised women from attending. Other women had put up a counter argument that the focus of this group was intellectual work, that the 'rights' agenda had not worked, had not delivered childcare, equal pay and so forth, so it was time to try something different—the politics of *difference* rather than the politics of equality. But, she found herself protesting, did that have to mean no longer actively supporting the campaign for more equitable access to on-campus childcare? To her horror and embarrassment, she had found herself offside with her poststructuralist feminist heroines and in agreement with a group of left-wing extremist puppets of the male revolution. After all, she too had a young daughter. She too had struggled with the inadequacy of childcare on campus. Did the realisation that intellectual work constitutes a crucial site of political struggle have to negate the socialist feminist political agenda?

She struggles with this dilemma for years. She works as a community activist, does community radio, organises gay conferences, women's conferences, writing conferences, writes submissions, attends marches, protests, gets arrested a couple of times, works for women's services, becomes a union rep—even joins the communist party for a while only to participate in the decision to disband the party in favour of the new left politics of coalition. She remains convinced, through all of this, that poststructuralisms, far from being elitist, are liveable and workable in spheres beyond academia, although she is not sure how to extend this possibility beyond personal politics into collective endeavour. Although in a way this is what she is already doing. After all, these poststructural ideas, as much as feminism, have helped her to 'make sense' (and non-sense) of her life.

> Poststructural theories raise critical concerns about what it is that structures meanings, practices, and bodies, about why certain practices become intelligible, valorised or deemed as traditions, while other practices become discounted, impossible or unimaginable. For post-structuralists, representation is always in crisis, knowledge is constitutive of power, and agency is the constitutive effect, and not the originator, of situated practices and histories... (Britzman, 2000, p. 30)

Poststructural theory has been defined as "thought which examines the notion of difference in all its facets" (Lechte, 1994, p. 95). Poststructuralism is generally associated with a group of mid to late twentieth century French theorists who were intellectually formed within a European philosophical tradition. Strongly influenced by the structuralist turn in linguistics, anthropology and psychoanalysis, they rejected both the humanistic and phenomenological centring of an originating, unified human subject, and the Hegelian/Marxist transcendental view of history. These poststructuralist thinkers also moved beyond structuralism by questioning its assumption of a deep and universal structure underlying language, culture and subjectivity.

Butler, however, problematises generalisations about poststructuralist theory, by questioning the alleged theoretical unity and purity of poststructuralism. She points out that the 'French Theory' within which she locates the ground of her own writing is a "curious American construction" (Butler, 1999, p. x). 'French theory'/poststructuralism brings together certain French intellectuals who for the most part do not perceive themselves as allied and do not share a domestic readership in France. Foucault and Derrida, amongst the most influential of poststructuralist thinkers, had substantive and at times vehement disagreements. Foucault accuses Derrida of "the reduction of discursive practices to textual traces" (Foucault, 2000d, p. 416). Given Foucault's emphasis on the materiality of discourse and the interrelation of discursive and non-discursive practices, he might well have dissented from Lechte's (1994) formulation of writing (or anything else) as 'the source'. Derrida utilises a notion of the undecidability of texts to problematise Foucault's critiques of Descartes' *cogito* and Freud's theory of instincts (Derrida, 1978, 1997). Foucault (2000e) not only refuses the description of himself as 'poststructuralist' but also questions the general usage of the terms 'postmodernism' and 'poststructuralism'.

It is clear, then, that poststructuralism is a contested term. While this could be regarded as an obstacle to the research, I prefer to regard it as an opportunity. The impure and contested status of poststructuralism exemplifies the proliferation of discourses (Foucault, 1980), the play of difference (Cixous and Clément, 1986; Derrida, 1978), and the rhizomic/horizontal movement of de-territorialized thought (Deleuze and Guattari, 1977, 1987). Rather than being an impediment to this research, the differences within and between poststructuralisms can be taken up as an invitation for creative appropriation and synthesis of those ideas most suggestive for an arts-based therapy.

From a poststructural theoretical perspective, the researcher is not 'outside' the research as in early positivism. As in other qualitative approaches to research, it is assumed that the researcher influences and is influenced by the data, but in poststructuralism influence extends to a notion of mutual constitution. The process of research constitutes the subjectivity of the researcher and also effectively constitutes the research data. Davies (2000) describes the subject's (here, the researcher's) engagement with the fleeting reflexive spaces of thought that figure 'agency' within the play of discourses. Donna Haraway's concept that "an optics is a politics of positioning" (cited in Meskimmon, 2003, p. 81) captures the significance, for poststructural research into art and narrative therapy, of the re-embodiment of the researcher's vision and point-of-view.

Introducing art therapies

(Is the body of my book a sexed body? What does the predominantly female profession of art therapy en-gender?)

She tries to remember—when and how did she meet 'art therapy'? Was it twenty years ago, when as a counsellor in a women's health centre, she offered art materials to women too bowed with shame and intimidation to give voice to the rapes, beatings and other humiliations they had endured? Was it a few years before that, when singing in a choir of like-minded queers had resurrected her spirits, added a femme flair to her wardrobe and reinvigorated her longings for justice and inclusion? Was it when she wrote a poem, aged ten, attempting to reconcile her deep homesickness for London and her maternal grandparents with her much-vaunted 'new life' on the other side of the world? Was it when she made huge visceral paintings in black and red, so dark and potent that her high school art teacher rang her parents to ask if she was depressed? (Shortly after this phone call, she had developed a penchant for painting miniatures, muted rural idylls bland enough to be hung in the annual school art show.) Was it in the early 1990s, when she was the clinical coordinator of a specialist sexual assault service and wanting to gain relevant postgraduate qualifications, but in a manner that enriched and extended her, rather than subjected her to the truths of a positivism from which she had long dissented? A friend had suggested that she contact the University of Western Sydney about their new Masters courses in drama therapy and art therapy. She had actually applied to do drama therapy but was offered a place in art therapy when the other course did not proceed. Until then, she had neither known about nor aspired to visual art therapy as a distinct profession. She is in this sense at least the accidental art therapist...

Art therapy can be broadly understood as a combination of visual art and psychotherapy (or more rarely family therapy) offered in the context of a therapeutic relationship by an appropriately trained and qualified specialist practitioner. Springing from a multiplicity of historical and theoretical antecedents, art therapies are diversely practiced in a range of countries, cultures and contexts.

It is often asked whether art therapy needs its own unifying 'theory' or should remain a collection of diverse theories and practices loosely derived from the 'parent' disciplines of art/aesthetics and psychoanalysis/ psychology (Rubin, 1987, 2001; Ulman, 2001). Moves toward articulating a theory specific to art therapy have tended, not surprisingly, to do so through a synthesis of existing psychological and/or aesthetic theories, one of the most extensive early projects being that of Schaverien (1992). While this research will respond to the question of theory by conceptualising art therapy from a poststructuralist perspective and examining the apparent theoretical opposition of art therapy and narrative therapy, the book will also necessarily call into question the possibility and desirability of locating or producing a 'true' theory of art therapy.

The questions and concerns that currently constitute the problematics of art therapy are generally based in and between a history of ideas and an analysis of psychological/subjective relations, thus enabling the re-constitution of the history of the profession as 'progress' and of the hermeneutic subject of art therapy as a self tied to the project of discovering its own identity, as a matter of personal 'freedom' (Rose, 2000). Both the history of ideas and the hermeneutics of the self tend to reconstitute binary oppositions such as those art and therapy, self and other, sick and well, conscious and unconscious, individual and social. These historicising and individualising modes of thought establish, within and between themselves, a role for critique, but this is a critique that tends to reverse hierarchies rather than to deconstruct binaries.

As Susan Hogan has pointed out in her history of British art therapy, the histories of disciplines generally serve to legitimise dominant trends or counter trends within that discipline (Hogan, 2001). Historical analysis emerges within relations of power to reinforce or challenge a particular paradigm, without necessarily exposing the processes by which certain beliefs and practices come to be 'truths'. Similarly, while self-questioning and reflexivity are arguably central to effective therapeutic practice, they do not in themselves guarantee the transformation of that practice. The 'ethical scenario' (Rose, 1998) of (art) psychotherapy requires techniques of self-examination and reflexivity, from both therapist and 'client', which (re)produce the responsible, self-governing subject of contemporary regimes of the self.

Nevertheless, as a relatively new profession, art therapy may be particularly accessible to a poststructuralist critique. Art therapy bears (and bares) the traces of how it is formed in a matrix of relations of power, disruptions and discontinuities—of how art therapists' struggles for professional re-cognition, historical coherence and theoretical consistency are intertwined with each other and riven with conflicting interests. In contrast, older and more established disciplinary and discursive formations may have constructed relatively seamless narratives of their origins and fields. It was, after all, with such an eye to the critical possibilities of studying the more recently formed disciplines that Foucault engaged on his genealogy of the social sciences, rather than studying the 'hard' sciences, whose epistemologies had 'hardened' into truths (Foucault, 2000a).

Art therapist in the spotlight:

Pet hates: *Colouring-in books. People who say "Oh yes I do a bit of art therapy too".* **Current love interest:** *Jung—he appreciates what I do. And I just adore the way he introduces me to his friends—"I'd like you to meet my better half".* **Favourite weekend:** *Time in the studio and Sunday brunch with friends at my local gallery cafe—freud eggs and francis bacon on sourdough toast.* **What are you enjoying?** *Sculpture by the Sea.* **Who are you listening to?** *Winnie Cott and the Re-Kleins playing covers of old favourites—'Mammy' and 'It's all over now, baby blue'.* **Who are you reading?** *Bowlby. And Harry Potter.* **Who would you most like to sit next to on a plane?** *Marion Milner and Frida Kahlo (I'll take the middle seat).* **If there were one word left to you in the world, what would it be?** *Transitional object.* **That's two words.** *Art, then. Or love.* [2]

Art therapy appears to me as an unsettled and contradictory enterprise—rich with extraordinary companionship, commitment and hope, yet painfully and personally conflicted; maverick in the extreme, yet aspiring to acceptance by the medical 'establishment'; based in intellectually challenging and even esoteric theory, yet attracting a number of practitioners so committed to art practice that they are reluctant to put down their brushes for long enough to pick up their books. Indeed, the bringing together of contradictions and binaries strongly marks the theoretical and historical antecedents of art therapy as well as its current constitution: the studio and the clinic, the artist and the clinician, psychiatry and antipsychiatry, realism and surrealism, aesthetics and psychoanalysis, the rationality of scientific positivism and the absurdist, critical potential of the visual arts. Moreover, the inter-disciplinarity to which some areas of academia aspire is a 'given' of art therapy, which brings together, in name and deed, the 'at least two' (Irigaray, 1981) of art and therapy.

Within this diversity, a hierarchy of knowledges nevertheless tends to reconstitute the primacy of psychoanalysis. The profession's first historians viewed psychoanalysis as the main intellectual precursor of art therapy (Waller, 1991; Junge, 1994), although Hogan's (2001) account of the history of art therapy in the U.K. challenges this perspective. The first published handbook of art therapy explicitly laid out a psychoanalytic basis for art therapy (Case and Dalley, 1992), although the opening chapter of another handbook published in the same year (Waller and Dalley, 1992) defined the field more broadly, in the context of an edited collection (Waller and Gilroy, 1992).

By the end of a particularly influential decade in the development of art therapy theory and pedagogy, the analytic psychology of Carl Jung and the object relations theory of Winnicott were the theoretical approaches most strongly taken up by art therapists in their clinical practice (Karkou, 1999). Psychoanalytic or psychodynamic concepts may also assume a truth status in approaches to art therapy that do not consider themselves to be primarily analytic. For instance, Harriet Wadeson's (2001) assertion that she takes an eclectic approach to art therapy appears to rest on the implicit 'truth' of the psychodynamic concept of transference. Although the centrality of art practice complexifies the process of art psychotherapy, both psychoanalysis and art therapy generally assume a psyche in excess of a subject, conceptualise therapy as 'working through', and understand the therapeutic relation in terms of transference and counter transference. Psychoanalysis is privileged as the historical and theoretical antecedent of art (psycho)therapy and 'diversity' is thereby relegated to a second order of consideration.

An intellectual engagement between art therapy and contemporary psychodynamic perspectives continues to be crucial in the current art therapy literature. Psychoanalysis thus remains central to an understanding of the intersubjective and intraspychic processes that come into focus when visual art making and psychotherapeutic practice are brought together. Drawing on postmodern, aesthetic and psychoanalytic theory in order to consider the epistemological position of the art psychotherapist, Leclerc suggests that

> the art therapist is both the subject and object of knowledge: the art therapist is the object of unconscious transmissions *and* the subject of deep intersubjective processes; and mostly, the art therapist is subjected to making them intelligible...This, in my view, accounts for the epistemological position of the art therapist, the "experienced other" in Bion's terminology (1962). (Leclerc, 2006, p. 133)

This is a formulation that is compelling for art therapists, who often look to the support of psychoanalytic and psychodynamic theory to sustain ourselves within the wordless intensity of an art-therapeutic relation. Nevertheless, I would want to place Leclerc's understanding of the art therapist's epistemological positioning 'under erasure', so that knowing is crossed with not-knowing. Otherwise, therapeutic certainty may re-emerge in the guise of 'experience'.

Irrationale

The art therapist is trying to keep herself clean. For all her skills in mixing and blending, she finds herself marked out from her clinical colleagues by bright, unregenerate flecks of paint. Clay clings to the soles of her imported leather shoes. Charcoal smudges her cheeks; crayon ingrains the lines of her hands; she feels a dark, oily resistance under her nails. The more she attempts to adhere to the relative uniformity of the professional classes, the more she is adhered to by feathers and stars. Glitter secretes itself like sedimented sunlight in the folds of her neatly scripted client files. As she rises from her chair in the clinical team meeting, she hopes no one will notice how the seat of her black wool trousers is matted with drying glue. In her art therapy studio, the scarified wooden and linoleum surfaces are dusted with chalky residues. Purple, scarlet, golden, cobalt, azure, jade, turquoise, cinnamon, yellow ochre, burnt sienna and deep madder, these pollens are waiting for an updraft of warm air, a door left accidentally ajar.

A turn, away from the 'clinification' of art therapy, towards aesthetics in some of the art therapy literature (e.g. MacLagan, 2001; Hyland Moon, 2002; Henzell, 2006) tends to reverse the hierarchy of psychotherapy and art, privileging aesthetics while suggesting the mutually enhancing potential of aesthetics and psychodynamics. A poststructuralist approach might extend upon and problematise this move by examining what is taken for granted in the notions of 'art' and 'therapy', thereby deconstructing the binary of art and therapy that has been variously configured as an opposition, a continuum or a dialectic. In a highly reflexive and ongoing intellectual project that troubles the philosophical underpinnings that keep reproducing one of art therapy's most longstanding debates, Sally Skaife has sought ways of challenging and going beyond the opposition of speech and art making in art therapy. Initially Skaife conceptualised a dialectical relationship between art making and speech in art therapy groups (Skaife, 1995, 2000). Later, she critiqued the tendency of dialectical theory to reconstruct the very binary of art and the verbal that she is committed to challenge, turning to Merleau-Ponty's theory of embodiment (Skaife, 2001), and more recently to Irigaray's attention to the sensory (Skaife, 2008), as a possible basis for a re-theorisation of art therapy. Skaife's most recent iteration of this project deconstructs, not just the binary of art and talk within art therapy practice, but also the binaries that are inevitably reconstituted when attempting to speak or write of art therapy. Skaife begins to take up the metaphor of performance, as a means to figure the interplay of complex intersubjectivities within art therapy, of bodies, imaginations, relations, symptoms, perceptions, images, and space (Skaife, 2008).

Poststructural ideas are selectively taken up in some of the other art therapy literature, although poststructural theory is radically under-represented in art therapy when compared to the literature on contemporary art. Lofts (2002) and Tipple (2003) take up discourse analysis in order make visible how discursive practices produce and reproduce the psychodynamic assumptions of art therapy. The notion of 'the gaze' has also been explored, particularly in relation to considerations of gender and power (Schaverien, 1995, 2003; Martin, 1997; Hogan, 1997, 2001). Rather than providing answers to current questions within frames that re-inscribe history as transcendence and the subject as origin, poststructural enquiry can trouble the divisions of thought that maintain and make invisible the relations of power and truth. A different order of questions becomes possible.

How is the subject constituted in this literature or practice? How is art constituted? What relations are constituted between art and the subject? How is change constituted in relation to artistic practice, therapeutic practice and the social?

Introducing narrative therapies

How did she meet narrative therapies? She remembers how, as a counsellor working in women's health services, she puzzled over the apparent contradictions between feminist theorisations of the social and political 'causes' of women's oppression, and the increasing popularity amongst feminist women of pathologising, victim-blaming discourses, for instance therapy groups for 'sex and love addicts' and 'women who love too much'. She remembers an early, uneasy intoxication with the 'insights' into herself and others that were made possible by psychotherapy training, and she also recalls her subsequent decoding of these understandings as practices of power. She remembers wondering why feminist counselling challenged so much of dominant practice only to reproduce its structure through inversion. She remembers her relief when, in the late 1980s, she received some training about the effects of sexual assault from Amanda Kamsler and Lesley Lang (see Kamsler, 1990; Lang and Kamsler, 1990) that introduced her to 'a text analogy' for therapy (Epston and White, 1989). She loved the narrative metaphor for therapy, ironically, not only for its centring of clients' multiple stories and for its deconstruction of therapy discourse, but because it enabled her to construct an autobiographical trajectory from her literary studies and writing practice through feminism, poststructuralism and community activism to her current practice as a therapist. Theoretical and political constructs that she held dear from her distant university days were being engaged in a reinvention of therapy and counselling. Familiars such as Foucault and Derrida had entered the therapy room, making visible and deconstructing its dominant assumptions and practices so that it, and she, could never be the same.

Narrative therapies emerged from a diverse field of disciplines and theoretical developments: feminist theory, literary theory, poststructural theory, anthropology, critical social theory, philosophy of science, and particularly the works of Gregory Bateson (in family therapy and anthropology) and of French philosopher-historian, Foucault (White, 1995). These therapies engage a narrative metaphor for the processes by which peoples' lives and identities are shaped and given meaning (White and Epston, 1990). The 'performative turn', as well as the narrative turn, in literature and ethnography has shaped the theory and practice of narrative therapies from their beginnings. The influence of the performative turn is apparent in how narrative therapists encourage the personification and dramatisation of externalised problems and/or preferences (e.g. Epston and Roth, 1998), and in the practice of reflecting teamwork as definitional ceremony (White, 1995, 2000).

Narrative therapies eschew the structural and systems metaphors that have guided much modernist therapy (e.g. the psyche as a structure for regulating instinctual energies, or the family as a system which seeks homeostasis), in favour of a discursive and relational understanding of identity. Narrative therapies assume that people both actively ascribe meaning to experience and have meaning ascribed within dominant relations of power and knowledge. Narrative therapy also assumes that people engage and are engaged in 'performances of meaning' that consolidate (and sometimes challenge) truth claims. Moreover, these therapies acknowledge that, in a culture in which normalisation, individualisation and rationalisation are effected through the technologies of the social sciences, therapy itself is a crucial site for the production of subjectivities and the performance of 'truth'. Just as the stories we live by, and which (en)live(n) us, are multiple and often contradictory, so the historical and theoretical antecedents of narrative therapies are many, and at times in contradiction. An influence from an ethnographic and interpretive perspective within the social sciences can sit a little uneasily with poststructuralism, especially when it comes to theorising subjectivity. The interpretive method assumes a phenomenological subject who is an active maker of meaning, whereas the agency of the poststructural subject is problematised as discursively produced within relations of power.

Rejecting an expert position, the narrative therapist takes a stance of 'co-authorship'. Co-authorship is understood not as a negation of therapeutic influence, but as an acknowledgement and taking up of the therapeutic conversation as co-production. Within the context of a 'co-authoring' relationship, narrative therapists pose questions characterised by an orientation to curiosity, unknowingness and the subjunctive mood, in order to facilitate a richer account of the person's life, relationships and identity. Given that people usually come to therapy because either they or others perceive something 'within' that person as a problem, narrative therapists' questions seek to locate someone's difficulties in narratives other than those that internalise, essentialise and pathologise the 'self'. The therapist poses questions which are oriented towards the deconstruction of dominant, often problem-saturated, personal and familial narratives—asking about these narratives' histories, current influence and possible future effects, and exploring the relationship between what is experienced as problematic and the 'grand narratives'/discourses of culture and identity.

As well as deconstructing 'dominant stories', the therapist invites the person coming to therapy to entertain the possibilities of 'insurrectionary', 'discontinuous' and local knowledges implicit in their narrative, which can be incorporated into preferred accounts of self and relationship. It is assumed that these preferred/alternative accounts can be generated from the subjugated stories of the person's (past, present, even hoped-for) life, from stories that others hold about the person and from marginalised narratives of the culture. Derrida's deconstruction and Foucault's genealogy inform the narrative approach to deconstructing the dominant story and making visible its relationship to dominant discourse/grand cultural narratives, and they also frame the notion of preferred stories as related to the indeterminacy of narratives and the mutual conditioning of power and resistance.

In an assumption borrowed from ethnography and parallel to the values of qualitative research, it is held that 'rich' stories of 'literary merit' (White and Epston, 1990)—detailed, specific and 'experience-near'—will offer opportunities for the development of preferred accounts of identity and meaning that are not available in 'thin' descriptions (i.e. unitary, reified and generalized accounts). These preferred stories, in narrative therapy, do not have an independent truth status but are regarded as contingent on the narrated and relational character of identity, the multiplicity and indeterminacy of narrative possibilities and the discursive context of the production of subjectivities. Preferred stories do not 'replace' previously dominant stories, but rather emerge alongside of, in relation with and/or in resistance to them. In narrative therapy it is also considered of primary importance not to disengage the notion of a co-authored conversation from other narrative therapeutic practices that de-centre the role of the therapist and open up space for the recognition and production of a multiplicity of other 'co-authoring' relationships within and beyond the therapy.

Michael White (1997) asserts that he has never claimed a truth status for alternative descriptions of identities and practices, and that his understanding is that "we are as multi-desired, multi-motived and as multi-intentioned in our lives as our stories are multi-storied" (p. 231). Identity in narrative therapy is conceptualised as fluid and relational, and much emphasis is put on the contexts and relationships that sustain a 'preferred story'. White (1995) anticipates the risk of (re)producing an authentic, humanist subject by recommending the deconstruction of positive as well as negative identity conclusions, the latter being understood as "emblems" adopted within contingent discourses of selfhood rather than as qualities intrinsic to a true self. The "unpacking" of identity conclusions is thus a means to counter the "naturalisation" of the subject of the preferred story.

However, there remains a sense in which such moves predominantly imply a volitional and conscious subject. Although not an autonomous individual, narrative therapy's subject is ascribed a sense of agency sustained by accounts of hopes, dreams, intentions, passions and conscious commitments. This raises the question of whether the self as narrative coherence is the aim of narrative therapy (Williams and Linnell, 2006). At the same time as the unpacking of identity conclusions interrupts the possibility of a seamless 'preferred story', the very possibility of unpacking, or critique, depends on a certain coherence of the intentional subject.

Narrative therapists are concerned with the ethics of co-authorship in the context of therapeutic privilege. They problematise the possibility of an equal partnership between co-authors and attempt to offset the possibility of therapist domination through practices of accountability to the 'client', with the therapist taking the position of a 'junior partner' in the collaboration. These ethics of co-authorship have also been carried into practitioner research, through an exploration of the rich interface between narrative therapy and narrative enquiry (Speedy, 2008).

However, a poststructural theoretical perspective also problematises co-authorship, not only through considerations of power relations, but also in terms of the radical indeterminacy of narratives. Scheurich suggests that the meanings and iterations of a co-authored research interview text is "a shifting carnival of ambiguous complexity, a moving feast of differences interrupting differences" (1995, p. 243)—a formulation very different from that of co-authorship as a production of shared meanings. At the same time as narrative therapy takes up the potential for transformations offered by the radical indeterminacy of texts, it underplays how the radical shifts and contradictions of such texts/conversations complexify relations of co-authorship (Williams and Linnell, 2006).

The discursive subject of narrative therapy remains at odds with the internalising accounts of unconscious motivation and authentic feeling that attend upon the predominantly psychoanalytic and humanistic subject(s) of art therapy. Following Foucault's suggestion that desire was the ethical substance in the early Christian era and that our feelings have become the ethical substance in contemporary times (Foucault, 2000c), narrative therapists are wary of the tendency of therapeutic discourses to fetishise feeling (in humanistic accounts) or desire/loss (in psychoanalytic accounts). This does not mean that narrative therapy conversations are unemotional or dispassionate—quite the contrary—but that narrative practitioners subscribe to an anthropology and a poetics of emotion rather than a psychodynamics of emotion, and to a discursive, rather than an intrapsychic, understanding of how particular emotions are privileged. Feeling and passion are located in relation to a person's embodied and lived narratives and to an emerging construction of preferred identity, rather than in relation to the effects of displacement and the surfacing of repression. The explicitly and/or implicitly psychoanalytic assumptions of much art therapy, such as repetition, transference and working-through, are challenged by narrative therapy which would focus on how such ideas are part of an internalizing discourse that can render invisible the ways in which discursive and institutional practices continually produce subjectivities. Narrative therapy is engaged in a project of contextualizing and deconstructing the discursive and institutional contexts in which subjectivities are produced and reproduced, and is in tension with more psychoanalytically oriented notions of subjectivity that speak in terms of the mechanisms of repetition, displacement and disavowal. Narrative therapists are interested in the co-construction of accounts of how people are both shaped by and subvert dominant discourses and narratives, rather than in making way for the re-entry of repressed stories of irrationality, loss, trauma and desire.

I propose, in this book, that in different ways narrative therapy and art psychotherapy have a critical potential to decentre the rational, autonomous subject (Linnell, 2008). Whereas art psychotherapy destabilises the subject through the psychoanalytic assumption of the primacy of unconscious and intersubjective processes, narrative therapy destabilises the subject by asserting that subjects are continually produced within discourse/relations of knowledge and power. The decentring of modern forms of the subject is a crucial and difficult project within therapy. The self-responsible subject of humanism is particularly difficult to challenge and is easily reconstituted within therapeutic practice, as the following, and final, 'introduction' for this chapter will suggest.

Introducing expressive therapies

How did she first meet the expressive therapies?

The answer to this question inevitably overlaps with her stories of art therapy. After all, the separation of these two modalities is partial, inconclusive and variable—as much about histories and politics as about theories and practices. A further and perhaps more controversial question occurs to her—is *she* an expressive therapist? Her answer to this, while indefinite, is also a matter of definition. She is formally trained and registered as an art therapist, but her practice is somewhat akin to expressive therapy in that she draws upon a broad range of art forms. She is also trained in psychodrama, which some people consider to be an expressive therapy, although she is unsure if this inclusion is appropriate. So she may have first formally encountered the expressive therapies at the beginning of the 1990s when, prior to training as an art therapist, she took a subject at university that explored drama in education and therapy, or perhaps it was almost ten years earlier...

She goes along to her first psychodrama training with a mixture of excitement and trepidation. The course is held in a magnificent federation Anglican church hall, on a tree-lined street not far from the waters of Iron Cove in inner western Sydney. It is a late summer evening; the air is warm and fragrant with frangipani. The occasion has brought together a motley assortment of inner city types with some Latin American people from the Evangelical church of the psychodrama director, who is also the 'progressive' pastor of a Spanish Baptist parish in the outer south western suburbs. They all sit around in a circle on the floor, talking about their apprehensions and anticipations.

She has come here with her colleague and friend, a Uruguayan lesbian feminist woman from the women's health centre where they both work. Neither of them is in concert with the orthodoxies made overt in the architecture of the building and in the dominant religious culture of this group. They have come because another colleague from their workplace has commended the psychodrama director and his approach to therapy, which brings together dance, drama and the visual arts, and is focussed more on the body and less on dialogue than contemporary North American psychodrama.

She looks around, beginning to take in the specificities, differences and deviations of bodies, genders, cultures, sexualities, beliefs, locations, privileges, marginalisations, histories, advantages, injustices, hopes, politics, relationships, ages and so forth that will make up this 'psychodrama group'. This unlikely diversity, even incompatibility, is to become, for her at least, the paradoxical condition for sublime moments of acceptance, connectedness and transport—moments that theory might limit to a concept of transcendence.

At some point the psychodrama director invites them to "come to the stage". It is a real stage, although this is not necessary for psychodrama—a semicircle raised a little above the main floor of the building, with its own domed ceiling and stained glass windows in the walls framing the half-circle. This stage, at first so strange and exposed, is to become, over the ensuing years of her training, a familiar point of entry into an alternative realm of experience. Here she will become a 'protagonist' in a drama. She will play, touch, dance, sing, laugh, cry, and be still. She will hold others, and she will be held. She will love and hate this large, soft, compassionate and arrogant man who calls himself a 'director'. Through entering the aesthetic, cultural and psychological space of the psychodrama, she will learn much about the possibility of accepting and transforming self and community. She will engage with a radical opening of herself to specific embodied others and to the Otherness of imagination. She will also learn how easily, and with what devastating consequences, the power and mystique of an alliance between therapy and the arts can be abused.

The separation of the aesthetic sphere and its division into specific art disciplines is a relatively recent phenomenon, and is again being challenged by contemporary art (Levine and Levine, 1999). Whereas (visual) art therapy is based in the specificity of the practitioner's background and ongoing practice in the visual arts, the approach of expressive therapy emphasises intermodality and a high sensitivity to aesthetic processes in and between a multiplicity of forms. Expressive therapy, with its emphasis on moving between expressive modalities, can thus claim a connection with ancient traditions of healing through creativity prior to the separation of the aesthetic sphere, and it can also claim a connection with postmodernism. This privileged relation with both the postmodern and the pre-modern lends great historical and current legitimacy to the expressive therapies. However, I suspect there is an unexamined tension in this claim, given that a slippage occurs between the pre-modern and 'universality', and that postmodernism disputes the possibility and/or desirability of the universal.

The work of Stephen K. Levine and his colleagues (Levine, 1996; Levine and Levine, 1999; Knill, Levine and Levine, 2005) towards a 'therapeutic aesthetics' of the theory, practice and pedagogy of expressive therapy constitutes a major philosophical shift, not only from classical assumptions of the separation of the aesthetic sphere (a shift that is also made in art therapy), but also from assumptions of the integrity of the subject. Both art and the subject are radically repositioned through a serious engagement with contemporary Western philosophies and the critique of modernism. Aesthetic theory is recast away from Kantian aesthetics as a progression of Cartesian logics and toward Nietzsche's figuration of a Dionysian *poiesis* (Levine, 1997). The theorisation of personhood within the reconceptualised field of expressive therapy seeks not to reinstate the autonomous and self-contained individual.

I am in agreement with the therapeutic aim of the expressive therapies to encourage expressive therapy participants, clients and trainee therapists alike to seek a shaping of art and 'self' that makes space for difference, disruption and particularity, rather than integration, and which is decentred through its obligation to the Other. However, I also wonder if this work reconstitutes aspects of the subject and of practice that it seeks to deconstruct. Levine notes the 'postmodern' fracturing of Eurocentrism and underscores the call of the Other, defined as "that class, race or gender that must serve ruling groups" (Levine, 1999, p. 19). However, although the subjects of therapy and pedagogy appear in these accounts as gendered and culturally different subjects, the politics and power relations of gender and culture seem to be marginalised by the (re)constitution of a generalised and self-responsible humanity. A vexed but crucial difference between postmodernisms and poststructuralisms marks this contemporary project of the expressive arts therapies. The authors courageously embrace the 'postmodern' possibilities of chaos and multiplicity, but do not emphasise the positivity of power, the tendencies of power relations towards domination, or the imbrication of power and knowledge—ideas that distinguish poststructural thought.

In setting out a philosophical framework for the expressive therapies, Levine also takes up aspects of Turner's (1969) ethnography, figuring therapeutic change as a contemporary rite of passage. This move from a psychological to an ethnographic paradigm is reminiscent of aspects of narrative therapy. However, in figuring the expressive therapist as responsible for structuring chaos, leading initiates into the unknown and conducting them back to safety, Levine does not extend the aesthetic process of 'decentring' from everyday reality to a decentring of the power of the therapist. This raises the question of whether these therapeutic processes rely on an elision of the power relations and cultural specificities of therapy itself. It is suggested, in this conceptualisation of the expressive therapies, that the position of the therapist becomes similar to that of persons trained and authorised in many cultural traditions to conduct rituals of transformation. The universal re-emerges in this comparison. The shaman is mapped onto the person of the contemporary expressive therapist. Such a person becomes an authentic expert/expert in authenticity, despite the authors' attempted refusal under the sign of the postmodern to equate authenticity with wholeness.

Narrative therapies challenge the expert position of the therapist by taking up a Foucauldian perspective of power, seeking to minimise the risk of domination by the therapist through practices of 'co-authoring'. Art psychotherapy complexifies the therapeutic relation in a different way, at least partially de-throning the therapist's authority through a theorisation of transference and counter transference. The expressive therapies, on the other hand, reinstall the therapist as a 'ritual master', one who is ironically responsible for managing the disintegration of the modern tropes of mastery and autonomy.

The assumed necessity of an active therapist with expert knowledge about when and how to move between artistic modalities is an interesting problem for an expressive therapist wanting to complexify and mediate relations of knowledge and power. As a facilitator of the aesthetic process, the therapist is reconstituted as a 'change agent'. In this metaphor, the therapeutic relation is acknowledged but relegated to a backdrop to the aesthetics of the client's explorations in art, whereas surely the messy intersubjectivity of therapeutic relations cannot be backgrounded in a poststructural understanding of therapy. The concept of therapist as 'change agent' engages with the possibilities of change for the client, but leaves a notion of the therapist's agency relatively unexamined.

The practice of decentring into an alternative reality, from what is generically described by the authors as the client's 'hopeless situation', runs a risk of marginalising the present/absent possibilities of hope within that person's stories of their everyday life. While taking some account of the social causes and conditions of hopelessness, this approach does not make visible the construction of hopelessness as a category of existence, or consider that deconstructing the production of this category, in therapy discourse as well as in popular understandings, might in itself be a therapeutic activity. Nor does it engage, as narrative therapy does, with the Derridean notion of the 'absent but implicit', in which a sense of hopelessness might gesture toward traces of subjugated histories of a person's disappointed yet honourable hopes for a more just and inclusive world (White, 2000). In assisting the client to transcend 'victimhood' through an engagement with imagination, chaos and creativity (Levine, 2009), the expressive therapies could marginalise the ways that the recipients of therapy are produced as needing a therapist to help them to become agentic subjects.

'Poiesis' (Levine, 1997), or the creative and shaping capacities of a person in relation to their world, is arguably not so much a largely unrealised potential of beings but a present/absent and marginalised subjective and social practice. I suggest that a kind of *poiesis* is always already embedded in the fabric of everyday, specific and situated subjectivities and socialities (Freedman and Combs, 2001), although often marginalised and made invisible through pathologising and impoverishing discourses and practices. It seems to me that a poststructurally oriented theory and practice of arts-based therapy needs, while it must enter into the space of the mysterious and the sublime, also to rehabilitate the poetry in and of the everyday by engaging the powers of art to search out and honour the marginalised arts of living of those who come to therapy. Otherwise, the ritualised space that the expressive therapies can offer for aesthetic experience/experimentation might ultimately re-stage the pathologisation and isolation of the subject, reinstate the therapist as expert, and reinforce the separation and mystification of the aesthetic sphere.

An outline of chapters

Following from the broad introduction to my fields of research and modes of enquiry in this chapter, chapters 2 and 3 offer an expanded and more specific account of the theories that (in)form this book. In these chapters, I introduce some poststructural theorists whose work is to be put into play in relation to my exploration of art therapy and narrative therapy. While I have engaged with a range of poststructural ideas and theorists in this book, I have not taken these up in an equal fashion, and that bias is reflected in these theoretical chapters/stories.

Chapter 4 extends the intellectual framework of the book through selectively engaging with questions of poststructural research methodology, especially the writing methodologies that have emerged from the work of a number of contemporary poststructural feminists. In this chapter I also engage with the discursive character of the visual in relation to this book project.

Chapters 5 and 6 engage, through poetry, story, visual images and discursive analysis, with two stories of arts-based and narrative therapeutic work with children and families. The first of these chapters considers my therapeutic engagement with a family whose stories have resonated closely with the biographies of myself and my family, while the second of these chapters tells of my therapeutic relations with a family whose legacies, positionings and narratives as Indigenous Australians pose questions about the politics and practices of working with the Other of ongoing colonisation.

Chapter 7 invites a further consideration of how writing *as* research calls for an ethics of uncertainty, unknowability, vulnerability and obligation to the Other (Butler, 2004b). In this concluding but necessarily inconclusive chapter, I bring together the threads of these accounts of the therapeutic and the theoretical, and of research and writing practice—accounts that push against the limits of therapeutic 'identity' and engagement. These threads continue to unravel and to escape into many different lines of flight towards ethical 'arts of existence'.

In the next chapter, I take the reader on a playful metaphorical excursion into the first stor(e)y of a vast department store of poststructural theory, in order to imagine what these philosophical ideas could open up for the practice of narrative, arts-based therapy.

---

[1] The description in words of a visual art form.

[2] See Karkou's (1999) survey, which concluded that Jung and Winnicott were the theorists favoured by the majority of U.K. art therapists.

REFERENCES

Britzman, D. (2000). The question of belief: Writing poststructural ethnography. In St Pierre, E. & Pillow, W. (Eds). *Feminist poststructural theory and methods in education,* (pp. 27–40). New York: Routledge.

Butler, J. (1997a). *Psychic life of power: theories in subjection.* California: Stanford University Press.

— (1997b). *Excitable speech: a politics of the performative.* New York: Routledge.

— (1999). *Gender trouble: Feminism and the subversion of identity.* New York and London: Routledge. (Original edition published 1990).

— (2000). *Antigone's claim: Kinship between life and death.* New York: Columbia University Press.

— (2001). Giving an Account of Oneself. *Diacritics*, 31(4), 22–40.

— (2004a). *Undoing gender.* New York and London: Routledge.

— (2004b). *Precarious life: the powers of mourning and violence.* New York and London: Routledge.

— (2005). *Giving an account of oneself.* New York: Fordham University Press.

Case, C., & Dalley, D. (1992). *The handbook of art therapy.* London: Routledge.

Clément, C. (1987). *The weary sons of Freud.* London: Verso.

Cixous, H. (1993). *Three steps on the ladder of writing.* New York: Columbia University Press.

— (1998). *Stigmata. Escaping texts.* London: Routledge.

— (2008). *White ink interviews on sex, text and politics*. Stocksfield: Acumen.

Cixous, H., & Calle-Gruber, M. (1997). *Rootprints: memory and life writing.* London & New York: Routledge.

Cixous, H., & Clément, C. (1986). *The newly born woman*. Minneapolis: University of Minnesota Press.

Davies, B. (2000). *A body of writing*. Walnut Creek, CA: AltaMira Press.

Deleuze, G., & Guattari, F. (1977). *Anti-Oedipus.* Minneapolis: University of Minnesota Press. (Original work published 1972).

— (1987). *A thousand plateaus.* Minneapolis: University of Minnesota Press. (Original work published 1980).

Derrida, J. (1978). *Writing and difference*. London: Routledge. (Original work published 1967).

— (1997). 'To do justice to Freud': The history of madness in the age of psychoanalysis. In A. Davidson (Ed.), *Foucault and his interlocutors* (pp. 56–96). Chicago: University of Chicago Press. (Original work published 1992).

Epston, D., & Roth, S. (1998). Consulting the problem about the problematic relationship: an exercise for experiencing a relationship with an externalised problem. In D. Epston, *Catching up with David Epston: a collection of narrative practice-based papers published between 1991 & 1996* (pp. 209–226). Adelaide: Dulwich Centre Publications. (Original work published 1996).

Epston, D., & White, M. (1989). *Literate means to therapeutic ends.* Adelaide: Dulwich Centre Publications.

Foucault, M. (1980). *The history of sexuality, Volume 1: an introduction.* New York: Vintage Books. (Original work published 1976).

— (1992). *The history of sexuality, Volume 2: The use of pleasure.* London: Penguin Books. (Original work published 1984).

— (2000a). An interview with Michel Foucault. In J. Faubion, (Ed.), *Essential works of Foucault 1954–1984, Volume 3, Michel Foucault: Power* (pp. 239–297). London: Penguin Books.

— (2000b). So is it important to think? In J. Faubion (Ed.), *Essential works of Foucault 1954–1984, Volume 3, Michel Foucault: Power* (pp. 454–458). London: Penguin Books.

— (2000c). On the genealogy of ethics: an overview of work in progress. In P. Rabinow (Ed.), *Essential works of Foucault 1954–1984, Volume 1, Michel Foucault: Ethics, subjectivity and truth* (pp. 253–280). London: Penguin Books. (Interview conducted 1983).

— (2000d). My body, this paper, this fire. In J. Faubion (Ed.), *Essential works of Foucault 1954–1984, Volume 3, Michel Foucault: Aesthetics, method and epistemology* (pp. 393–417). London: Penguin Books. (Original work published 1972).

— (2000e). Structuralism and poststructuralism. In J. Faubion (Ed.), *Essential works of Foucault 1954–1984, Volume 3, Michel Foucault: Aesthetics, method and epistemology* (pp. 433–458). London: Penguin Books. (Original work published 1983).

Freedman, J., & Combs, G. (2001, February). *Bringing forth the poetry in 'little sacraments of daily existence'*. Paper presented at the International Narrative Therapy and Community Work Conference, Adelaide, Australia.

Freeman, J. C., Epston D., & Lobovits, D. (1997). *Playful approaches to serious problems: narrative therapy with children and their families.* New York: W.W. Norton.

Henzell, J. (2006). Unimaginable imaginings: fantasies and works off the margin. *Inscape*, 11(1), 13–21.

Hogan, S. (1997). Problems of identity: deconstructing gender in art therapy. In Hogan, (Ed.), *Feminist Approaches to Art Therapy* (pp. 21–47). London: Routledge.

— (2001). *Healing arts: The history of art therapy.* London: Jessica Kingsley.

Hoshino, J., & Cameron, D. (2008). Narrative art therapy within a multicultural framework. In C. Kerr *et al.*, *Family art therapy: foundations of theory and practice* (pp. 193–219). London & New York: Routledge.

Hyland Moon, C. (2002). *Studio art therapy: cultivating the artist identity in the art therapist.* London: Jessica Kingsley.

Irigaray, I. (1981). That sex that is not one. (C. Reeder, Trans.). In E. Marks & I. de Courtivron (Eds.), *New French feminisms: an anthology* (pp. 107–110). Great Britain: The Harvester Press. (Original work published 1977).

Junge, M. (1994). *The history of art therapy in the United States.* Mundelein, Ill.: American Art Therapy Association.

Kamsler, A. (1990). Her-story in the making: therapy with women who were sexually abused in childhood. In M. Durrant & C. White (Eds.), *Ideas for therapy with sexual abuse* (pp. 9–36). Adelaide: Dulwich Centre Publications.

Karkou, V. (1999). Findings from a nationwide survey in arts therapies. *Inscape,* 4(2), 62–69.

Knill, P., Levine, E. G., & Levine, S. K. (2005). *Principles and Practice of Expressive Arts Therapy: towards a therapeutic aesthetics.* London & Philadelphia: Jessica Kingsley.

Laing, L., & Kamsler, A. (1990). Putting an end to secrecy: therapy with mothers and children following disclosure of child sexual assault. In M. Durrant & C. White (Eds.), *Ideas for therapy with sexual abuse* (pp. 159–181). Adelaide: Dulwich Centre Publications.

Lechte, J. (1994). *Fifty key contemporary thinkers: from structuralism to postmodernity.* London & New York: Routledge.

— (2006). The unconscious as paradox: impact on the epistemological stance of the art psychotherapist. *The arts in psychotherapy,* 33, 130–134.

Levine, S. K. (1997). *Poiesis: the language of psychology and the speech of the soul.* London & New York: Jessica Kingsley.

— (1999). Poiesis and post-modernism: The search for a foundation in expressive arts therapy. In S. K. Levine & E. G. Levine (Eds.), *Foundations of Expressive Arts Therapy: theoretical and clinical perspectives* (pp. 19–36). London & New York: Jessica Kingsley.

— (2009). *Trauma, tragedy, therapy: the art of human suffering.* London & New York: Jessica Kingsley.

Levine, S. K., & Levine, E. G. (Eds.). (1999). *Foundations of Expressive Arts Therapy: theoretical and clinical perspectives.* London & New York: Jessica Kingsley.

Linnell, S. (2008). Found wanting and becoming undone: a response to Eva Bendix Petersen's 'Passionately attached: academic subjects of desire'. In B. Davies (Ed.), *Judith Butler in conversation: Analysing the texts and talk of everyday life.* London & New York: Routledge.

Linnell, S., & Cora, D. (1993). *Discoveries: a group resource guide for women who were sexually abused in childhood.* Sydney: Dympna House.

Linnell, S., Hanslow, I., & Rummery, L. (2006, March). *Arts of connection: bringing together visual arts practice, art therapy training, and narrative therapy and community work.* Conference paper and performance presented at the Inaugural International Festive Conference: working with the stories, songs, drama and poetry of people's lives: linking narrative therapy and community work with the fields of drama, song, film, fiction, and poetry, Adelaide, Australia.

Lofts, J. (2002). The application of social constructionism and discourse analysis to the examination of art therapy with people with learning disabilities. *International Journal of Arts Therapies,* 1. Retrieved October, 2009, from http://www.derby.ac.uk/research/v-art/journal/articles/jlofts/

Martin, R. (1997). Looking and reflecting: returning the gaze, re-enacting memories and imagining the future through phototherapy. In S. Hogan (Ed.), *Feminist Approaches to Art Therapy* (pp. 150–176). London: Routledge.

McLagan, D. (2001). *Psychological aesthetics.* London: Jessica Kingsley.

Meskimmon, M. (2003). *Women making art: History, subjectivity, aesthetics.* London & New York: Routledge.

Milner, M. (1950). *On not being able to paint.* London: Heinmann.

Riley, S. (1999). *Contemporary art therapy with adolescents.* London & Philadelphia: Jessica Kingsley.

Riley, S. & Malchiodi, C. (2003). Solution focussed and narrative approaches. In C. Malchiodo (Ed.), *Handbook of art therapy* (pp. 82–92). New York & London: The Guilford Press.

Rose, N. (1998). *Inventing ourselves: Psychology, Power and personhood.* Cambridge University Press.

— (2000). Power in therapy: Techne and ethos. *Academy for the study of psychoanalytic arts.* Retrieved March, 2003, from http://www.academyanalyticarts.org/rose2.html

Rubin, J. (Ed.). (1987). *Approaches to art therapy: Theory and technique.* New York: Brunner-Mazel.

— (Ed.). (2001). *Approaches to art therapy: Theory and technique. 2nd Edition*. Philadelphia: Brunner-Routledge.

Said, E. (1975). *Beginnings: Intention and method.* New York: Basic Books.

Scheurich, J. (1995). A postmodernist critique of research interviewing. *International Journal of Qualitative Studies in Education*, 8(3), 239–252.

Sellers, S. (Ed.). (2004). *The writing notebooks of Hélène Cixous.* New York: Continuum.

Shaverien, J. (1992). *The Revealing Image: Analytical art psychotherapy in theory and practice.* London: Routledge.

— (1995). *Desire and the female therapist: engendered gazes in psychotherapy and art therapy.* London and New York: Routledge.

— (2003). Inaugural lecture, University of Sheffield. The eye of the beholder: Eros and art in psychotherapy. *Inscape*, 8(1), 2–16. (Original lecture 2001).

Skaife, S. (1995). The dialectics of art therapy. *Inscape,* 1(Summer), 2–7.

— (2000). Further thoughts on the dialectics of art therapy. In A. Gilroy & G. McNeilly (Eds.), *The changing shape of art therapy* (pp. 115–142). London: Jessica Kingsley.

— (2001). Making visible: Art therapy and intersubjectivity. *Inscape,* 6(2), 40–50.

— (2008). Off-shore: a deconstruction of David Maclagan's and David Mann's 'Inscape' papers. *International journal of art therapy (Inscape)*, 13(2), 44–52.

Speedy, J. (2008). *Narrative inquiry and psychotherapy.* New York: Palgrave Macmillan.

Swartz, S. (2005). Can the clinical subject speak? Some thoughts on subaltern psychology. *Theory and psychology,* 15(4), 505–525.

Tipple, R. (2003). The interpretation of children's artwork in a paediatric disability setting. *Inscape,* 8(3), 48–59.

Turner, V. (1969). *The ritual process.* New York: Cornell University Press.

Ulman, E. (2001). Art therapy: a problem of definition. *American journal of art therapy*, 40(1), 16–27.

Venn, C. (2000). *Occidentalism, modernity and subjectivity.* London: Sage.

— (2002). Refiguring subjectivity after modernity. In V. Walkerdine (Ed.), *Challenging subjects: critical psychology for a new millennium* (pp. 51–71). Houndsmills, U.K.: Palgrave.

Wadeson, H. (2001). An eclectic approach to art therapy. In J. Rubin, (Ed.), *Approaches to art therapy: Theory and technique* (2nd ed.) (pp. 306–317). Philadelphia: Brunner-Routledge. (Original work published 1987).

Waller, D. (1991). *Becoming a Profession: The History of Art Therapy in Britain: 1940–82.* London: Tavistock/Routledge.

Waller, D., & Dalley, T. (1992). Art therapy: a theoretical perspective. In D. Waller & A. Gilroy (Eds.), *Art therapy: a handbook* (pp. 3–24). Buckingham: Open University Press.

Waller, D., & Gilroy, A. (Eds.). (1992). *Art therapy: a handbook.* Buckingham: Open University Press.

White, M. (1992). Deconstruction and therapy. In D. Epston & M. White, *Experience, contradiction, narrative and imagination: selected papers of David Epston and Michael White 1989–1991* (pp. 109–152). Adelaide: Dulwich Centre Publications. (Originally published 1991).

— (1995). *Re-authoring lives: Interviews and essays.* Adelaide: Dulwich Centre Publications.

— (1997). *Narratives of therapist's lives.* Adelaide: Dulwich Centre Publications.

— (2000). *Reflections on narrative practice.* Adelaide: Dulwich Centre Publications.

— (2003). Narrative Practice and community assignments. *The International Journal of Narrative Therapy and Community Work*, 2, 17–55.

White, M., & Epston, D. (1990). *Narrative means to therapeutic ends.* New York & London: W.W. Norton & Co.

Williams, C., & Linnell, S. (2006). When the doctors consulted the narrative therapist…an experiment in questioning dominant stories of PhD pedagogy. *The International Journal of Critical Psychology,* 18, 56–80.

CHAPTER 2

BROWSING THE STORE OF POSTSTRUCTURAL THEORY: RETHINKING THE SUBJECTS AND PRACTICES OF ART THERAPY AND NARRATIVE THERAPY THROUGH DERRIDA, DELEUZE AND GUATTARI, AND ESPECIALLY FOUCAULT

> *...not to be confined by theory, but for theory to appear as what it is, useful and traversable...*
>
> (Cixous, 1988, p. 144)

Abstract: Following from the broad introduction to my fields of research and modes of enquiry in chapter 1, chapter 2 is the first part of an expanded and more specific account of the theories that inform this book. In this chapter, I introduce some of the poststructural theorists, particularly male French philosophers from the second half of the 20th century, whose work is to be put into play in relation to my exploration of art therapy and narrative therapy. I do this in a playful and writerly way through an extended metaphor of browsing through the men's clothing section of a large department store, trying on various garments/ theories to see if they fit. While I engage a range of poststructural ideas and theorists in this book, I do not take all up in an equal fashion. My bias is reflected in this chapter, which concludes with an extended consideration of Foucault's philosophy and an exploration of how his late work on ethical subjectivities, ethical substances and arts of self can inform my enquiry into the subjects and practices of art therapy and narrative therapy.

As she walks up the wide Travertine marble steps to the entrance of the Store of Poststructural Theory, she passes a picket line. In an eerie echo of the anti-globalisation movement, two elderly gentlemen in shabby evening dress are waving placards that declaim, with the clarity of socialist materialism and the biblical force of prophesy:

> CULTURE TODAY
> IS INFECTING EVERYTHING
> WITH SAMENESS

and

> INDUSTRY IS INTERESTED IN HUMAN BEINGS
> ONLY AS ITS CUSTOMERS OR EMPLOYEES
> & HAS IN FACT REDUCED HUMANITY AS A WHOLE
> TO THIS EXHAUSTIVE FORMULA [1]

Sheridan Linnell

These messages are clearly urging her to reconsider the capitalist and consumerist implications of her current metaphor. But she is here now, outside the store, and it has taken her a long time to get here. She steps through revolving glass doors into the orange and black 1970s retro interior.

The entire ground floor is taken up with the Men's Section. A man, only a few years younger than she, asks if he can assist her. He has shaved his head to disguise a receding hairline and is wearing one silver earring, deeply distressed Levis and an old leather bike jacket over an inside-out faded black T-shirt with the seams showing. Perhaps, he enquires casually, she is looking for a little something for the current man in her life? She says that she is just looking. As he walks away, she wonders if anything on the 'specials' rack of last season's men's continental intellectual fashions will actually fit her.

She flicks through the rack of fine garments, some bright and richly embellished, others darkly elegant and subdued. A pair of mahogany slacks from the House of Bachelard reverberates with memories of dark interiors, the drawers and wardrobes of her childhood. (She wonders if this item has been put back on the wrong rack, but the nostalgic image projected by the Bachelard line has after all been a major influence on later designers of the 'po-mo' school.) The exquisite suit by Lacan is simply impossible—even gazing at it, let alone trying it on, is enough to underscore the disillusion most people encounter in the changing room mirror. And it's so tiny that it must surely have been made for an 'hommelette' (see Grosz, 1990). She flicks past the shining gold buttons and matching eyelets adorning a camouflage-green Bataille jacket. Catches herself wondering if a sleek, synthetic waistcoat is an *original* Baudrillard or one of the numerous imitations around the place, all virtually indistinguishable from the real thing.

She lingers over the intricate textu(r)al weave of a Derrida hand printed linen dress shirt. She is attracted and disconcerted by its *differance* in relation to the shirts on either side of it—by her sense that the garment is not quite, and never could be, finished. She touches the surface, noticing how the print has registered differently in different places, as though an image or idea has begun to find traction only to slide off, leaving a trace of that which cannot quite be erased. She really likes this one, but it's difficult. She isn't sure how to wear it, so she defers judgement; after all, with this particular creation, she is not compelled to 'decide'...

Jacques Derrida

> [I]f you were to bide your time awhile in these pages you would discover that I cannot dominate the situation, or translate it, or describe it. I cannot report what is going on in it, or narrate or depict it, or pronounce it or mimic it, or offer it up to be read or formalised without remainder. I would always have to renew, reproduce and reintroduce into the formalising economy of my tale—overloaded each time with some supplement—the very indecision I was trying to reduce. (Derrida, 1987, p. 2)

The ideas of Derrida are difficult to define/confine. His notions of deconstruction, 'writing', 'differance' and the 'undecidability' of texts—of the irreducible multiplicity of language, the non-identity of signs and deferral of meaning—suggest a refusal to foreclose on (im)possibilities, a continual dissolution of binaries and opening of space.

Derridean 'differance' (Derrida, 1978)—difference and deferral—is not unlike a Freudian displacement that has escaped from its marriage to psychosexual determinism, into an intense and indeterminate textual erotics, or *jouissance*.

Spivak explains how Derrida takes up, from Heidegger, the concept of *sous rature* (under erasure):

> This is to write a word, cross it out, and then print both the word and its deletion. (Since the word is inaccurate, it is crossed out. Since it is necessary, it remains legible.) ...In examining familiar things we come to such unfamiliar conclusions that our very language is twisted and bent even as it guides us. (Spivak, 1997, p. xiv)

Derrida's 'deconstruction' has sometimes been viewed as a nihilistic project for the destruction of order and reason, or, alternatively, as a methodology that could be 'reasonably' 'applied' to a text, although Derrida makes it clear than neither of these options capture a deconstructive mood. Deconstruction is neither destructive nor dispassionate: as Derrida said in his last interview, deconstruction is always on the side of the *yes,* on the side of the affirmation of life (Derrida, 2007, p. 51).

The metaphor of 'writing under erasure' (Derrida, 1997) has been taken up within a broad poststructural and deconstructive project of writing between and beyond binaries (e.g. Davies, 2000). White (2003) follows Derrida's refusal of 'presence', through a close and subversive attention to how the subjugated stories of people's lives are 'absent but implicit' in the dominant narratives of those who come to therapy, although arguably this refusal of presence is undone when White's work is taken up as the work of reconstructing the agentic subject (see Carey, Walther and Russell, 2009). Skaife (2008; see also chapter 1) deconstructs the art/therapy binary, entering into and laying bare the structuralist and patriarchal truth claims that produce this binary and that structure both sides of an ongoing debate. These ways of taking up the work of deconstruction in therapy are a matter, not of applying a deconstructive technique to an object of research outside oneself, but of inhabiting and subverting existing structures and discourses *from the inside:*

> The movements of deconstruction do not destroy structure from the outside. They are not possible and effective, nor can they take accurate aim, except by inhabiting those structures. Inhabiting them *in a certain way,* because one always inhabits, and all the more when one does not suspect it. Operating necessarily from the inside, borrowing all the strategic and economic resources of subversion from the old structure, borrowing them structurally, that is to say without being able to isolate their elements and atoms, the enterprise of deconstruction always in a certain way falls prey to its own work. (Derrida, 1997, p. 24)

Derrida's work inscribes a profoundly ethical uncertainty, so that a radical openness to the Other lies at the heart of this book. Derrida continually unhinges the assumed unity of sign and signified, word and thing, writing and voice, presence and absence, refusing the nostalgia (Spivak, 1997) of unified presence and being. But this undoing is also the undoing of the one who is doing the undoing. Deconstruction is always an 'inside job', and as such cannot be the work of something or someone in a meta-relation to that which is under erasure. Thus deconstruction is not critique. It is not even a critique of critique, but rather an undoing of the deciding agency assumed in taking up a critical position (Derrida, 1995).

Perhaps she might begin to imagine herself wearing both the garment of deconstruction and the deconstructed garment—inhabiting it, unravelling it, being unravelled by it—'in an (un)certain way'.

And so, with Derrida held close to her heart yet indefinitely deferred, she continues to search through the rack of extraordinary 'specials'. As for this shimmering invention from the studio of Deleuze and Guattari, what is it? Why is it in the Men's Section when it looks like a ball gown, or a sunrise, or an exotic bird? And what is that nomadic melody drifting on the air? "There's no place like rhiz-home..." Held up to the light, the fabric(ation) is infinitely changeable, becoming the rippling cerulean of the ocean, the stark reds and oranges of the desert, now black and velvety as a bat's wing on a moonless night, now silvery and slippery, indefinite as autumn mist. She desires this chimera more than anything. She is sure, too, that it would be very 'becoming', but she also knows it is not to be had.

Gilles Deleuze / Felix Guattari

Rather than cutting off possibilities through the linear organization of the book, I am challenged by Deleuze and Guattari's notions of horizontal/ rhizomatic thought and of deterritorialisation to follow potentially productive lines of flight, to bend lines of enquiry, to follow the subtle curves of horizons of thought as they arc into previously unimagined landscapes (Deleuze and Guattari, 1977a, 1987).

Guattari and Deleuze undertake a 'de-territorialisation' of the Oedipal organisation of self, family and culture to be found in Freud (Deleuze and Guattari, 1977a, 1977b). Their work challenges the Freudian hermeneutics of depth and reduction, playing on the possibilities of proliferation across surfaces, enacting a philosophy of difference and a politics of desire.

Deleuze's philosophy of difference frees difference from the strictures of 'difference from', suggesting a serious ethic of decentred playfulness and a transcendental yet embodied specificity to practices of self-dissolution and becoming-other (Deleuze, 1994). His theory of desire is productive and decentralised, leading Patton (2000) to suggest that Deleuzian desire is comparable with and complementary to Foucault's analytic of power.

Deleuze has written extensively on the arts, including cinema, music and painting (Bogue, 2003), and he elaborates many of his ideas through an exploration of the aesthetics of these different art forms. In an extended study of Francis Bacon, rich with possibilities for art therapy, Deleuze (1981) analyses the facture (mark making/aesthetic properties) of Bacon's paintings in terms of sensation, rhythm and an intense interplay between corporeality and a desire for becoming-other. "For Deleuze, the visible holds a particular fascination. To think differently is to see differently..." (Bogue, 2003, p. 194). Visual art, as the embodiment of sensual perception, and as counterpoint to the transcendental gestures of music, holds a privileged place in Deleuze's philosophy.

In art therapy, there is a need to theorise complex subject and object relations between the therapist, the person coming to therapy, and the artwork. In attempting to understand these relations as mutually constitutive rather than simply representational, I follow a long tradition of artists and art therapists who argue for the creative, as well as the expressive and hermeneutic, significance of art (e.g. Milner, 1950; Fuller, 1980; Waller and Dalley, 2006). Art making, in this view, is not only the making of art; it is also what art makes of its maker in relation to the world. The proposal of Nicholas Rose (1998), following Deleuze and Guattari, that our 'selves' do not necessarily stop at our skins but are extended or become other through our use of 'technologies', could inform an account of how artwork may not simply reflect, but may also constitute, the capacities and identities of those who engage with art therapy.

The notion of the psyche in Deleuze is that an enfoldment of the outside produces an interiority. This radically challenges essentialising theories of intrapsychic phenomena and troubles the widespread assumption that therapy is about an unfolding of inner essence. John Winslade (2009) reminds us that from a Deleuzian perspective it is more interesting to follow the folds themselves. Remembering this, it becomes possible to (re)locate the notion of the fold as a line that both produces and separates inner and outer worlds. Bending this line a little, I find I can follow its trajectory into new territories of existence beyond the binary of the psychic and the social.

Narrative therapists such as Winslade have only just begun to touch upon the possibilities of Deleuzian philosophy for narrative therapeutic practice. Winslade suggests this shifts narrative therapy thinking, initially by a small degree, by moving toward a geopolitical metaphor for the territories of life, and asking what difference a philosophy of difference may open up in therapy, when difference is thought prior to the subject. Winslade also gives an intriguing and touching account of how, on the day of Michael White's final teaching workshop, Winslade was expecting to go out to dinner with White to discuss their mutual interest in the possibilities of Deleuze for narrative therapy, except that during the afternoon Michael was taken to hospital (Winslade, 2009). A few days later he died. In this instance, 'expect the unexpected' has a tragic resonance.

For a long moment she thinks about Michael. Then she picks up a deep purple jacket circa 1960, a stylish, contemporary creation cut on the bias from a classic blend of European wool and silk. The label reads 'Experience' per Michel Foucault. She slips it on. This one she will certainly take with her. It's a bit broad for her, but very well cut, and the colour really suits her complexion. Perhaps she'll grow into it, a little.

Michel Foucault

> There are two meanings to the word "subject": subject to someone else by control and dependence, and tied to his own identity through a

> conscience or self-knowledge. Both meanings suggest a form of power that subjugates and makes subject to. (Foucault, 2000a, p. 331)

> [The subject] is not a substance. It is a form, and this form is not primarily or always identical to itself...Undoubtedly there are relationships and interferences between...different forms of the subject; but we are not dealing with the same type of subject. In each case, one plays, one establishes a different type of relationship to oneself. And it is precisely the historical constitution of these various forms of the subject in relation to the games of truth that interests me. (Foucault, 2000b, pp. 290–291)

Foucault suggests that the modern 'self', rather than being conceptualised as universal or 'given', might be thought of as recent, and continually produced or created through historically and culturally specific relations of knowledge and power. Much of this book is a response to the radical implications of that suggestion.

Truth and the subject

For Nietzsche, "truth was the greatest lie" (Foucault, 2000c, p. 476). Following Nietzsche, Foucault "would like, in short, to resituate the production of true and false at the heart of historical analysis and political critique" (2000d, p. 230). The kind of history that can facilitate such a task is one that refuses the twin myths of origin and progress, recognising that power and conflicting interests are present at the inaugural moments of 'reason'. Such an 'effective history', or genealogy, examines what is closest to it and gives consideration to what might be considered 'below' notice, even the body itself. This emphasis on the analysis of objects that are marginalised by their very closeness to us is something that Foucault's genealogy shares with his earlier metaphor of archaeology. Both the 'archaeological' suggestion that implicit knowledges give rise to formal knowledges (Foucault, 2003a), and the related 'genealogical' suggestion that knowledge is constituted through relations of power, implicate therapy in processes of dominant knowledge formation and subjectification. In this view, therapy cannot be assumed to be either an innocent vehicle for progress and healing or a conservative force that 'represses' freedom and pacifies the desire for social change.

Foucault's genealogy recognises that it is a perspectival knowledge, grounded in the particularities of time, place, preference and passion (Foucault, 2000e). As a situated knowledge, genealogy does not claim to operate outside of the relations it seeks to analyse. However, it does offer powerful tools for unsettling what would otherwise remain taken for granted.

Foucault defines his overall project as a 'genealogy' of the subject: a critical and historicising account of how human beings in modern Western culture are constituted as both subject and object (Foucault, 2000f). By analysing the historical conditions of emergence and the theoretical antecedents of the modern subject, Foucault suggests that our understandings of our 'selves' and of our lives are more recent and less inevitable than we might otherwise assume. Foucault poses the question of 'what we are', and also the question of how we might refuse what we are. Foucault emphasised that the positivity of contemporary criticism must entail "an historical investigation into the events that have led us to constitute ourselves and recognise ourselves as subjects of what we are doing, thinking and saying" (Foucault, 2000g, p. 315). As archaeology, this criticism will "treat the instances of discourse that articulate what we think, say and do as so many historical events" (2000g, p. 315). As genealogy, this criticism will "separate out, from the contingency that has made us what we are, the possibility of no longer being, doing, or thinking what we are, do, or think" (2000g, p. 315–316). Foucault specifies three major and interrelated areas for consideration: the discourses of the human sciences, the disciplinary practices of Western democracies and the self's relation to the self in Western culture. His work offers methodological suggestions for the analysis of discourses, power relations and ethical/subjective formation. Foucault's research led him to critique what he describes as the "repressive hypothesis" (Foucault, 1980, p. 15) and to formulate an "analytics" (1980, p. 82) of modern power as productive, decentralised and mutually implicated with knowledge.

Foucauldian genealogy can highlight issues of significance for the ongoing development of a critical and reflexive praxis of art therapy. Foucault's critique of the truth claims of the human sciences can invite us to historicise and deconstruct taken-for-granted ideas and practices within art therapy. A Foucauldian analytic of power (Foucault, 1980) poses fresh questions about our discipline's relationship to 'governmentality' (Foucault, 2000h) and normalising judgement, thereby giving impetus to the current and historical discussion around the 'clinification' of art therapy. A view of power as both disciplinary and productive invites a consideration of how our clinical and pedagogical practices may engage our clients, our students and ourselves in certain ways of constituting identity. A view of resistance as an always-present response to power might provide an alternative framework for considering our own stories and images, as well as those of the people who come to meet with art therapists.

I find Foucault's work highly suggestive for challenging the binaries that mark much debate within and between therapeutic modalities. Rather than choosing between binary positions, it seems to be more useful, following Foucault, to enquire into the production and maintenance of such binaries, into the history and effects of the unhinging of thought and emotion, the formation and divisions of the disciplines, the problematisation and separation of psychic and social spheres. Foucault offers ways of challenging or undoing the art/science binary that has marked art therapy and research methodologies alike. Rather than 'siding' with the possibilities of proof through scientific method, or valorising irrationality as giving privileged access to emotional (as opposed to intellectual) 'truth', Foucault questions the production of such a binary.

Foucault's later work on ethical subjectivity, with its emphasis on modern 'techniques' and 'technologies' of the self, is particularly rich in suggestions for an ethics and aesthetics of therapy. However I think it is important not to isolate Foucault's ethics from other aspects of a genealogy of the subject. Foucault pointed out that new forms of power (and, one could add, new forms of knowledge and subjectivity) emerge and may become dominant in different times and contexts, but that they do not replace existing forms, which may also become more or less influential (Foucault, 2000h). The 'ethics' of art therapy are necessarily informed by a critical ontology of the present—by a continual questioning of what is otherwise taken for granted in clinical theory and practice.

Problematisation

Foucault speaks of problematisation as "the set of discursive or nondiscursive practices that make something enter into the play of the true and false, and constitutes it as an object for thought" (1996a, pp. 456–457). In this sense of the word, problematisation is one of the ways that historically specific knowledges and practices come to be accepted as 'normal, natural and true'. Problematisation is therefore a practice of dominant power, but it can also be a practice of resistance. Since Foucault exposes the political and historical contingencies of any supposedly disinterested claim to knowledge, a Foucauldian/poststructuralist ethics would require the researcher to openly 'locate' her interests and investments. In this view, a researcher can generate a strategic starting point from within the narrative of her own experience: a 'problematisation' that in turn connects with relevant issues for a wider community of interest (Foucault, 2000i). This proposal extends the radical feminist assertion that 'the personal is the political', drawing attention to the discursive work involved in the mutual constitution of individual and collective concerns.

For Foucault (2000j) critical thought is itself a difficult and necessary practice of freedom. Thought is "freedom in relation to what one does, the motion by which one detaches oneself from it, establishes it as an object, and reflects on it as a problem" (2000i, p. 117), "the act that posits a subject and an object, along with their various possible relations" (2000k, p. 459). It is important to analyse, rather than take for granted, the formation and mutually constitutive relationship of both the subject and the object of thought within a field of practice—to understand how things become problematised and how they thereby enter a domain of thought in which they can be considered as either true or false.

In tandem with problematisation, a method of 'eventalisation' disrupts self-evidence and undoes necessity by rediscovering the singularities and specificities of a particular occurrence/event. As a researcher breaks down an event into its specifics, it becomes more possible and indeed obligatory to relate the specifics of the event to other social and discursive practices, so that attention to discontinuities and idiosyncracies paradoxically increases the researcher's capacity to locate the proliferating tendencies and effects of power. (Foucault, 2000d). Foucault's emphasis on local as well as upon broad categories of thought is indicative of how one might attempt a study of art therapy that disrupts and displaces the profession's dominant theoretical and practical assumptions.

Knowledge

Foucault's interest in the human sciences—a field that incorporates the psychotherapies—is of significance for a poststructurally oriented book about art therapy because it provides a frame within which to locate the profession historically and discursively and, in the process, unmasks powerful implicit assumptions. For Foucault, the human sciences become objects of investigation because these disciplines occupy an anomalous zone between 'pure' science and 'mere' opinion. Foucault suggests that it is both more possible and more strategic to study the historical contingency of truth claims in the recently formed 'sciences of man' than in the more established 'hard' sciences (Foucault, 2000l).

For Foucault, the human sciences did not *inherit* 'man' as the object of their investigations (and hence as both the subject and object of 'his' own thoughts)—they *constituted* him. And if 'man' in this sense could be invented, he could also disappear (Foucault, 1994a), in order to be re-invented (2000l). Much of Foucault's later work could be seen as an attempt to reconstitute, differently, the relation of subject to object—of ourselves to ourselves. Therapy, in this view, rather than being a refinement of an historical and universal practice of healing, is only made possible through its relatively recent mutual constitution with the invention and problematisation of 'man'. Similarly, a subjective and reflexive practice of art is only a possibility when a theory of subjectivity complicates the assumption of pure and transparent representation. Thought this way, art psychotherapy is an inevitably 'modern' practice. If the modern age invented 'man', then modernity is continually constituting what it means to be human, and shaping who is included and excluded from humanity. Therapy plays a crucial role in this constitution. Therapy, as a discursive practice within expanding modern rationalities, is constitutive of subjectivities, socialities and truths. Such modern practice is marked with a self-consciousness and reflexivity that it is necessary to go beyond, a project in which Foucault's refusal of a hermeneutics of the subject and his ethic of critique become crucial. Such a refusal could lead to an ongoing critique and transformation of the ethics of therapeutic practice. By locating the apparently individual question of therapeutic transformation in relation to power and the social, and by dethroning 'objectivity' and its dominating effects, therapy can contribute, little by little, to the shaping of a more inclusive and just sociality, or at least to a greater alertness to the strategic tendency for forms of power to become domination.

Following Foucault's focus on the human sciences and his method of disrupting and reorganising disciplinary categories, Rose (1998) has studied the constitution of what he calls the 'psy' disciplines. By grouping together psychology, psychiatry, psychotherapy and psychoanalysis, Rose can describe the common discursive features of areas that often appear in opposition to each other. He can account for the emergence and proliferation of these disciplines, which take the modern 'self' as their object. By breaking up and regrouping these disciplines, Rose makes visible how they are imbricated in practices of governmentality and normalising power. This analysis situates art therapy—for all its emphasis on the unconscious and the recuperation of irrationality—as part of an expansion of forms of rationality that shape a self-governing neoliberal subject of 'choice'. This is an important frame for the more localised stories of therapeutic work that form the central chapters of this book.

In his early work on the discourses of the human sciences, Foucault (1994a) gives a privileged status within the human sciences to both psychoanalysis and ethnology because of their critical capacity in relation to their fields of knowledge. Psychoanalysis radically decentres the truth of the subject it seeks to investigate, while ethnology historicises and culturally contextualises that truth. This privileging of both psychoanalysis and ethnology holds considerable interest for me because of their influence, respectively, on the constitution of art therapy and narrative therapy. My research for this book has underlined for me that, despite their apparent incompatibility, narrative therapy and art therapy share a radical potential for destabilising the truth of positivism. Foucault's analysis has assisted me to understand this shared potential, while Butler's theories (see chapter 3) have enabled me to understand the opposition of narrative therapy and art therapy as an effect of/productive of the binary of the psychic and the social.

Discourse analysis

Within a Foucauldian framework, the word 'discourse' is asked to do the work of suggesting that a range of signifying and social practices, such as writing, speech and art, act at a local and immediate level to produce our experience and constitute the realities within which we live (Abu-Lughod and Lutz, 1990). For Foucault, discourses have real/material effects that constitute subjectivity and truth. Textual work within the Foucauldian frame identifies how dominant cultural discourses shape specific narratives and signifying practices, which in turn constitute (without fully determining) those dominant discourses. Differences within and between discourses and narratives open space for 'resistance'. According to Foucault, the statements or units of discourse—graphs, tables *etcetera* as well as written statements—that make up a discursive formation or archive do not merely describe knowledge: they regulate, produce, and distribute it as truth. Their operation is characterised as a 'positivity'. The notion of productive signifying texts that are not only linguistic but include art and social acts expands the notion of discourse in a manner useful to a critique of art therapy, which is distinguished among therapies for its emphasis on the visual and non-verbal. The idea that what is sayable and visible is historically conditioned is suggestive for a revised problematics of art therapy. Art therapy often concerns itself with an opposition of seeing and saying—with the idea that art makes visible that which cannot be spoken. This gives rise to a hermeneutics of the art therapy product. From a Foucauldian perspective, I am at least equally concerned with how the sayable and the visible are produced, through historical relations of power, in binary opposition to the unspeakable and the invisible. I am also concerned with what art therapy does as well as with what it 'means'.

Gazes and critical visualities

Foucault, having taken up the theme of the psychiatric/clinical gaze in *Madness and civilisation: A History of Insanity in the Age of Reason* (2001), extends his analysis of gazes and visualities in *Birth of the Clinic: an Archaeology of Medical Perception* (1994b). The constitution of the medical gaze through the practice of dissecting corpses in clinical anatomy renders disease visible and divisible below the envelope of skin. This inaugurates a positivist science that analyses life from the point of view of death, or the analytic of finitude. The medical model is formed and then mapped onto an understanding of emotional and psychological ills. The image of the corpse and its dissection speaks eloquently to the effects of pathologising, categorising and objectifying practices within psychology and psychotherapy. The clinical gaze is a particular and dominant visuality that may be either reproduced or challenged by the visualities of art therapy, given a notable tension in art therapy theory and practice between the certainties of scientific positivism and the notion of therapy as a form of art.

The specificity of Foucault's accounts of ways of seeing breaks up the empire of the gaze into local and embodied visualities. Gary Shapiro (2003) claims that Foucault often parallels his major works with shorter expositions in terms of the visual, so that, for instance, his analysis of the visual practices of Manet composes an alternative to panopticism.

Gillian Rose (2001) offers a useful account of Foucauldian discourse analysis in relation to the emerging field of visual culture and the development of a critical visual methodology. As a visual methodology, discourse analysis can ask what is made visible through the signifying practices of art, what is made visible or obscured in the exegesis or ekphrasis of an image, and how specific visualities interrelate with specific signifying practices. Discourse analysis can also highlight specific visualities and signifying practices as forms of resistance. Gillian Rose suggests that, while one dimension of discourse analysis focuses on art as a signifying practice, another dimension focuses on the social and institutional production of visualities. This may be a useful schematic separation, although Foucault emphasised a relationship of mutual constitution between social and signifying practices. I agree with Gillian Rose that researchers need to reflect on "how you as a critic of visual issues are looking" (Rose, 2001, p. 16). However, I do not agree that Foucauldian work fails to meet this criterion for a critical visual methodology because "discourse analysis refuses to be reflexive" (Rose, 2001, p. 142). A contemporary Foucauldian approach does not refuse to acknowledge reflexivity, but it does complicate the assumption of an essential, humanist subject who 'looks', reflects and reflexively acts.

According to Gillian Rose visual imagery can never be innocent; it is always constructed, through various practices, technologies and knowledges. The meaning of an image or set of images is made at three sites: production, the image itself, and its audiencing (Rose, 2001). The practices, technologies and knowledges involved in the construction of visual images and their meanings in art therapy are a complex interplay of the psychological, the aesthetic and the social. They encompass the implicit and the explicit, and span the professional cultures of both therapy and art and the cultures of those individuals and groups who come to therapy. The construction of images within the context of art psychotherapy is usually based in, and reproduces, a theoretical assumption that 'art' is an expression

—albeit often in a disguised or displaced form—of an 'authentic' aspect of the interiority of its maker(s).

This assumption is structured by, and also perpetuates, modern humanistic and psychological discourses about the 'nature' of both art and therapy. The art of art therapy is often also thought to express its maker's relationship to significant others, including the therapist. It is less frequently thought to express a relation to the social and to culture, including visual culture, or these cultural and social relations are relegated to a second order. Even when a broad account is offered of the expressive possibilities of art therapy, an implicit hierarchy may operate to suggest that the expression of interiority (perhaps drawn out through the relationship to the therapist as well as to the artwork) is the primary purpose of art therapy. If the therapeutic frame is psychodynamic, the art making might be regarded as a partly unconscious product that repeats historic and current patterns of personality and relationship through a three way transference to both the artwork and the therapist (Schaverien, 1992; Case and Dalley, 1992). If the framework is existential or humanistic, then the artwork may be regarded as an expression of authentic (or inauthentic) consciousness (Moon, 1995, 2001; Garai, 2001). The notion of art as purely an expression, rather than also as a production, of feelings, stories and relationships, tends to mask operations of power and the potential for relations of either co-construction or domination in the art therapeutic context.

When therapeutic art making is viewed as primarily the expression of a person's interior world in relationship to a supportive and/or containing Other, then conditions for the production of such an image are likely to be established to facilitate this form of expression. For instance, 'expressive' and plastic media may be preferred technologies and may be given priority over photography, film, video and computer generated imagery. A room and furniture may be set up to encourage an alternation between one to one interpersonal engagement and attention to the processes of making art, perhaps with some comfortable chairs at angles to each other (or in a circle for a family or group) in one part of the room and art tables and materials in another part of the room. The person(s) coming to therapy may be engaged, through explicit and implicit messages, in a view that an intense or absorbed attitude and expressive rather than conceptual forms of art making are to be understood as appropriate therapeutic engagement and authentic self-expression. They may then produce an image in such a way that the image itself authenticates the notion of expressing the inner world of the maker, and the therapist, as audience to this production, may confirm this through her responses—perhaps with subtle and even unintended signs of interest or encouragement. Such an account, while over-simplified, draws attention to how theory and practice work together to reproduce and create each other, and even to construct the work of art itself.

Yet at the same time as the truths of art therapy are reproduced and documented at multiple sites of construction of the art therapy image, these truths are also challenged and perverted. Each citation and performance of the subjects, relations and images of art psychotherapy is as much an unravelling as a performance of truth. 'Resistance', in all its multiple and overlapping meanings, comes into play. Art therapy is implicated in the citation and reproduction of dominant discourses in relation to both art and psychology, and in an associated reproduction of the subject of modernity. However, this reproduction is never total. There are always and inevitably subtexts, slippages, variations, excesses, 'mistakes', rebellions and so forth that signal the potential to move beyond the taken-for-granted truths of art therapy.

Hence art therapists work, knowingly and unknowingly, at the sites of production, audiencing and the image itself, and this work both reconstitutes the known and true, and opens a space for difference. Art psychotherapists have argued to varying degrees that art therapy is the creation of something new as well as the reflection of something deeply inscribed in the psyche (see Case and Dalley, 2006). This position mediates the tendency for the work of art to be subjugated to the psychological in theorisations of art therapy. However, the view of art therapy as creative as well as expressive does not generally entail a consideration of the positivity of social and intrapsychic relations of power. The notion is still one of art making as an expression and refinement of interiority, rather than as a production or enfoldment of the space of interiority itself.

Power relations

> If power were never anything but repressive, if it never did anything but to say no, do you really think one would be brought to obey it? What makes power hold good, what makes it accepted, is simply the fact that it doesn't only weigh on us as a force that says no; it also traverses and produces things, it induces pleasure, forms knowledge, produces discourse. It needs to be considered as a productive network that runs through the whole social body, much more than as a negative instance whose function is repression. (Foucault, 2000a, p. 120)

When Foucault critiques the human sciences he is speaking not only of theories, but also of disciplines, as assemblages of discourses and practices (Milchman and Rosenberg, 2000). According to this view, 'truth' is produced not only in formal theoretical writing, but also at the everyday, administrative level of documentation. Such documentation—course leaflets, the public documents of professional associations, case files—can be seen as producing implicit knowledges that are mutually reinforcing with more formal academic and clinical discourses. Discourses and practices are also considered to be mutually conditioning and constituting. In these ways, 'higher knowledge' is thoroughly implicated with disciplinary power.

Foucault has sometimes been misunderstood as claiming that power and knowledge are the same thing, whereas he tells a nuanced story of an historically changing relationship between knowledge and power wherein power is implicated in what forms of knowledge become dominant and are seen as having legitimate claims to truth (Foucault, 2000m). For Foucault, power exists "only as exercised by some on others"; it is "an action upon the actions of others" (2000f, pp. 340–341). In contemporary scenarios of ethical subjectivity, power is also an action upon the actions of one's self. Modern power is thus simultaneously individualising and tending toward domination. According to Foucault, modern power does not primarily operate through repression, but through the decentralised production of what will count as truth and normality. In liberal democracies, surveillance by the State is increasingly replaced by practices of management of the self and others according to a proliferating range of norms. Pastoral power becomes secularised and invested in the disciplines of the human sciences, giving these disciplines' theories, practices and practitioners a particularly authoritative status in peoples' lives. This insight troubles the liberatory claims of progressive therapies, since the pursuit of freedom through self-knowledge serves to tighten the noose of (self) subjectification.

Foucault's analysis of power relations invites a consideration of the extent to which my theories and practices as an art therapist might collude with or challenge the expansion of normalising power (and its distressing consequences for people who are diagnosed or labelled, or who label themselves, as abnormal or deficient) (Foucault, 2003b). It prompts a consideration of those ideas and practices within art therapy that assist people to resist the totalisation of their identities that can sometimes be the consequence of contact with helping professionals and institutions. While the power relations invested in therapeutic authority cannot be avoided, neither are they inherently good or bad (Rose, 2000a). An understanding of power as productive suggests that art therapy can assist in the development of capacities that assist people to negotiate relations with themselves and others. An acknowledgment that therapists are involved in constituting the identities of those who come to art therapy enables therapists to aim to exercise therapeutic authority as consultatively as possible and with a minimum of domination.

A Foucauldian perspective of power's positivity can give rise to a number of questions in relation to those who come to art therapy as 'clients'. How does art therapy describe/constitute its clients? How is 'clienthood' understood in art therapy literature and in other documentation? How does art therapy state its aims for the client's relationship with his/herself, with the therapist, with the art process and product? What aspects of the client are problematised in the documentation? How does art therapy 'enrol' clients in the process of therapy? How is meaning attributed to the client's experience of therapy and to the artwork? What part is played in the constitution of the client by the therapeutic relationship including the three way transference (here considered as a 'technology') and the activity of making of art? How are the therapist's listening practices engaged in constituting the hermeneutics of the subject of therapy (Foucault, 2005), including art therapy?

Discipline

Whereas domination leaves the subject no choice, disciplinary power works by coercion. It organises space, activities, time, and an integration of all of these (McHoul and Grace, 1993). While prison provides an extreme and formative instance, disciplinary power also operates in other institutions such as barracks, hospitals and schools. According to the perspective of disciplinary power, the clinical setting is composed of spaces, times and practices that act on art therapists and their clients to produce the professional and clinical subjects of art therapy (cf. Tipple, 2003; McHoul and Grace, 1993). Training courses could also be viewed through this disciplinary lens, by analysing timetabling, assessment processes, the supervision of practicums, etcetera.

It would be far-fetched to assume an equivalence between the regularities of therapy—discursive practices which punctuate rather than define either a community or institutional life—and the totality of life in prison. Nevertheless, therapy is administrated in ways which regulate the subjects of therapy (both therapist and client) in time and space—the therapeutic hour, the regularity of appointments, the arrangements of furniture and bodies in space—and includes practices of surveillance such as the one way mirror, case conferencing, duties of care and protection, and various systems for assessment and record keeping. Therapy practices can be 'double-edged': therapeutic confidentiality and therapeutic abstinence, for instance, are important protections, and they may also operate as technologies of hierarchisation, individuation and isolation—as dividing practices. Even the formation of the art therapy training or therapeutic group, with participants and leader/conductor seated in a circle, each participant's image laid out before her, might mirror something of the architecture of surveillance exemplified (although never practically realised) in the Panopticon (Foucault, 1991, 1996b). Such groups substitute a more apparently open and egalitarian form of observation for the hierarchical discipline of the prison: the disciplinary gaze democratised, circulated, 'ethicalised', turned towards the normalisation of others and oneself.

The repressive hypothesis

Foucault proposes that repression is only one of the modes by which an aspect of human existence becomes an object of attention. He traces the rise of the repressive hypothesis in relation to the problematisation of sexuality (1980) [2]. He is interested in how repression becomes a dominant hypothesis to the extent that the supposed repression of 'the truth of sex' comes to be taken as a sin, and as the repression of the truth of ourselves.

Through this repressive hypothesis, a form of transgression and revolt is made possible, but this revolt is itself an inversion, caught up in the same discursive terms as that which it seeks to resist. Whereas once one confessed the sins of the flesh and aspired to purity, now one confesses the sin of sexual repression and aspires to sexual liberation. The technologies of pastoral power, in particular the practices of Christian confession, are expanded and then secularised. A continuing imperative to examine oneself and to confess the truth shapes and is shaped by the domains of psychoanalysis and the psychotherapies, such that (art) psychotherapy is inextricably implicated in this incitement to confess 'the truth of ourselves'.

Foucault acknowledges practices of liberation from oppression, giving the example of a colonised people liberating themselves from their colonisers, but he also suggests that, just as repression is only one mode of power, so processes of liberation do not define all the possible practices of freedom (Foucault, 2000b). Moreover, frameworks which derive their explanatory and critical capacity from a notion of power as primarily repressive can be seen as discursively producing the very lack of freedom they would wish to either explain as inevitable or challenge as unjust. Foucault's critique of the repressive hypothesis thus constitutes a radical criticism of both the psychodynamic and humanistic underpinnings of art therapy, which rest in the first instance on a theory of intrapsychic repression, and in the second instance on a theory of liberating a true and authentic self.

An analytic of power

Although Foucault initially saw Freudian psychoanalytic theory in terms of its radical potential for decentring dominant conceptions of a rational subject, in his later work he became more concerned with the subjugating/ subjectifying effects of Freudian theory. I understand this shift, not as 'progress' in relation to the 'truth' about Freud, but as a critical and historical comment on the differing discursive effects of Freudian psychoanalysis. The contradictory potential of psychoanalysis to disrupt rationality and yet to rationalise the hermeneutics of the modern subject is very much in accordance with my own clinical and personal therapeutic experiences, and it is a dilemma that haunts the territory of this book.

In relation to the effects on the subject of the deployment of sexuality, Freudian psychoanalysis becomes an occasion for the further rationalisation of the repressive hypothesis. However, Foucault does not read Freud as simply an architect of a theme of repression. Lacan's account of Freudian psychoanalysis substitutes a law of desire for the repression of instincts. Lacanian desire is 'produced' rather than repressed, but it is also always already governed by 'the father's no'. In this way, Lacan and Freud share a negative representation of power in which you are "always already trapped" (1980, p. 83). Foucault sketches out this dominant representation of power in order to establish the basis for an alternative explanation. Such a power works in the negative by specifying limit or lack, it creates binaries, and it lays down rules for what can be said, so that the object is only intelligible within an understanding of that object's relation to the law.

In contrast to this dominant, 'juridico-discursive' representation of power, Foucault offers an analytics of power's positivity. This is not an alternative theory of power because Foucault asserts that power does not exist separately from being exercised. Since power has no separate ontological status, rather than saying what it is, Foucault attempts to specify how it works. As "a mode of action upon the action of others" (2000f, p. 341), power is distinct from, although often tending towards, domination. Foucault (1980) elaborates an analytics of modern power as productive, decentralised and mutually constitutive with knowledge. Power relations are conceptualised as tending towards but never achieving totalisation because they are always creating and responding to resistances.

Foucault (1980) offers some suggestions for analysing relations of power. In taking up these points in relation to my book, I could be attentive to the following considerations:

- a sensitivity to discontinuities, sudden breaks and multiple trajectories within accounts of art therapy;
- a consideration of anecdotal accounts of art therapy as mutually constitutive with formal claims to truth;
- a consideration of how case studies and other accounts of specific clinical practices of art therapy are mutually constitutive with art therapy theory;

- a focus on the subject positions made available to clients, practitioners and trainees within the literature and within clinical and pedagogical art therapies;
- a consideration of how art therapists actively participate in the discursive construction of their own and their clients' subjectivities; and/or
- reconceptualisation of intrapsychic resistance as resistance to power-knowledge.

Ethics

Ethics, in Foucault's sense, concerns the production of ethical subjects through particular practices of the self. These 'technologies of the self' do not replace other modes of power, although they do come to prominence in modernity, particularly through the rise and popularisation of the psychological disciplines. Accordingly, the ethical constitution of the subjects of therapy is mutually constitutive with the discursive production of the clinical subject of therapy in the literature, and with the disciplinary production of therapists and their clients through pedagogical, clinical and professional relations of power.

Foucault makes a distinction between morality and ethics. Ethics is that part of morality which constitutes an ethical subject through practices of the self in relation to the self. No one is simply an agent of a moral code, since there are different ways of conducting oneself in relation to moral precepts. Just as moral codes differ widely, so do the various aspects of ethical formation. The relative importance of moral code and ethics can also differ—some moralities have highly prescriptive codes while others are more open and ethically based. In relation to the training and regulation of therapists, for instance, there can be a conflict of 'moralities' between educational and professional institutions. The professional associations may consider themselves obliged to focus more strongly on prescribing rules and standards, while educational courses may focus more strongly on producing self-regulating ethical subjects (Linnell, 2003).

Foucault (2000m, pp. 263–269; 1992, pp. 27–28) offers four points to consider in mapping the constitution of the self as an ethical subject. This map raises questions about the ethical self-constitution of the subjects of art therapy:

- *Ethical substance*: the aspect of self that is considered relevant to moral conduct. (What do art therapists, trainees and clients understand to be the aspect of themselves that art therapy works on in order to transform?)

- *Mode of subjection*: the way in which the individual establishes her relation to the moral code and recognises herself as obliged to put it into practice. (How do these subjects of art therapy come to recognise that these ethics are 'truly' applicable to them?)
- *Ethical work* or *self forming activity*: practices which one performs, not only to change behaviour, but also to attempt to transform oneself into the ethical subject of one's behaviour. (What techniques of the self must be practiced in order to achieve and sustain competence in relation to this aspect of selfhood?)
- *The telos*: a commitment not only to moral action but also to attaining a particular mode of being. (What mode of being do these subjects aspire to attain through the acceptance and practice of these ethics?)

The constitution of the 'ethical substance', or the aspect of the self that is problematised as in need of transformation, changes across time and contexts. Whereas in Christian theology the dominant ethical substance tended to be 'desire', for Kant and the Enlightenment it was 'intention', and in the mid to late 20th century it seemed to be 'feelings' (Foucault, 2000m). Within a Western, consumer-based democracy, Rose (1992, 1998) suggests that the dominant contemporary ethical substance is our capacity to make choices.

It seems to me that different therapies promote different conceptions of ethical substance, and therefore make different assumptions about what kind of therapeutic transformation, or telos, is to be achieved. If the ethical substance differs, so too do the subjective state to which one aspires, and the skills one must practice to attain that way of being. Rose (2000a) suggests that 'behaviour' is the ethical substance to be transformed in contemporary positivist psychology, although I would add that 'thinking' as well as 'behaviour' is the ethical substance of the cognitive-behavioural models that are considered best practice in Australia at present. Similarly, instincts and unconscious desires are the ethical substance of psychoanalysis, and our 'feelings' are the ethical substance of humanistic approaches.

Both Rose (2000a, 2000b) and White (2002) invoke the relevance of Foucault's ethics for the theory and practice of therapy. Rose and White concur that therapy is constitutive of clients' identities, and that therapists are privileged and influential in the power relations of therapy—therefore an ethical obligation of therapists is to participate in power relations with a minimum of domination. Although both Rose and White focus primarily on the ethical constitution of clients, both authors also acknowledge the relevance of considering the ethical constitution of therapists, with White (1997) dedicating a volume to the lives of narrative therapists.

However, there are significant differences between the ways that Rose and White engage with a Foucauldian perspective. Rose (2000b) follows Foucault in using the classical Greek concept of *techne* to draw out the pedagogical relationship between therapist and client made explicit in cognitive behavioural therapy but implicit in all psychotherapies, even psychoanalysis. Rose suggests that it is not a matter of whether, but of how, a transmission of life skills is effected between therapist and client. White and other narrative therapists have preferred a 'co-authoring' metaphor for the therapeutic relationship (White and Epston, 1990). For these therapists, an heuristic use of Foucault's notions of resistance and the proliferation of discourses, and of Derrida's deconstruction, provide a basis for locating, narrativising and amplifying those 'preferred' ways of doing (action) and being (identity) which are marginalised and/or implicit in the stories of people coming to therapy. While in a broad sense this might imply a pedagogical relation, such a pedagogy would eschew the teaching of life skills in the conventional sense. From the perspective of narrative therapy, the 'life skills' discourse is implicated in the construction of norms associated with a discourse of personal failure. A 'life skills' approach (even if these skills involve foregoing 'outcomes' in favour of the dance of transference and counter transference) assumes a lack on the part of a client that reinforces the expert position of the therapist.

It seems to me that the ethical substance of therapists' lives closely parallels the ethical substance assumed to be relevant for the 'clients' of particular approaches to therapy (Linnell, 2004). Indeed, the application of these ethics to themselves is a primary means by which therapists come to understand and embody the historically and culturally contingent theories and practices of their discipline as 'normal, natural and true'. Cognitive-behavioural therapists learn and apply systematic thinking and behavioural intervention, thereby transforming themselves into the subjects of rational thought and reasonable action. Psychoanalysts undergo a training analysis in order to develop 'insight' into their own psychic topographies, and humanistic therapists engage in experiential training in order to gain self-awareness and cultivate high levels of empathy and intuition. Both psychoanalytically informed and humanistic therapists thus become subject to the requirement to 'know themselves' (Foucault, 2005). I have found myself wondering to what extent the ethical substance might differ between a psychodynamically and/or humanistically based, and an aesthetically based, practice of art therapy. In the former approach, the ethical substance might be unconscious processes and/or feelings, whereas in an aesthetic approach it might be something like 'imagination' or 'creativity'. Since narrative therapists regard their task as the co-authoring of lives and relationships, for a narrative practitioner the ethical substance to be transformed is the landscape of her own narratives of 'action' and 'identity' in connection with the life narratives of significant others, including those who come to therapy.

These different ethics of therapy are all predicated on the assumption of a psychological subject. According to Rose:

> Psychology has participated in the invention of a variety of procedures by means of which individuals, using the techniques elaborated by psychological experts, can act upon their bodies, their emotions, their beliefs and their forms of conduct in order to transform themselves, in order to achieve autonomous selfhood...Overarching all these differences, psychological techniques of the self seek to instill in the subject a constant and intense self scrutiny, an evaluation of our personal experiences, emotions and feelings in relation to psychological images of fulfilment and autonomy. Within this psychological ethics, the self is obliged to live its life tied to the project of its own identity. (Rose, 2000a, p. 18)

While narrative practice is mediated by an acknowledgement and decentring of therapeutic privilege, and by an understanding of the self as constructed in relation to discourse and the other, narrative practitioners are not separate from the discourses we attempt to critique. Narrative therapies are necessarily implicated in the broader project of modern psychology, social science and therapy. In particular, intention, which Foucault identified as an ethical substance associated with the Enlightenment, is often a privileged category in narrative therapy, suggesting a tendency in such therapy to reconstitute the rational subject of Enlightenment. If narrative therapy is to continue to take up a Foucauldian ethic of critique, then the critical potential of narrative therapy to disturb the constitution of an autonomous self-regulating individual must, paradoxically, remain in question.

Refusing what we are: an ethic of permanent critique

> Maybe the target nowadays is not to discover what we are but to refuse what we are...to imagine and to build up what we could be in order to get rid of this kind of political 'doublebind' which is the simultaneous individualisation and totalisation of modern power structures...We have to promote new forms of subjectivity through the refusal of the kind of individuality which has been imposed on us for several centuries. (Foucault, 2000f, p. 336)

Foucault has me wondering—what would constitute a refusal of "what we are" as art therapists? How could we refuse to incite our clients to discover who they 'truly' are? How can we refuse what we are as researchers, as educators? What 'becomings' are made possible by such a refusal? What freedoms are thus engendered? If the dominant contemporary ethical substance is choice (Rose, 1998), within a contemporary biopolitic that makes us the economic subjects of a diversity of choices that nevertheless fold us back into a neoliberal rationality (Foucault, 2008), then it becomes crucial to problematise self-awareness and agency in order to "refuse what we are". This ethic informs the particular notion of freedom in Foucault, and in this book.

Foucault asserted that he wrote "experience book[s]", as opposed to "truth book[s]" or "demonstration book[s]" (2000l, p. 246). Such books are inspired by a personal experience of the writer that the book makes accessible to others. They render current social and political mechanisms intelligible, thus enabling a detachment from and a different perception of the present. They invite a change in modes of thinking, and open onto the possibility of collective practices of transformation. Foucault is worth quoting at length on the inseparability of practices of critique and transformation. Rather than critical thought being a precondition for a deferred moment of trans-formation, such thinking *is* the work of transformation:

> [A]bove all, I don't think criticism can be set against transformation, "ideal" criticism against "real" transformation. A critique does not consist in saying things are not good the way they are. It consists in seeing on what types of assumptions, of familiar notions, of established, unexamined ways of thinking the accepted practices are based
>
> ...Thought does exist, both beyond and before systems and edifices of discourse. It is something that is often hidden but always drives everyday behaviours...Criticism consists in uncovering that thought and trying to change it: showing that things are not as obvious as people believe, making it so that what is taken for granted is no longer taken for granted. To do criticism is to make harder those acts that are now too easy.
>
> Understood in these terms, criticism (and radical criticism) is utterly indispensable for any transformation...[A]s soon as people begin to have trouble thinking things the way they have been thought, trans-formation becomes at the same time very urgent, very difficult and entirely possible.
>
> So there is not a time for criticism and a time for transformation...As a matter of fact, I believe the work of deep transformation can be done in the always turbulent atmosphere of a continuous criticism. (Foucault, 2000j, pp. 456–457)

An aesthetics of existence

In his late work, Foucault (2000m, 1990) challenges the separation of the aesthetic sphere by elaborating an aesthetic metaphor for the ethical shaping of our selves and our relationships. As an alternative to the frequently invoked concepts of self-knowledge and self-discovery, Foucault suggests that the ongoing work of ethical subjectivity might consist in 'making' ourselves as a work of art, and that this might be our major contemporary ethical and aesthetic task: "From the idea that the self is not given to us, I think there is only one practical consequence: we have to create ourselves as a work of art" (Foucault, 2000m, p. 262). To me, this is a beautiful instance of how Foucault opens space for refusal and creation within and against the contemporary discursive order. Despite Foucault's differences with Derrida, the ethical substance of 'choice' could be seen as coming 'under erasure' in Foucault's work, in that choice is both discursively constructed and the work of thought.

Reading Foucault according to his own notion of experience/experiment, his work is as much a performance as an exposition of an ethic of permanent critique and an aesthetics of existence. His writing embodies the art of engaging the reader in an experience of the transformative possibilities of resistance.

Foucault's ethics/aesthetics of existence could fit with a recent turn, or return, to aesthetics within art therapy theory and practice. I am struck by the consonance between Foucault's suggestion of an aesthetics of existence and the 'aesthetic turn' in art therapy, and between the metaphor of making our selves and the experience and expertise in art making that is necessary to arts-based therapy. Accordingly, it is tempting to turn from what Rose (1998) calls the 'psy' disciplines, from the association of art therapy with psychology, psychiatry, psychoanalysis and psychotherapy, toward an aesthetic basis for art therapy practice. There is a risk in this turn, however, of romanticising and essentialising art, and thereby reproducing an historical and ongoing binary which in art therapy literature is expressed as a tension between 'art psychotherapy' and 'art as healing'. Just as one can engage Foucauldian genealogy to explore the relation of the self to the self, one can similarly situate the concept of 'art as healing', a concept which often suggests that there is a universal and transcendent character to art's healing powers. While some commentators identify precursors of art therapy in earlier times or different cultures (McNiff, 1992; Junge, 1994), I suggest it would also be unwise to assume any equivalence between these phenomena and contemporary art therapy. What European culture designates as 'art' may not exist as such within those Indigenous cultures that do not separate the aesthetic, cultural and social spheres.

Foucault suggests that, rather than mapping a colonising sameness of subjectivity and culture over the face of difference, we could practice an art of making ourselves strange to ourselves. Such an ethics and aesthetics—one might say an (a)e(s)th(et)ics of existence—avoids the binary of the aesthetic and the psychological by bringing poststructural notions of ethics and subjectivity into play. Having argued that Foucault's late suggestion for a contemporary *telos* tends to reconstitute the Enlightenment subject he is wishing to destabilise, some poststructural feminist commentators propose an 'ethico-politics' based in the differences within and between embodied subjects (e.g. Diprose, 1994). However, Foucault's notion of his works as books of experience (2000l) and his ethic of permanent critique (2000j) arguably construct a very different ethics and aesthetics of existence to that of the Enlightenment subject. For Foucault, rather than either 'we' or 'I' being transcendent or prior, both are mobile and unstable. Just as the 'I' is not I-dentical with itself, 'we' signifies not a diverse though relatively stable and developing sociality, but a nomadic and strategic coming together around particular points of resistance (Foucault, 2000i).

I am nevertheless interested in what is made available to thought by these feminist practices of 'reading Foucault against himself' (Butler, 1999). In particular, I am interested in the further destabilisation of the self that can come from close engagement with notions of the Other. Moroever, in engaging with the slipperiness and discontinuities of Foucault in the context of this book, I have become aware of my tendency to try to 'make sense' of Foucault in ways that are reductive of the Other of his text. Thus, even my suggestion that Foucault's work could be thought as a performance of his ethic of permanent critique and an art of engaging the reader in an experience of the transformative possibilities of resistance is a move that threatens to unify disunity and to fix the unfixable. Of course, Foucault always escapes my attempts at capture. Speaking after his death, his friend Hélène Cixous asked:

> He is a nomad, even in his work: do you believe that he has built his house? Not at all. 'That's not it', he said to me about his last volume, 'I've been mistaken. I have to re-cast everything. Go elsewhere. Do it otherwise'. (Cixous, cited in O'Leary, 2002, p. 171)

She is settling into the weave and cut of her new jacket, almost as if it might become a second skin. Yet, catching a glimpse of herself in the mirrored surfaces of the art deco interior, she mistakes herself momentarily for someone else, as though this Other, both familiar and strange, is walking toward her.

Drifting now from an imagined world to the more subtle fictions of memoir, she remembers a conversation with a colleague that took place only this morning. Michelle Cherubin had recently presented her work to an audience of her peers in the local community health centre. Searching for a quotation—just *one* quotation that would do justice to the immensity of Foucault and his influence on her practice as a therapist—Michelle had chosen this question:

> What can I become in the contemporary order of being?

It is such a beautiful question.

Sheridan plays with the question, considering for a moment whether the 'I' is, and must remain, I-solated from the Other.

> What can 'I' become in the contemporary order of being?
>
> What can 'I' become in the presence of the Other?
>
> How might my/our becomings disorder the contemporary order of being?

The metaphor of fabric/fabrication that I have taken up in this chapter is suggestive of the paradox that an individual subject is, at once, citational and different, material and imagined, closely determined and emergent. A garment is fabricated from existing materials, belongs to a recognisable genre of clothing or fashion, and yet can simultaneously be the creation of something new. Similarly, the individual's fabrication within discourse is paradoxically the condition of subjectivity. Subjectivity, in this view, implies the creation of something, or rather someone, who emerges and is recognisable within an existing sociality and relations of power, yet is also unique and unsubstitutable (Bansel, 2008). The writing subject, myself in this instance, is also produced and limited by existing discourses. At the same time, the writing subject can fabricate, from those discourses, different possibilities for the subjects and practices of therapy.

The next chapter is a companion piece to the one you have just read. Chapter 3 dramatises my engagement with several theorists who work at the intersections of poststructural theory with feminism and postcolonialism, thereby troubling the autonomy of the modern individual and refusing to privilege Western and patriarchal discourses. I extend the metaphor of fabrication into a consideration of the critical and transformative potential of marginalised narratives and subjugated categories of being. I then explore how these theories, particularly the work of Butler, open up the possibility of thinking narrative therapy and art psychotherapy together, so that the subjects of therapy emerge in response to the ethical call of the Other.

---

[1] From Horkheimer and Adorno (2002, p. 95 and p. 118).
cont.

[2] The problematisation of sexuality, if not often the overt focus of contemporary therapy, remains implicit in its Freudian psychodynamic legacy. Moreover, the liberation of this problematised sexuality is intrinsic to the project of the humanistic therapies. From a Marxist-humanistic perspective in therapy—the perspective, for instance of Wilhelm Reich—it is as much our task to liberate the truth of our sex and of our authentic selves from sexual and emotional repression as it is to liberate our working lives from economic oppression. However Foucault's critique of the repressive hypothesis positions such 'liberatory' politics as implicated in the reproduction of the very operations of power that they would hope to critique.

REFERENCES

Abu Lughod, L. & Lutz, C. (Eds.). (1990). *Language and the politics of emotion.* Cambridge: Cambridge University Press.

Bansel (2008). *Subjectivity at work.* Unpublished doctoral dissertation, University of Western Sydney.

Bogue, R. (2003). *Deleuze on music, painting and the arts.* New York: Routledge.

Carey, M., Walther, S. & Russell, S. (2009). The absent but implicit: a map to support therapeutic enquiry. *Family Process,* 48(3), 319–331.

Case, C. & Dalley, D. (1992). *The handbook of art therapy.* London: Routledge.

— (2006). *The handbook of art therapy.* (2nd ed.). London & New York: Routledge.

Cixous, H., & members of the Centre d'Etudes Feminines. (1988). Conversations. In S. Sellers (Ed.), *Writing differences: readings from the seminar of Hélène Cixous* (pp. 141–154). Milton Keynes: Open University Press. (Original interview recorded 1986).

Davies, B. (2000). *A body of writing.* Walnut Creek, CA: AltaMira Press.

Deleuze, G. (1994). *Difference and repetition.* New York: Columbia University Press. (Original work published 1968).

— (1981). *Francis Bacon: logique de la sensation* (Vol. 1). Paris: Editions de la difference.

Deleuze, G., & Guattari, F. (1977a). *Anti-Oedipus.* Minneapolis: University of Minnesota Press. (Original work published 1972).

— (1977b). May 14, 1914. One or several wolves? *Semiotexte. Anti-Oedipus: from psychoanalysis to schizopolitics,* 2(3), 137–147.

— (1987). *A thousand plateaus.* Minneapolis: University of Minnesota Press. (Original work published 1980).

Derrida, J. (1978). *Writing and difference.* London: Routledge. (Original work published 1967).

— (1987). *The truth in painting.* Chicago: Chicago University Press. (Original work published 1978).

— (1995). Ja, or the faux-bond II. In E. Webber (Ed.), *Points...Interviews, 1974–1994* (pp. 30–77). California: Stanford University Press.

— (1997). *Of grammatology.* Baltimore & London: John Hopkins University Press. (Original work published 1967).

— (2007). *Learning to live finally: The last interview.* Australia: Allen & Unwin.

Diprose, R. (1994). *The Bodies of Women. Ethics, Embodiment and Sexual Difference.* London and New York: Routledge.

Foucault, M. (1980). *The history of sexuality, Volume 1: an introduction.* New York: Vintage Books. (Original work published 1976).

— (1990). *The history of sexuality, Volume 3: The care of the self.* London: Penguin Books. (Original work published 1984).

— (1991). *Discipline and punish: the birth of the prison.* London: Penguin. (Original work published 1975).

— (1992). *The history of sexuality, Volume 2: The use of pleasure.* London: Penguin Books. (Original work published 1984).

— (1994a). *The order of things: An archaeology of the human sciences.* New York: Vintage Books. (Original work published 1966).

— (1994b). *The birth of the clinic: an archaeology of medical perception.* New York: Vintage Books. (Original work published 1963).

— (1996a). Clarifications on the question of power. In *Foucault live: collected interviews 1961–1984* (pp. 255–263). New York: Semiotexte. (Original interview conducted 1978).

— (1996b). The concern for truth. In *Foucault live: collected interviews 1961–1984* (pp. 455–464). New York: Semiotexte. (Original work published 1984).

— (2000a). Truth and power. In J. Faubion (Ed.), *Essential works of Foucault 1954–1984, Volume 3, Michel Foucault: Power* (pp. 111–133). London: Penguin Books. (Original interview conducted 1976).

— (2000b). The ethics of the concern of the self as a practice of freedom. In P. Rabinow, (Ed.), *Essential works of Foucault 1954–1984, Volume 1, Michel Foucault: Ethics, subjectivity and truth* (pp. 281–301). London: Penguin Books. (Interview conducted 1984).

— (2000c). Life, experience and science. In J. Faubion (Ed.), *Essential works of Foucault 1954–1984, Volume 3, Michel Foucault: Aesthetics, method and epistemology* (pp. 459–463). London: Penguin Books. (Original work published 1985).

— (2000d). Questions of method. In J. Faubion (Ed.), *Essential works of Foucault 1954–1984, Volume 3, Michel Foucault: Power* (pp. 223–238.) London: Penguin Books. (Original work published 1980).

— (2000e). Nietzsche, genealogy, history. In J. Faubion (Ed.), *Essential works of Foucault 1954–1984, Volume 3, Michel Foucault: Aesthetics, method and epistemology* (pp. 369–392). London: Penguin Books. (Original work published 1971).

— (2000f). The subject and power. In J. Faubion (Ed.), *Essential works of Foucault 1954–1984, Volume 3, Michel Foucault: Power* (pp. 326–348). London: Penguin Books. (Original interview published 1982).

— (2000g). What is Enlightenment? In P. Rabinow (Ed.), *Essential works of Foucault 1954–1984, Volume 1, Michel Foucault: Ethics, subjectivity and truth* (pp. 303–319). London: Penguin Books. (Original work published 1984).

— (2000h). Governmentality. In J. Faubion (Ed.), *Essential works of Foucault 1954–1984, Volume 3, Michel Foucault: Power* (pp. 201–222). London: Penguin Books. (Original work published 1978).

— (2000i). Polemics, politics and problematizations. In P. Rabinow (Ed.), *Essential works of Foucault 1954–1984, Volume 1, Michel Foucault: Ethics, subjectivity and truth* (pp. 111–120). London: Penguin Books. (Original interview conducted 1984).

— (2000j). So is it important to think? In J. Faubion (Ed.), *Essential works of Foucault 1954–1984, Volume 3, Michel Foucault: Power* (pp. 454–458). London: Penguin Books. (Interview conducted 1981).

— (writing as Maurice Florence). (2000k). Foucault. In J. Faubion (Ed.), *Essential works of Foucault 1954–1984, Volume 3, Michel Foucault: Aesthetics, method and epistemology* (pp. 459–463). London: Penguin Books. (Original work published early 1980s).

— (2000l). An interview with Michel Foucault. In J. Faubion (Ed.), *Essential works of Foucault 1954–1984, Volume 3, Michel Foucault: Power* (pp. 239–297). London: Penguin Books. (Original interview conducted 1980).

— (2000m). On the genealogy of ethics: an overview of work in progress. In P. Rabinow, (Ed.), *Essential works of Foucault 1954–1984, Volume 1, Michel Foucault: Ethics, subjectivity and truth* (pp. 253–280). London: Penguin Books. (Interview conducted 1983).

— (2001). *Madness and civilisation: The history of insanity in the age of reason*. London & New York: Routledge. (Abridged version published 1964. Original work published 1961).

— (2003a). *The archaeology of knowledge*. London: Routledge. (Original work published 1969).

— (2003b). *Abnormal: Lectures at the College de France 1974–1975*. (G. Burchell, Trans.). London & New York: Verso. (Original work published 1999).

— (2005). *The hermeneutics of the subject: Lectures at the College de France 1981–1982*. (G. Burchell, Trans.). New York: Palgrave Macmillan.

— (2008). *The birth of biopolitics: Lectures at the College de France 1978–1979*. (G. Burchell, Trans.). London & New York: Verso. (Original work published 1999).

Fuller, P. (1980). *Art and psychoanalysis*. London: Writers and Readers.

Garai, J. E. (2001). A humanistic approach to art therapy. In J. Rubin (Ed.), *Approaches to art therapy: theory and technique (*2nd ed.) (pp. 149–162). Philadelphia: Brunner Routledge. (Original work published 1987).

Grosz, E. (1990). *Jacques Lacan: a feminist introduction*. Australia: Allen & Unwin.

Horkheimer, M., & Adorno, T. (2002). *Dialectic of enlightenment: philosophical fragments*. USA: Stanford University Press. (Original work published 1987).

Junge, M. (1994). *The history of art therapy in the United States.* Mundelein, Ill.: American Art Therapy Association.

Linnell, S. (2003, October). *The making of art therapists.* Paper presented at 14th Annual Conference of the Australian National Art Therapy Association, Sydney.

— (2004). Towards a 'poethics' of therapeutic practice: extending the relationship of ethics and aesthetics in narrative therapies through a consideration of the late work of Michel Foucault. *The International Journal of Narrative Therapy and Community Work,* 4, 42–54.

McHoul, A., & Grace, W. (1993). *A Foucault primer: discourse, power and the subject.* Australia: Melbourne University Press.

McNay, L. 1992: *Foucault and feminism.* Cambridge: Polity Press.

McNiff, S. (1992). *Art as medicine: creating a therapy of the imagination.* Boston & London: Shambala.

Milchman, A., and Rosenberg, A. (2000). A Foucauldian analysis of psychoanalysis: A discipline that 'disciplines'. *Academy for the study of psychoanalytic arts.* Retrieved May, 2003, from http://www.academy analyticarts.org/milch&rosen.html

Milner, M. (1950). *On not being able to paint.* London: Heinmann.

Moon, B. (1995). *Existential art therapy: the canvas mirror.* Springfield, Ill.: Charles C. Thomas.

— (2001). II Humanistic approaches: commentary. In J. Rubin (Ed.), *Approaches to art therapy: Theory and technique* (2nd ed.) (pp. 189–190). Philadelphia: Brunner-Routledge.

O'Leary, T. (2002). *Foucault and the art of ethics.* London & New York: Continuum.

Patton, P. (2000). *Deleuze and the political: thinking the political.* London: Routledge.

Rose, G. (2001). *Visual methodologies: an introduction to the interpretation of visual materials.* London: Sage.

Rose, N. (1992). Governing the enterprising self. In P. Heelas & P. Morris (Eds.), *The values of the enterprise culture* (pp. 141–164). London: Routledge.

— (1998). *Inventing ourselves: Psychology, Power and personhood.* Cambridge University Press. (Original work published 1996).

— (2000a). Power and subjectivity: critical history and psychology. *Academy for the study of psychoanalytic arts.* Retrieved March, 2003, from http://www.academyanalyticarts.org/rose1.html

— (2000b). Power in therapy: Techne and ethos. *Academy for the study of psychoanalytic arts.* Retrieved March, 2003, from http://www.academyanalyticarts.org/rose2.html

Shapiro, G. (2003). *Archaeologies of vision: Nietzsche and Foucault on seeing and saying.* Chicago: The University of Chicago Press.

Schaverien, J. (1992). *The Revealing Image: Analytical art psychotherapy in theory and practice.* London: Routledge.

Spivak, G. (1997). Translator's preface. In J. Derrida, (1988). *Of grammatology* (pp. ix–lxxxvii). Baltimore & London: John Hopkins University Press.

White, M. (2002). Addressing personal failure. *The International Journal of Narrative Therapy and Community Work*, 3, 33–76.

— (2003). Narrative Practice and community assignments. *The International Journal of Narrative Therapy and Community Work*, 2, 17–55.

White, M., & Epston, D. (1990). *Narrative means to therapeutic ends.* New York & London: W.W. Norton & Co. (Expanded from original work published 1989).

Winslade, J. (2009). Tracing lines of flight: implications of the work of Gilles Deleuze for narrative practice. *Family Process* 48(3), 332–346.

CHAPTER 3

AnOther Stor(e)y: Imagining Narrative Therapy and Art Psychotherapy Together Through the Works of Kristeva, Clément, Cixous, Spivak, Venn and Butler

The real question is: can there be otherness? Does philosophy accept otherness or does it reduce it to the Hegelian space that does nothing but dialecticise, annul, cancel, or incorporate it...

(Cixous, 1991, p. 90)

Abstract: This chapter raises a set of philosophical puzzles that calls into question what therapy is and does. The theoretical and fictocritical explorations of the previous chapter are taken, metaphorically and philosophically, to another level. I explore the possibilities of the Women's and Other departments of the Store of Poststructural Theory, extending the notion of the fabrication of subjectivity and playfully critiquing the practice of 'shopping around' for ideas. I introduce theorists working at the intersection of poststructuralism with feminist and postcolonial theory, and consider what their work might offer to an exploration of art psychotherapy and narrative therapy. As suggested by the leading quotation from Cixous, an acceptance of the Otherness within others and oneself becomes crucial, in this chapter, for thinking beyond the binary of the psyche and the social, particularly as it is staged in the apparent opposition of art psychotherapy and narrative therapy. Butler's work in particular becomes central to my project of thinking art psychotherapy and narrative therapy together. I note how something akin to Butler's insight that the reiteration of the subject and of language is both citational and productive of difference informs both narrative therapy and (art) psychotherapy, but informs them very differently.

Going up, madam?

The wrought iron door creaks closed across the front of the old fashioned lift. Her tummy lurches and then settles as she begins to ascend.

1st floor Women's clothing, haberdashery, cafe, bookshop & homewares.

She steps out across a gap that reveals a little too much of the giddy chasm of the lift shaft, into a high ceilinged room with tall windows overlooking a park laid out with curving paths and Moreton Bay figs. There is something simultaneously homely and exotic about this light-filled space. She is about to set off in the direction of the dress section to find something French and feminine to wear close to the skin, under her new Foucault 'Experience' jacket, when the aroma of coffee and freshly baked bread reminds her that it's time for lunch.

Sheridan Linnell

The cafe is crowded with women and men pausing for refreshment before launching themselves back into the aisles. Looking around for a free table, she catches the eye of someone familiar sitting at a north-facing window. The dark-haired woman smiles in recognition and beckons her to the table. She feels a faint ripple in the surface of time, as fiction and reality again converge...

"I've read what you've been writing," Bronwyn Davies says, "and it seems to me that, although you say you don't know what you will do with this project, you are creating a poststructural conceptual framework for art therapy—you are already quite some way along that path. I look forward to seeing where it might take you.

"I'm glad to meet up with you here in the women's section," Bronwyn adds, "because, up to this point in the text, your work has relied a bit too much on 'boy theorists'...and by the way, the rocket salad here is very good" . As the waiter approaches to take their order, time shudders back into its narrative path.

Suitably nourished, Sheridan wanders over to a table strewn with all manner of fine and colourful fabrics and threads. Here are the materials she needs to stitch together theory, experience and imagination into something of her own. She runs her fingers across a Chinese satin, pale as milk, its circular design etched in delicate embroidery. There is a fine tension here. Revolutions of multicoloured threads break free from the regularities of the pattern and run off in multiple trajectories, only to be caught up with a strong gold thread and cross-stitched into other, more vibrant circles.

Julia Kristeva

The work of Julia Kristeva, a semiotician and psychoanalyst, is highly influential within visual arts, cultural theory and psychoanalysis (Moi, 1990). Kristeva's work offers a response to the psychoanalysis of Lacan. Many concepts within Kristeva's work are suggestive for art therapy, including her notions of the speaking subject (1990) and subject-in-process (1984), abjection (1982), the semiotic (1984, 1990), and her general privileging of artists and aesthetics (1980, 1989, 2000).

Kristeva's 'analytic of revolt' can be critiqued for the terms upon which it establishes a dialectical relationship between the symbolic and the semiotic. While suggesting that the sterility of the symbolic order must and will be challenged and modified by revolt, Kristeva ultimately subjugates irrationality to the rational, madness to reason, the feminine to the masculine and the maternal to the paternal, restoring the Lacanian 'law of the father' as the universal condition of individual sanity and social order (Grosz, 1989; Butler, 1999). Nevertheless, many of Kristeva's concepts can be heuristically engaged in an expansion of the cultural and therapeutic significance of embodiment, aesthetics and artistic experience. These themes are most commonly examined in psychoanalytic art therapy through Klein's child analysis (1988) and Winnicott's development of object relations (1965), and the interest of both of these psychoanalysts in art and play (see Klein, 1991; Winnicott, 1971).

Each of Kristeva's concepts could be more fully explored for their implications for the theorisation of art therapy. For instance, Kristeva's theory of abjection could enable art therapists to conceptualise the revulsion to 'mess' which often characterises responses to an invitation to make art and can position art therapists as 'lowly' in a hierarchy of professional standing. Considered as a state of abjection, 'mess' could suggest the liminal status of art making, 'in-between' psychic and bodily processes, or the symbolic and semiotic orders. The notion of abjection can also challenge the mother-blaming tendencies of art therapy and many other therapy discourses, by identifying these tendencies as manifestations of fear of the maternal chora (Kristeva, 1984). The concept of the semiotic and the linkage of artistic and analytic revolt (Kristeva, 2000, 2002), are richly suggestive for a reconciliation of aesthetic and psychodynamic perspectives in art therapy.

Kristeva's notion of the subject-in-process informs an understanding of a decentred/irrational dimension to my subjective experiences of writing this book. Her theorisation of the semiotic and its relationship to art and literature suggests that bringing artistic and literary processes into the methodology of this book offsets the possibility of my explorations hardening into a rigid conventional structure.

Kristeva's thought could form a basis for theorising art psychotherapy by highlighting the critical capacities of both art and psychoanalysis and offering an intellectual framework for bringing these terms together. However, I remain wary of the tendency for Kristeva's writing to support a liberalised patriarchal hierarchy by offering a dialectical 'solution' to, rather than a dissolution of, binary oppositions (Grosz, 1989; Butler, 1999). It seems to me possible to take up/appropriate some of Kristeva's ideas, alongside questioning how aspects of modernity are reconstituted both through her theories and through the practice of art psychotherapy.

Despite this attempt at ordering disorder, things are becoming a little disarrayed in the women's section. The table promising 'substantial reductions' is succumbing to opposite tendencies. Its vast surface is spilling over with the expansive possibilities on offer. Whole garments are tumbled together with fabrics and threads. She pulls an opera jacket of deep indigo velvet from among the tousled remnants. Something for a cool summer evening perhaps, when she might put aside her daily apparel and bathe in moonlight.

Catherine Clément

Clément's work is an extraordinary philosophical and rhetorical performance, drawing on mythologies, anecdotes, histories, autobiographies, quasi-fictions, political critiques and cultural commentaries. She re-establishes feminist and class issues within her textual practice, without reconstituting the rational claim to truth or the biological essentialism which poststructuralist theory has respectively problematised in Marxism and radical feminism. With Hélène Cixous (Cixous and Clément, 1986), she imagines and writes the feminine transformation of culture in a collaboration that exemplifies differences between (these two, and all) women as much as it celebrates the difference of women.

Clément (1987) romps seriously through what could only be an intimate's critique of Freud and Lacan, refusing to deny the social responsibility of psychoanalysis to heal. Moreover, she shares art therapists' affinity with Winnicott, and on similar grounds. Writing of women in opera, Clément recalls the childhood tale of the little match girl who freezes to death in the snow: each match she strikes to warm a long night brings momentarily to life an intense image of a joy she has longed for but has been denied. Clément continues:

> I like the English psychoanalyst Winnicott. He was an old man who knew a lot about childhood. He noticed that for a long time—sometimes until they are grown up—children go to sleep with stuffed animals or bits of cloth. He called these "transitional objects". Well, what do you expect, after all, he was a psychoanalyst and he was not worried about being understood by his peers. A transitional object is a temporary support, a support for the duration. It is an object which the child brings to life when he pleases, one he attacks and destroys and that is strongly resilient…It guarantees the transition into the world…
>
> The matches are the opposite of this transition. They flame and there is nothing left. The women, whose eternal story I have told you, blaze up all at once and there is nothing left. Nothing is left but the music. Yes, finally, the music, like a transitional space; the music that is

> neither outside nor inside, but elsewhere and surrounding you. The music where love and hatred can interact without vital risk, and where the light of passion burns and immediately goes out. Life is different, nothing in it happens that way. But opera still endures with its limited stories because music plays the blessed role of the stuffed animal in it. (Clément, 1989, p. 179)

Here Clément both takes up and deterritorialises Winnicott's notions of transitional objects and transitional spaces. The women who flame up and burn out are not the resilient and putatively male child subject who—unlike the match girl—transitions to adulthood through play. The (im)possibility, the virtuality, of these passionate and doomed women finds a register only in the nowhere and everywhere of music, itself a transitional space.

Clément's writing exemplifies the operatic range of discursive possibilities and stylistic registers available to a broadly poststructuralist and feminist writing, thereby inspiring the writing of this book. She is committed to the pleasurable fullness of sound, passion and movement, and she is also devoted to asceticism and the void. To reach toward the inexpressible, Clément turns to music, and to poetry, the form of language closest to music. She is just as interested in silence as in sound. Music and poetry are an interplay, a mutual interpellation, of sound and silence.

Clément devotes a whole book to syncope (Clément, 1994): to the faltering of time, a moment 'out of time', a rapture in which the self is elsewhere. In linguistics, syncope is the suppression or elision of a syllable or letter. "The most familiar language produces syncope spontaneously: "m'sieur", "mam'selle", "p'tit" " (Clément, 1994, p. 5); in the Australian vernacular it would be o'right, c'mon, g'day. In the body, syncope is a faint or passive fit, a trance, a moment of unconsciousness, a falling down/out of awareness, a being temporarily elsewhere. In dance, syncope is a suspended moment, the swoon and hold of the tango. In music, the rhythm falters and sways, holding a note over, producing dissonance. Similarly, in poetry, the line is enjambed, carried over by and producing an excess.

We are, says Clément,

> obsessed with the autonomous and aware Subject, and even if nowadays we force it to follow the path of the unconscious (like a policeman tailing a suspect) we never doubt its existence, even less its fundamental validity, without which no democracy, no individualism is ever possible. (Clément, 1994, p. 5)

Clément laments how the social and the individual are dependent on and subordinate to an I-solated self that is tied to the project of discovering its true nature. Thankfully, in syncope, there is the promise of 'nothing' to be found.

She is/is not browsing among fragments of fabric, poetry and philosophy. She is/is not in the present moment of writing this text. She is/is not in the presence of a dream. She is walking and not walking on a summer's evening in her opera jacket, holding and not holding in her arms an elusive veil of moonlight. She wanders dreamlike among the syncopated shadows of the scribbly gums, running her fingers across their greywhite limbs. She touches the scarified trunk of one particular tree, tracing the scribbles that give this tree its name, the wayward and authorless inscriptions of its irreducible otherness.

Hélène Cixous

Cixous w(h)(r)ites out, or puts under erasure, such binaries as head/heart, active/passive, nature/culture, logos/pathos, high/low, slave/master, man/woman and, one might add, philosophy/fiction and discursive/poetic. These are "dual hierarchised oppositions" (Cixous and Clement, 1986, p. 63–64) by which logocentrism organises the thinkable, and phallocentrism achieves and retains dominance at the cost of the repressed/marginalised feminine/Other.

Cixous' textual practice of 'feminine' writing releases/produces the conditions of possibility of the otherwise unthinkable and unimaginable. Through a restitution of the feminine Imaginary, she offers a 'de-subjectivised' and re-embodied woman/humanity, a hyperbolic Utopia that radically destabilises the current organization of self, relationship and the social. Cixous (1981) incites women to write, to repaint our half of the world. She calls upon an embodied, discursively produced and productive notion of 'the feminine' that is ironically marginalised within the predominantly female profession of art therapy. Without the provocation and support of such poststructuralist feminist writers, the feminine could be similarly disavowed within the writing of this book. Cixous' call to write ourselves and each other into existence invites a feminist, fictocritical response to the question 'but what would poststructuralist art therapies (and therapists) look like/feel like/do/be/become?'.

At the same time, Cixous' writing cannot be strictly defined by an early (although by no means currently irrelevant) and polemical project of creating an alternative to the dominant patriarchal structure of discourse. Although the body of Cixous' writing is feminine, the feminine/poetic is not tied to gender. It is not 'tied' to anything. Yet it is always in an ethical relation of generosity and openness toward the Other (Blyth, 2004; Cixous, 2008). This is the otherness of both others and oneself.

For Cixous, the 'I' in writing is not I-dentical with herself; s/he is always other. Writing is "writing what you cannot know before you have written" (Cixous, 1993, p. 38), and writing is also writing what you cannot know. The first other is oneself: through writing, 'I' become more than my known self and yet cannot be fully known (Cixous and Calle-Gruber, 1997; Sellers, 2004). Drawing, too, for Cixous, is the art of drawing what you cannot know, or cannot see.

> It's not a question of drawing the contours, but of what escapes the contour, the secret movement, the breaking, the torment, the unexpected. The drawing wants to draw what is invisible to the naked eye. (Cixous, 1998, p. 23)

The brushstrokes of a painting, the lines of a drawing or written text are traces of an otherness that can be sensed, but cannot be captured (or arrested, or 'apprehended'). These gestural strokes and lines, like dreams, are imbued with a "feeling of the secret" (Cixous and Calle-Gruber, 1997, p. 85), with the shape of that which is unknowable and infinitely deferred.

In a portrait of Cixous' writing as "writing-thinking", Mireille Calle-Gruber suggests that a "relation of uncertainty" and "the undecidable" are crucial to Cixous' work. The reading of such writing "*puts* everything *into questions*" (Cixous and Calle-Gruber, 1997, p. 137, italics in original), as well as bringing everything into question. Cixous plays upon the consonance, in French, of death *(mort)* and the word *(mot):*

> It's so dark here where I am searching for a language that makes no noise to whisper what is neither living nor dead. All words are too loud, too rapid, too sure, I'm searching for the names of the shadows *between the words*... (from *Déluge,* in Cixous and Calle-Gruber, 1997, p. 152, italics in original)

Art is at once a welcoming and a departure, a 'going without saying': loss forms a space between the words, a door in the picture, and we pass through.

As she walks away from the overflowing table with her arms full of richly textured linens, fine wools and subtle silks, she is hopeful that she at last has the makings of something, although of just what, she is less sure than ever. She is walking back to the lifts at the rear of the building when she notices an out-of-the-way shelf labelled 'Other Fictions'. She begins to flick through an assortment of titles.

She picks up a volume with a curiously folded dust jacket and a cover image of two overlapping spheres. The design is reminiscent of distant high school geometry classes—could it be something like a Venn diagram, but with more dimensions? *Becoming-other than what we are. She mutters the title suspiciously to herself, supposing she has picked up another one of those ubiquitous New Age, self help guides to how to heal yourself and change your life in twelve easy steps. But there is nothing easy about this one. It's an invitation to (re)think Western poststructuralisms together with the death of neo-colonial privilege, to leave the 'shore' behind and dance a two-step out along the jetty of postcolonial theory (Derrida, in Venn, 2002), as a prelude to diving into some very deep water.*

Couze Venn

Venn (2000, 2002) seeks to create a space outside the Western privileging of the autonomous and rational individual from which to pose the question 'who comes after modernity?'. Venn's question complements Foucault's question 'what are we today?'. For Foucault, the work of critiquing the present is the work of transformation (Foucault, 2000a), but Venn proposes that Foucault's question "exceeds genealogy, since the subject is located by reference to a memory and an historicisation, as well as to a narrative of emancipation, and to a sense, therefore, of futurity" (Venn, 2002, p. 56). According to Venn, it is necessary to both memorialise our pasts and critique our presents in order to imagine our (im)possible futures.

While Venn (2000) acknowledges that Western poststructural theories offer a radical break with many modernist assumptions he also suggests that, in subtle ways, these theories can tend to reproduce a separation of self and other, individual and social, inadvertently reproducing the modern, Eurocentric ideal of autonomy. Venn agrees with Foucault that power is productive, but argues that the latter's frequent foregrounding of the subjugating effects of power can reproduce an opposition of the individual and the social. For Venn, it is important to also consider how non-coercive forms of power produce sociality and intersubjectivity [1]. He suggests that one paradigm of how non-coercive power can apprentice us to the other and inscribe us as social beings can be found in the (symbolic configuration of) the relationship of women and their children.

Challenging the occidental tendency, even within poststructuralisms, to reproduce binaries of self and other, individual and social, Venn proposes the possibility of becoming-other through processes of apprenticeship and choreography. These metaphors suggest that the self is formed always in relation to the other, not only through learning and self-reflection, but also through an aesthetic and embodied experience of connection that Venn calls "autopoesis" (Venn, 2002, p. 58). Apprenticeship to the other is thus

> the self-reflective, but learned, autopoetic character of the figuration and refiguration of subjectivity, not reducible to the model of internalisation or Nietzschean willing…in part a way of appropriating, making one's own what belongs to the 'we' or intersubjective domain of culture, a way of folding the outside inside one's self, that changes the self. (Venn, 2002, p. 58)

This concept of apprenticeship has an affinity with Foucault's ethics and aesthetics of the self, while avoiding what Venn calls the "volitional slippages in Foucault" (Venn, 2002, p. 59). For Venn, the 'we' of culture becomes part of every embodied and storied 'I'. Transformation of selves and relationships cannot be reduced either to an active and conscious 'will' for change, or to a passive and unconscious 'internalisation' of early experience or family and social mores. Transformation is a complex dance of self and other, in which we appropriate that which belongs to the "intersubjective domain of culture" (2002, p. 58) into our selves. What Venn is proposing here has an affinity with, but goes beyond, Foucault's ethics and aesthetics. Foucault (2000c) himself points out that 'intention' as an ethical substance is a rational, Enlightenment ideal, and yet Foucault's 'art of self' can be critiqued for seeming to suggest that we could each consciously and intentionally give form to our lives. Venn offers a reconfiguration of an ethics and aesthetics of existence that cannot be reduced to the individual subject's intention.

Venn suggests that we are 'heteronomous beings'—intersubjective, self-reflective, emotional, embodied and embedded—and as such are neither autonomous nor simply intentional. Venn chooses the word 'being' for this refigured story of who we might be, because he wants to interrupt the Western philosophical opposition between the self as either 'embodied existence' or 'socially constructed'. Both language, in particular narrative, and embodied experience entwine us with others. Our sense of an 'interiority' (or psyche) can be understood as a fold in the social fabric, established, embodied and maintained through relations with others. Our bodies are archives of, and monuments to, both personal and collective memory and experience. Our stories are entangled with the stories of others, emplotted in culturally available ways, and 'stitched' into wider historical narratives.

Venn offers four cornerstones to his account of embodied, narrated and relational 'ways of being':

- *Being in time*

Temporality is fundamental to our ability to question our ways of being. Our relation to time is one of becoming rather than one of linearity, since our sense of the present, our memory of the past and our anticipation of the future 'leach' into each other.

- *Narrativity*

Following Ricoeur, Venn suggests that it is through narrative that we come to know ourselves as being-in-time, so that "every self is a storied self…mingled with the stories of other selves" (2002, p. 57).

- *Being-with*

Following Merleau-Ponty, Venn suggests that being is intersubjective. As narrated and embodied beings we are always already interconnected with the stories and bodies of others and with objects in the physical world. Being-with (or intersubjectivity) is not directly representable, but is intimated in experiences of liminality, mystery and the sublime.

- *Emplotment*

The plots with which we make sense of our experience are 'givens' within the culture. We figure and reconfigure our stories of self through the 'interlocution' or mediation of others within broader cultural and historical discourses of identity, themselves open to reworking.

Bringing together many strands from phenomenology, psychoanalysis and poststructuralism, and particularly from the philosophies of Foucault, Merleau-Ponty, and Ricouer, Venn (2002) offers a sustained reading of the politics and poetics of Fanon's (1970) *Black Skin, White Masks.* Venn points out that the production of "dissident discourses" is a necessary, but not a sufficient, condition for subjective and social change (Venn, 2002, p. 60). It is through a poetics of practice, an apprenticeship to otherness and a choreography of intimate relations that we can become 'Other-wise'. From this perspective, therapeutic change could involve *both* a refusal of dominating and subjugating relations of power *and* a privileging of non-coercive relations of power.

A foregrounding of the poetics as well as the politics of therapeutic relations seems to me to be highly significant for an ethics and aesthetics of poststructural therapeutic practice. The work of therapy might be thought of as an apprenticeship to the unending stories, and as a dance with the myriad ways of being, of those others who come to therapy, including the Otherness within one's self.

She tucks the book under her arm and continues browsing, but is immediately distracted by the silken-red tassel of what must be a bookmark, wedged in between the selected works of Foucault and Derrida. *These two get around,* she mutters to herself, having seen them in the Men's Section as well. Pulling on the tassel, she finds herself desperately attempting to reel in an apparently endless stream of illuminated characters on a finely woven textile scroll. It unravels around her in loops and whorls. Soon she is at sea in a veritable ocean of text, whipped into peaks and troughs by a prevailing wind from the East.

Gayatri Chakravorty Spivak

Spivak is an uncompromisingly brilliant and difficult writer, whose texts twist and turn, advocating for marginalised cultures and subjectivities, while refusing to be positioned as the postcolonial and feminist Other of Western poststructuralisms. Spivak notes the tendency to "assign a static ethnicity to the Other in order to locate critique or confirmation of the most sophisticated thought or act of the West", suggesting that "it is necessary for all of us to watch out against the curious politics of this all-too-seductive move". She goes on to say that elsewhere she has called this kind of vigilance, within the necessity of what one writes, "a critique of what we cannot not want" (1999, p. 110).

Spivak seeks to writes (out of) a deconstructive space between and beyond the individual voice and its effacement in a collective politic, between and beyond "the itinerary of the ethico-political in authoritarian fictions...the complacent apath(ies) of self centralisation...and the bigoted elitism (theoretical or practical) conversely possible in collective practice" (Spivak, 1996a, p. 101). For Spivak, Western postcolonialisms run the risk of reproducing the elitism of other and more conservative Western 'isms', effacing the names of specific others under the sign of a generalised "native informant" (1999). Her preference is therefore to take up the "gymnastic(s)" (Spivak, 1996, p. 158) of a deconstructive positioning. For Spivak, deconstruction is committed to transformation without being Utopian, approaching the promise of change

> in the language of persistent effort and deferred fulfilment, in a future that is not simply a future 'present'...This way of working, half in and half out of what is at hand, negotiating with pre-existing structures of violence, is the way that works, the way things work… (Spivak, 1999, p. 110)

Spivak is a major translator of Derrida. Derrida's writing is both an inspiration and a 'pedagogy' for Spivak (Landry and MacLean, 1996), but she is nevertheless never his subaltern. Spivak cannot simply 'repeat' Derrida, according to the notions of alterity and iterability, since "every repetition is an alteration (or iteration)" (Spivak, 1999, pp. 86–7), and her translations and interpretations of his work have been formative for the understandings of an English language readership. For Spivak, critics of Derrida's emphasis on writing miss the texture of his writing—the material and creative possibilities of text as textile. Her own iterations of/in/through Derrida make possible an ethics of 'unlearning' the privileged confines of the autonomous Western subject, whether this subject is figured through colonial and patriarchal dominance, or in the inverted form of an identity politics that paradoxically denies the capacity and responsibility of the subject to hear, speak with and respond to the Other.

Part of Spivak's project is to refuse the (Anglo-American) assimilation of Derrida's deconstruction into a kind of neo-Romanticism, and the normalisation of Foucault's ethics of the care of the self into the program of a Western liberal humanism. Reading Foucault by way of Derrida's interest in the interrelationship/rift between the general and the narrow, Spivak considers how Foucault's "bestowal of the name power upon a complex situation produces power 'in the general sense'" (1996b, p. 144). Spivak restores a productive 'narrowness'—a cultural situatedness and even a kind of domesticity—to Foucault's concept of *pouvoir-savoir,* or power/ knowledge. She surfaces the vernacular "can-do-ness" of the French verb *pouvoir* and the "homely verbiness" of *savoir*, highlighting the common occurrence of such verb couplets in French (e.g. *savoir-faire, savoir-vivre*).

In Spivak's reading, power/knowledge takes on the radical ordinariness of "being able to do something—only as you are able to make sense of it" (1996b, p. 151). People act within/against their permissible narratives; their agency is both made possible and limited by discourse. Spivak gives the example of what is made possible for a woman within different narratives of marriage. The 'knowing'/*savoir* of the practice of exogamous marriage, as the passing of a woman from the protection of her father to that of her husband and eventually to that of her son, makes it possible that this woman can preserve the stability of marriage. Conversely, the 'knowing' of marriage as a presumed site of reciprocity, intimacy, and emotional and sexual fulfillment makes it possible that a woman not met in these ways can seek her fulfillment elsewhere. (Lest this example seem too much the province of a Western feminism, I remind myself of Spivak's ongoing engagements with the terrible fact of the self-immolation of Hindu widows.)

Spivak prefers an ontic, rather than ontological, version of Foucault's *pouvoir/savoir*. This is not a move away from theory in the direction of empirical practice, but a call to remember the historical and cultural specificities of language. Spivak destabilises the tendency to reincorporate Foucault's idea of power/knowledge into naturalised systemic notions of power. Consistent with Foucault's insistence on the heterogeneity of power relations, Spivak restores a heterogeneity to power that the general naming of power threatens to remove.

Spivak is concerned to challenge 'applications' of Foucault and Derrida, to read their texts by way of "the deconstructive theorizing of practice" in which "theory brings practice to crisis, and practice norms theory, and deviations constitute a forever precarious norm" (1996b, pp. 153–4). Foucault slashed with Derrida prevents Foucault being normalised, turned into a blueprint for social justice movements and made fit for liberal academic and political consumption. For Spivak it is crucial to preserve a critical rather than a dogmatic basis for a philosophy of action: to be aware of the limits of knowing rather than to shape a generalising program for 'freedom' in Eurocentric terms. Proposing that it is necessary to resist the normalisation of ethics in the program of a liberal humanism, Spivak suggests giving the proper names of Foucault and Derrida in to each other, even against their lack of endorsement for such a move. She writes an asymmetrical and difficult 'Derrida/Foucault', slashed apart and brought together, as a condition of possibility of being able to 'give in' to both.

For Spivak, as for Venn, writing contorts in the persistent attempt to memorialise colonial injustices and transfigure future possibilities. Contextualising her infamous claim that the subaltern cannot speak (Spivak, 1985), Spivak has said that she was then at the beginning of something, where the suicide of the young woman Bhubaneswari Bhaduri posed the problem of "trying to find a way of putting this woman as a lesson for me that was more complicated and more apposite than Foucault or Deleuze" (Spivak, 1996c, p. 288).

> So, "the subaltern cannot speak", means that even when the subaltern makes an effort to the death to speak, she is not able to be heard, and speaking and hearing complete the speech act. That's what it had meant, and anguish marked the spot. (Spivak, 1996c, p. 292)

Then the wind drops. The churning ocean of text subsides into silvery ribbons, twisting around her feet. For an instant, she fears that it might catch fire. As she steps out of the charmed and dangerous circle of discourse, a streamer of letters is still tangled in her hair. Returning to the shelf of books, she picks up a thick volume with a lurid cover. She loves detective novels, especially if they don't take themselves too seriously. This one has a really terrible title, but the cover-notes promise that the author has subverted the genre through her citation and disruption of a dominant literary theme.

The book is called *The Butler Did It*.

A bit of light reading for late at night after a long day at the computer, she tells herself.

Later she will remember this thought with an ironic sigh as she rereads the concluding chapter for the third time. She will still be uncertain about whose Face that was at the window, still doubt whether the terrible words scrawled on the glass could really be held responsible for the chain of gruesome murders that propels the mystery. The narrator, to her knowledge the first transgender detective in the genre, won't have the answers either. The redoubtable Shirley Locque and her philosophically minded offsider Ms Whatsonia will, however, respond admirably to the threat of death and the indeterminacy of the plotline. They will engage the reader in an intelligent questioning of the authenticity of various conflicting accounts of whodunnit. Despite the persistence of their uncertainties, they will engender in her/the reader a keen sense of obligation to the most vulnerable, marginalised and abject of the other characters. Rather than suspecting these abject souls of inhuman acts of cruelty, and subsequently 'entertaining' ideas of retaliatory violence, she will detect anOther possibility, make a novel response.

Judith Butler

> You may think that I am in fact telling a story about the prehistory of the subject, one that I have just been arguing cannot be told. And there are two responses to this (1) that there is no final or adequate narrative reconstruction of the prehistory of the speaking subject does not mean we cannot narrate it. It only means that at the moment when we narrate we become speculative philosophers or fiction writers. And (2) it is this prehistory that has never stopped happening and, as such, is not prehistory in any chronological sense. It is not done with, over, relegated to a past, which then becomes part of a causal or narrative reconstruction of the self. On the contrary it is that prehistory that interrupts the story I have to give of myself, which makes every account of myself partial and failed...The I is the moment of narrative

> failure in every attempt to give an account of myself. (Butler, 2001, pp. 36–37)

Butler's writing not only gives an intellectual 'account' of, but enacts, discursive agency (1997a) together with an ethics of vulnerability, accountability and gratitude to the Other. The indeterminacy of narrative and of the 'I' who narrates become occasions for opening our selves radically to Other possibilities. We do not cease to tell our stories. We continue to attempt to narrate the un-narratable. We will try to make sense of our selves and we will seek recognition from the Other, because, as Spivak might say, this is something we cannot not do. Even Butler, while questioning the limits of narrativity, continues to tell us her stories. What does it mean, I wonder, that 'I', in the context of this book, am trying to make sense of multiple and inevitably partial accounts of 'Butler'?

I go back to the first thing of hers that I ever read, to those well-known opening words about her childhood. (I am a therapist, after all.)

> To make trouble was, within the reigning discourse of my childhood, something one should never do precisely because that would get you *in* trouble. The rebellion and its reprimand seemed caught up in the same terms, a phenomenon that gave rise to my first critical insight into the subtle ruse of power: the prevailing law threatened one with trouble, even put one in trouble, all to keep one out of trouble. Hence I concluded that trouble is inevitable and the task how best to make it, what best way to be in it. (Butler, 1999, p. xxvii)

Butler is quick to point out that this childhood story is an allegorical construction of sorts, although based in memory. Reading on, I am reminded of the kind of trouble Butler makes or gets herself into: feminine trouble, troubling the feminine, engendering desire, undoing gender, contesting boundaries. In the 1999 edition of *Gender Trouble* from which I have quoted here, the original 1990 preface containing these words is preceded by a new preface that, with hindsight, situates the book as a form of 'immanent critique' that sought to promote more inclusive forms of feminist theory. Butler's critique is a particular type of 'trouble', made in the service of expanding the possibilities of feminist theory, of social worlds and, indeed, the categories of who and what can be regarded as 'human'.

Butler is prominent amongst those poststructuralist feminists who question the historical and philosophical bases of Foucault's 'art of self', thereby producing an account of ethico-politics that emphasises relationship and is sensitive to differences within and between subjects (Williams, 1996). Butler "reads Foucault against himself" (1999, p. 124), not only in the cited instance of critiquing a contradictory call to sexual emancipation in the journals of Herculine Barbin, but in numerous engagements which draw from, critique and extend Foucauldian theory. Butler's poststructural critique of theories of the unconscious and subjectivity (Butler, 1997b), and her imagination of an historically and culturally contingent unconscious (Butler, 2000), could transform both psychoanalytic and Foucauldian perspectives of therapy.

In this book I am deeply curious about what might come from bringing together Foucault's account of the subject and Butler's (2001, 2005) critical engagement with the limits of accountability itself. In pursuing the notion of a non-narrativisable excess, I am cautious of the dangers of falling into yet another metaphysics of the subject, or myth of origins. From my practice as a narrative and art therapist, interested in how therapy is itself implicated in the production of abnormal and pathological subjects, I am constantly reminded of just how much of that which appears either self-evident or mysterious about the processes of subjectification can be painstakingly historicised, narrativised, and thereby made available for question. Nevertheless, I am also interested in how the ethics of accountability and the genre of narrative may themselves shape subjectification, and from what borderlands they may be questioned.

Butler's notion of performativity (Butler, 1997a) is a brilliant metaphor for how truth claims are continually produced, embodied and "spoken into existence" (Davies, 2003, p. 1). The trope of performance furthermore suggests that a space of difference opens up through each citation/performance of a claim to truth. Butler gives an example of the performative power of what, following English theorists Austin and Searle, she calls speech acts, when she describes critical response to her book, *Antigone's claim: Kinship between life and death* (2000). Butler explores what possibilities might be opened up by placing the story of Antigone, Oedipus' daughter, at the centre of psychoanalysis, rather than the myth of Oedipus himself. As the offspring of Oedipus' crime, and as a woman within a Greek culture where only freeborn men were accorded the rights of citizens, Antigone is already positioned as forbidden to speak. She commits an unspeakable act by even speaking of, let alone carrying out, an intent to bury her brother inside the city walls against the edict of her uncle, Creon, the king. In doing so, she challenges the limits of the law: not only the specific, social law of the Athens of her time, but the Law of symbolic order which Lacanian psychoanalysis, following Freud, asserts to be a universal truth.

Butler analyses the treatment of Antigone in the work of three philosophers. According to Hegel, Antigone's defiance symbolises an act of kinship at the limits of the sphere of viable cultural norms. According to Irigaray, Antigone signifies the violent 'remaindering' of the feminine at the point of transition from matriarchy to patriarchy. According to Lacan, Antigone signifies the border between the imaginary and the symbolic, and the limits of the speakable. Butler's reworking of this myth engages with and goes beyond Hegel, Irigaray and Lacan to suggest that we could radically reconfigure both the unconscious and sociality. Rather than treating the nuclear, patriarchal, heterosexual family as a symbolic norm from which we are at best sufficiently enlightened to tolerate social and cultural deviations, Butler's work expands the liminal area between the psychic and the social into a platform for a different understanding of subjectivity and culture. The point here is not to create a new psychoanalytic ontology by replacing one myth with a 'better' one. Rather, the effect is a destabilisation of the truth of origins and an opening out of possibilities for subjectivity itself. One critical response from a psychoanalytic position to Butler's work was to tell her that it, like Antigone's crime, was unspeakable, that it posed a threat to the stability of human culture, and that Butler could not challenge the symbolic order because it was the Law. Noting this, Butler writes:

> Those who disagree with me tend to claim, with some exasperation, "But it is the law!" But what is the status of such an utterance? "It is the law!" becomes the utterance that performatively attributes the very force to the law that the law itself is said to exercise. "It is the law" is thus a sign of allegiance to the law, a sign of the desire for the law to be the indisputable law, a theological impulse within the theory of psychoanalysis to put out of play any criticism of the symbolic father, the law of psychoanalysis itself. (Butler, 2000, p. 21)

Thus Butler, like Foucault, engages critically with what the latter philosopher calls 'the father's no', the basis of the dominant, negative representation of power that Foucault calls 'juridico-discursive' (Foucault, 1980). Foucault's critique moves from a negative representation of power to an analytic of power's 'positivity', from a centralised representation of power towards its deterritorialisation, and from psychoanalytic discourse towards an (a)e(s)th(et)ic of the subject. Butler, too, engages with power's positivity, analysing how citations and performances of truth claims consolidate 'the truth'. Butler also confirms Foucault's view of the inevitability of resistance to power, noting how each citation and performance, each repetition, is also an undoing of what it does, since no citation can be identical with that which it seeks to reproduce. However, for Butler, it is less a matter of refusing psychoanalytic discourse than of troubling it deeply. Butler's critique leads her to radically reconceptualise the basis of psychoanalysis, reinventing its myths of origin, co-opting its explanatory powers, and undoing the force of repression so that 'outlawed' forms of sociality, connection, and subjectivity become more possible and more fully liveable.

Butler draws on the explanatory powers of psychoanalysis in an account of the subject's passionate attachment to that which constitutes its subjection. She asks, "how are we to understand, not merely the disciplinary production of the subject, but the disciplinary cultivation of *an attachment to subjection*?" (Butler, 1997b, p.102, italics in original). In responding to this question, Butler works with and against Foucault's account of subjectification and of resistance as an effect of power. For Butler, the resources of the discursive are not in themselves sufficient to account for attachment to subjection or for resistance to its totalising tendencies.

Butler proposes that a constitutive 'loss' of the body founds the disciplinary subject in Foucault, and that this body is remaindered/becomes a constitutive outside to discourse. Butler further suggests that if

> according to psychoanalysis, the subject is not the same as the psyche from which it emerges, and if, for Foucault the subject is not the same as the body from which it emerges, then perhaps the body has come to substitute for the psyche in Foucault—that is, as that which exceeds and confounds the injunctions of normalisation. (1997b, p. 94)

If so, against Foucault's notion of the soul imprisoning the body stands a psyche that precedes, exceeds and destabilises discourse and signification. For Butler,

> the psyche, which includes the unconscious, is very different from the subject: the psyche is precisely what exceeds the imprisoning effects of the discursive demand to inhabit a coherent identity, become a coherent subject. (1997b, p. 86)

On this basis, Butler asks whether resistance is always and only (as Foucault would suggest) an effect of power within discourse.

> More precisely, is the resistance upon which psychoanalysis insists socially and discursively produced, or is it a kind of resistance to, an undermining of, social and discursive production *as such*? (1997b, p. 88, italics in original)

Butler's work inspires questions that are crucial for the work of therapy, and indeed for the work of subjectivity itself. How are we, who are constituted over and over again as autonomous, doomed to fail so miserably at this independence? Is it because we are always already linked to others through gratitude, through debt, through an embodied connectedness that predates and survives the myriad modern forms of constituting self and knowledge as singular and impregnable? Is our vulnerability a consequence of how we are formed in discourse, how we are obliged to perform over and over again, each time risking that to which we have become passionately attached? Or are we vulnerable to our formation in discourse because life is precarious, even before our precarious subjectivity is precariously formed and performed? And if these positions are not mutually exclusive, and these questions not fully answerable, what are the ethics associated with such insights? (Butler, 1997a, 1997b, 2001, 2004, 2005).

In Butler's view, an originary vulnerability to the Other haunts the subject from its horizons, such that s/he is always and inevitably a subject of both power and desire (Butler, 1997b, 2004a). This vulnerability can lead, defensively, to a psychodynamics and politics of aggression against the perceived threat posed by the Other and by particular marginalised and abjected others. Alternatively, it can be realised as the very basis of an ethics of non-violence and care toward these others (Butler, 2004).

By bringing together Foucault and Freud, Butler's work has been crucial to the theoretical framework of this book. Butler's work assists me to analyse the opposition and connection between a psychoanalytically informed art therapy and a poststructurally informed narrative therapy, through a consideration of their theoretical antecedents. Narrative therapy and psychoanalytically informed art therapy can seem almost mutually exclusive, although there have been some reconciliatory moves (McFayden, 1997; White, 2004). I find this polarisation interesting and sometimes baffling, given that both narrative therapy and psychoanalysis attempt to theorise a decentred subject and to understand the possibilities for subjective and social transformation inherent in this subject's instability. In both narrative and psychoanalytic therapies, language, relationship and embodiment are key terms in the constitution and destabilisation of the autonomous, self-identical individual.

Something like a Butlerian insight that the reiteration of the subject and of language is both citational and productive of difference (Butler, 1997b) informs both narrative therapy and psychoanalytic therapies, but it informs them very differently. Narrative work eschews a consideration of psychodynamics and transference, focussing instead on deconstructions, retellings and audiencings of people's stories, in relation to other socially and culturally constructed and embodied/embedded narratives, as sites for subjective and social transformation. Psychoanalysis, on the other hand, is concerned with the scene of therapy itself and with the therapeutic relation as a repetition and reparation of that which cannot be directly thought or remembered, that which cannot directly enter a time-based narrative. The transformational potential of psychoanalysis and the psychodynamic therapies, including art psychotherapy, depends largely on the premise that repetition within a different relational frame is healing. Extending this psychoanalytic precept through Butler's notion of performativity, each repetition is both a citation and a discursive production of difference. In this way, there is no 'pure' repetition. This is underlined in art psychotherapy by the material production of the artwork. The making of art within therapy could be said to make visible and available to a therapeutic process some of the ways in which a discursive production always exceeds its re-presentational and citational qualities.

Since there can never be a pure repetition, are the re-citation of narratives, and the performance of a choreographed dance of the Otherness within the self of the 'client' with the Other of the therapist, therapeutically sufficient? Or is it is necessary to actively challenge the discursive reconstitution of the modern subject within therapy? Psychoanalytically oriented therapies tend to take the former position, whereas narrative therapy takes the latter.

In narrative therapies, the therapist as co-author engages in a collaborative deconstruction and production of multiple narratives (White, 1992). She asks questions that help tease out, from the discursive complexities of the subject's formation in power, distinctions between that subject's constitution through dominant discursive practices and the subject's taking up of positions and narratives in ways that challenge or exceed dominant prescriptions. In psychoanalytic therapies, the therapist as ally and Other makes herself available for projections and allows herself to become implicated, but not absorbed, in a different form of reiteration, whereby a ghostly non-narrativisable realm of early connection and loss appears in the present narrative as a transference.

The preferred position of the narrative therapist is decentred although influential, perhaps reflecting an ethnographic heritage in which the therapist attempts to leave the smallest possible footprint in the culture of the family, whereas the psychoanalytic therapist must be centred in order to incite a series of displacements.

The practices and ethics, indeed the ethicalisation of the therapist, within the different approaches of narrative therapy and psychoanalysis, are at times in contradiction. A move that is recommended within one approach would often be considered as unwise, and possibly even harmful, within the other. From the perspective of psychoanalysis, I become obliged to question the kinds of reiterations produced within narrative therapy: to ask if the more active and questioning style of the narrative therapist could be defensive and likely to further the client's defences, if the collaborative position of the narrative therapist promotes an exclusively positive transference and maintains an illusion, and if the generation of a 'preferred story' risks a 'flight to health' at the expense of psychoanalytic insight or 'self-knowledge'. And as a narrative therapist, I become obliged to question the sorts of reiterations produced within psychoanalytic therapies: seeing transference as an effect of a set of technologies of power (White, 2000) that produce the subject of therapy as regressed and resistant, and privilege the therapist's knowledge of the shape, if not the content, of what the 'patient' cannot by definition know. These examples not only highlight the incommensurability of different therapeutic ideas and practices; they also draw attention to the 'work' that therapists do in policing the boundaries of their own and others' subject positions and subjectivities (cf. Davies, 2000).

Psychoanalysis, of course, is not outside the discursive and narrative construction of knowledge and reality simply because it posits a formative prehistory to the subject's formation in language. Psychoanalysis cannot be other than yet another story, albeit one with powerful claims to universality. As Søndergaard (2002) has pointed out, perhaps it is precisely the theoretical and discursive dominance of psychoanalysis that makes its truths seem so self-evident. Moreover, psychoanalysis can sometimes play the devastating trick of labelling as denial or repression any attempt to critique its truth status, although it would be unfair to hold this to always be the case, given the persistence of psychoanalysis' immanent critique. From a Foucauldian perspective, psychoanalysis is implicated in creating the normal through a production and abjection of the abnormal, and in problematising instinct and desire, thereby giving rise to an expansion and consolidation of technologies of regulation, normalisation and self-government (Foucault, 2003). In my areas of work, faced with the normative and pathologising practices of much psychoanalytically oriented therapy, I have taken up, in relation to psychotherapy, to psychoanalysis and to my own profession of art psychotherapy, a Foucauldian critique of the repressive hypothesis and of juridico-discursive power (Foucault, 1980). Whether this constitutes an immanent or extrinsic critique of psychoanalysis on my part must perhaps remain undecidable since, in the deconstructive tradition, I both inhabit and subvert the various genres of therapy.

Similarly, narrative therapy is not, by virtue of taking up the narrative metaphor in its poststructural dimensions of multiplicity and indeterminacy, exempt from a poststructural critique of subjectification. An attempt to bring poststructural research methodology together with narrative therapy led my colleague Carolyn Williams and myself to raise some questions about just who *is* the subject of narrative therapy, and to ask whether "the self as narrative coherence is the aim of such therapy" (Williams and Linnell, 2006, p. 72). Thinking this further through Butler's intervention, I begin to wonder whether this problem might flow from *any* therapeutic take-up of narrativity. Clearly 'narrative' is not the sole province of 'narrative therapy': it was after all Anna O., a patient of Freud's colleague, Joseph Breuer, who first named 'the talking cure' (Breuer, 1995). In all therapies we have ways of making you talk, and to talk in ways we are trained to hear. When narrative therapy makes space for the wordless and metaphorical dimensions of the therapeutic encounter (White, 1995, 1997, 2000), it turns towards the liminal and the poetic, and this turn may mark a limit of narrative itself.

Butler (2001, p. 34) expresses a concern with "the way in which narrative coherence may foreclose upon an ethical resource, namely, an acceptance of the limits of knowability in oneself and others". In its appreciation of the significance and limits of narrativity, Butler's work creates further 'ground' for both the theory and practice of narrative therapy while offering a poststructural critique of its limits. To me, this kind of critique is crucial in sustaining narrative therapeutic practice as a form of enquiry, rather than allowing it to solidify into received knowledge. Meanwhile, Butler's close questioning and re-visioning of the founding myths of psychoanalysis assist me to reconsider my ambivalent relationship to this tradition. It becomes possible to maintain a Foucauldian critique of how psychoanalytic discourse and practice enables normalising power, while simultaneously drawing upon the critical potential of psychoanalysis in order to trouble the figure of a self-identical, self-reflexive, and autonomous subject.

The discursive subject of narrative therapy appears far less at odds with the psychoanalytic subject of art therapy from a perspective that analyses the intricate mutual constitution of social and psychic realms and acknowledges intrapsychic suffering as an effect of power (Butler, 1997b). The deconstructive questioning associated with narrative therapy can make this mutual constitution and these effects of power available to the therapeutic conversation, at the same time that psychoanalytic and art psychotherapeutic practices provide space for the eruption, intensification and containment of emotions and memories that appear 'out of time'. Although different therapeutic practices invite different narratives of self, and although what is available to be 'storied' changes across time and context, there is arguably always a non-narrativisable excess. Failure to recognise this implicates therapy in the reconstitution of the autonomous subject of rationality.

Butler's work incites me to question the 'I', not only in therapy, but also in this book, since for Butler, as for Foucault, the subject cannot be a point of origin. Hence (to reprise the point that inaugurates this section of my chapter), the subject cannot ever give a full and reliable account of its origin:

> I would have to say that I can tell the story of my origin and even tell it again and again, but the story of my origin I tell is not one for which I am accountable, and it cannot establish my accountability. At least, let's hope not, since, over wine usually, I tell it in various ways, and the accounts are not always consistent with each other. (Butler, 2001, p. 26)

My acts, my speech, my thoughts and feelings as a therapist and researcher are in Butler's terms citational, and even my sense of myself as an agential subject is itself a citation of predominantly humanist and modernist notions of agency. A space of difference opens up within these citations, and I actively 'take up' these possibilities of difference. Yet even as 'I' 'take myself up' within these possibilities, there is an opacity and indeterminacy to such acts and to the subject that commits them, and who is committed to, or by, them. This suggests a limit to my reflexivity in my work as a therapist, and to the accounts I offer in this book. I am of course not without the possibility, the necessity and even the inevitability of performing 'agency'. But if I propose or assume that I can 'exercise' even a poststructural version of agency as perhaps I *must* propose in order to do my work, am I not already undone?

My effectiveness as subject of whatever order is always somewhat mysterious to me, displaced from intention, played out in layers of histories and memories and relations and bodies. Nor, having attempted to dethrone the self-identified agency of a phenomenological subject, can I rely on the intervention of a critical theory to pull the wool from my eyes. Sovereign theory is as problematic as any other sovereignty. The effect of this realisation, as Butler points out, need not be nihilism, paralysis, unbounded relativism, amorality or despair. Humility, connectedness, open-endedness, might rather be the implications of such radical uncertainty (Butler, 2001, 2005). And perhaps I cannot even afford to be certain of uncertainty, or grounded in an assuredness of ungroundedness. At the limits of reflexivity I do not so much turn as become the turn itself, that which is always forming through turning towards the Other, losing myself at the moment of self-consciousness, finding myself only in that which I must strive to, but cannot, know (Butler, 1997b).

Well, she thinks to herself a little crossly, perhaps the Butler didn't do it after all, because that would be incompatible with an ethics of non-violence. What is it, anyway, that the Butler is supposed to have done?

Given an ethics of uncertainty, how could she ever know? Perhaps it's more a question of what the Butler undid? While she loves her excursions into the wonderland of Philosophy, they often make her head spin. Perhaps it is better to eschew such vast ontological questions in favour of specifics. For instance, what is it that the Butler has done/undone for her? But after all this reading about obligation and responsiveness to the Other, that sounds like a selfish question.

She puts down her bags and sits for a while on a new, 'old fashioned' bench in an internal courtyard. She is tired, a bit grumpy, and somewhat overwhelmed. She has all this exciting 'stuff', but what is she going to do with it? As the sunlight fades from the courtyard, she sighs and gathers her things together.

And so, for a time at least, she leaves the Store of Poststructural Theory, still wearing her new 'Experience' jacket, her green bags overflowing with exquisite colours, textures and fabrications, her new books tucked under her arm. She passes the same two protesters whom she encountered when she first entered the store at the beginning of chapter 2. She notices that this time one of them is playing the fiddle, a mournful yet uplifting improvisation, while the other is simultaneously weeping and holding a placard, different to the one he was holding before. She stops to read it.

> THE MAN WHO SURRENDERS TO TEARS IN MUSIC THAT NO LONGER RESEMBLES HIM AT THE SAME TIME ALLOWS THE STREAM OF WHAT HE HIMSELF IS NOT—WHAT WAS DAMMED UP BACK OF THE WORLD OF THINGS—TO FLOW BACK INTO HIM. IN TEARS AND SINGING, THE ALIENATED WORLD IS ENTERED. "TEARS POUR, THE EARTH HAS TAKEN ME BACK"—THIS IS THE GESTURE OF MUSIC. THUS THE EARTH RECLAIMS EURYDICE. THE GESTURE OF RETURNING, NOT THE FEELING OF WAITING, DESCRIBES THE EXPRESSION OF ALL MUSIC, EVEN IN A WORLD WORTHY OF DEATH.

Her eyes fill with tears. She passes him a wisp of silk, from her other-wor(l)dly treasures, to wipe his eyes.

The words on the placard are those of Theodor Adorno, a foundational figure in the post-Marxist philosophical tradition of critical theory, and the internal quotation is from Goethe's *Faust 1*, line 784 (cited in Leppert, 2005, p. 107). Have I made a Faustian bargain with poststructural theory in this and the preceding chapter, a pact with the devil of moral relativism, as critical theory might imply? I don't think so. In the chapter you have just read, the vulnerability and uncertainty that accompany a crisis of representation and a questioning of absolute truth do not necessarily lead to moral relativism. Uncertainty does not automatically lead to an ethical indecisiveness in the face of injustice, including the injustices that may inadvertently be perpetuated through the pathologising and dividing practices of therapy. Vulnerability does not inevitably lead to a defensive shoring up of the power and knowledge of the therapist. Rather, an acknowledgement of vulnerability and uncertainty becomes the precondition for an ethical relation to the Other and an expanded notion of the human. In the domain of therapeutic practice, acknowledgement of vulnerability and uncertainty on the part of the therapist enables the therapist to become Other-wise, and thus to engage in a therapeutic practice of recognition and restitution with those subjects who are Othered by dominant discourse.

In the next chapter, I ask what approaches to research and writing about art therapy and narrative therapy—what methodologies—will carry forward the critical concerns and radical possibilities that have opened up through the theories I have just explored.

---

[1] I do not entirely agree with Venn's critique of Foucault who, in my opinion, does explore the possibilities of non-coercive relations, particularly through his consideration of friendship (Foucault, 2000b).

REFERENCES

Blyth, I. (2004). *Hélène Cixous: Live theory.* New York & London: Continuum.

Breuer, J. (1995). Case 1: Fraulein Anna O (Breuer). In P. Gay (Ed.), *The Freud reader* (pp. 61–78). London: Vintage. (Original work published 1895).

Butler, J. (1993). *Bodies that matter: on the discursive limits of 'sex'.* New York: Routledge.

— (1997a). *Excitable speech: a politics of the performative.* New York: Routledge.

— (1997b). *Psychic life of power: theories in subjection.* California: Stanford University Press.

— (1999). *Gender trouble: Feminism and the subversion of identity.* New York and London: Routledge. (Original edition published 1990).

— (2000). *Antigone's claim: Kinship between life and death.* New York: Columbia University Press.

— (2001). Giving an Account of Oneself. *Diacritics*, 31(4), 22–40.

— (2004a). *Precarious life: the powers of mourning and violence.* New York and London: Routledge.

— (2004b). Bracha's Eurydice. *Theory, Culture and Society*, 21(1), 95–100.

— (2005). *Giving an account of oneself.* New York: Fordham University Press.

Cixous, H. (1981). The laugh of the Medusa. In E. Marks & I. de Courtivron (Eds.), *New French feminisms: an anthology* (pp. 245–264). Great Britain: The Harvester Press Ltd. (Original work published 1975).

— (1991). *Readings: the poetics of Blanchot, Joyce, Kafka, Kleist, Lispector, and Tsvetavev.* Minneapolis: The University of Minnesota Press.— (1993). *Three steps on the ladder of writing.* New York: Columbia University Press.

— (1998). *Stigmata. Escaping texts.* London: Routledge.

— (2008). *White ink interviews on sex, text and politics*. Stocksfield: Acumen.

Cixous, H., & Calle-Gruber, M. (1997). Rootprints: memory and life writing. London & New York: Routledge. (Original work published 1994).

Cixous, H., & Clément, C. (1986). *The newly born woman.* Minneapolis: University of Minnesota Press.

Cixous, H. & members of the Centre d'Etudes Feminines (1988). Conversations. In S. Sellers (Ed.), *Writing differences: readings from the seminar of Hélène Cixous* (pp. 141–154). Milton Keynes: Open University Press. (Original interview recorded 1986).

Clément, C. (1987). *The weary sons of Freud.* London: Verso. (Original work published 1978).

— (1989). *Opera, or the undoing of women.* London: Virago Press. (Original work published 1988).

— (1994). *Syncope: the philosophy of rapture.* Minneapolis: University of Minnesota Press.

— Davies, B. (2000). *A body of writing.* Walnut Creek, CA: AltaMira Press.

Fanon, F. (1970). *Black skin, white masks.* London: Paladin.

— (1996b). Subaltern talk: interview with the editors. In D. Landry & G. MacLean (Eds.), *The Spivak reader: selected works of Spivak* (pp. 141–174). New York & London: Routledge. (Original work published 1993).

Foucault, M. (1980). *The history of sexuality, Volume 1: an introduction.* New York: Vintage Books. (Original work published 1976).

— (2000a). So is it important to think? In J. Faubion (Ed.), *Essential works of Foucault 1954–1984, Volume 3, Michel Foucault: Power* (pp. 454–458). London: Penguin Books. (Original interview conducted 1981).

— (2000b). Friendship as a way of life. In P. Rabinow (Ed.). *Essential works of Foucault 1954–1984, Volume 1, Michel Foucault: Ethics, subjectivity and truth* (pp. 135–140). London: Penguin Books. (Original interview 1981).

— (2000c). On the genealogy of ethics: an overview of work in progress. In P. Rabinow (Ed.), *Essential works of Foucault 1954–1984, Volume 1, Michel Foucault: Ethics, subjectivity and truth* (pp. 253–280). London: Penguin Books. (Interview conducted 1983).

— (2003). *Abnormal: Lectures at the College de France 1974–1975.* (G. Burchell, Trans.). London & New York: Verso. (Original work published 1999).

Grosz, L. (1989). *Sexual subversions: three French feminists.* Australia: Allen & Unwin.

Klein, M. (1991). The psychoanalytic play technique: its history and significance. In J. Mitchell (Ed.), *The selected Melanie Klein* (pp. 35–56). Harmondsworth: Penguin. (Original work published 1952).

— (1988). *Envy and gratitude and other works 1946–1963.* London: Virago.

Kristeva, J. (1980). *Desire in Language: A Semiotic Approach to Literature and Art.* (T. Gora, Trans.). New York: Columbia University Press.

— (1982). *Powers of horror.* New York: Columbia University Press. (Original work published 1980).

— (1984). *Revolution in poetic language.* New York: Columbia University Press.

— (1989). *Black sun: depression and melancholia.* New York & Oxford: Columbia University Press.

— (1990). The system and the speaking subject. In T. Moi (Ed.), *The Kristeva reader* (pp. 24–33). Oxford: Basil Blackwell Ltd. (Original work published 1972).

— (2000). *The sense and non-sense of revolt: the powers and limits of psychoanalysis.* New York: Columbia University Press. (Original work published 1996).

— (2002). *Revolt, she said.* Los Angeles: Semiotext(e).

Leppert, R. (2005). Music 'pushed to the edge of existence' (Adorno, listening, and the question of hope). *Cultural critique.* 60(Spring), 92–133.

Landry, D., & Maclean, G. (1996). Introduction: reading Spivak. In D. Landry & G. MacLean (Eds.), *The Spivak reader: selected works of Spivak.* New York & London: Routledge.

McFayden, A. (1997). Rapprochement in sight? Postmodern family therapy and psychoanalysis. *Journal of Family Therapy,* 19, 241–62.

Moi, T. (Ed.). (1990). *The Kristeva reader.* Oxford: Basil Blackwell Ltd. (Original work published 1986).

Sellers, S. (Ed.). (2004). *The writing notebooks of Hélène Cixous.* New York: Continuum.

Sondergard, D. (2002). III. Theorising subjectivity: contesting the monopoly of psychoanalysis. *Feminism and psychology,* 12(4), 445–454.

Spivak, G. (1985). Can the subaltern speak? Speculations on widow-sacrifice. *Wedge,* 7/8(Winter/Spring), 120–130.

— (1997). Translator's preface. In J. Derrida, (1998). *Of grammatology* (pp. ix–lxxxvii). Baltimore & London: John Hopkins University Press.

— (1996a). Revolutions that as yet have no model: Derrida's 'Limited Inc'. D. Landry & G. MacLean (Eds.), *The Spivak reader: selected works of Spivak* (pp. 75–107). New York & London: Routledge. (Original work published 1985).

— (1996b). Subaltern talk: interview with the editors. In D. Landry & G. MacLean (Eds.), *The Spivak reader: selected works of Spivak* (pp. 141–174). New York & London: Routledge. (Original work published 1993).

— (1996c). More on power/knowledge. In D. Landry & G. MacLean (Eds.), *The Spivak reader: selected works of Spivak* (pp. 287–308). New York & London: Routledge. (Original work 1992).

— (1999). *A critique of postcolonial reason: toward a history of the vanishing present.* Cambridge & London: Harvard University Press.

Venn, C. (2000). *Occidentalism, modernity and subjectivity.* London: Sage.

— (2002). Refiguring subjectivity after modernity. In V. Walkerdine (Ed.), *Challenging subjects: critical psychology for a new millennium* (pp. 51–71). Houndsmills, UK: Palgrave

White, M. (1992). Deconstruction and therapy. In D. Epston & M. White, *Experience, contradiction, narrative and imagination: selected papers of David Epston and Michael White 1989–1991* (pp. 109–152). Adelaide: Dulwich Centre Publications. (Original work published 1991).

— (1995). *Re-authoring lives: Interviews and essays.* Adelaide: Dulwich Centre Publications,.

— (1997). *Narratives of therapist's lives.* Adelaide: Dulwich Centre Publications.

— (2000). *Reflections on narrative practice.* Adelaide: Dulwich Centre Publications.

— (2004). Working with people who are suffering the consequences of multiple trauma: a narrative perspective. *The International Journal of Narrative Therapy and Community Work,* 2004(1), 45–76.

Williams, C., & Linnell, S. (2006). When the doctors consulted the narrative therapist…an experiment in questioning dominant stories of PhD pedagogy. *The International Journal of Critical Psychology,* 18, 56–80.

Winnicott, D. W. (1965). *The maturational processes and the facilitating environment.* London: Hogarth Press.

— (1971). *Playing and reality.* London: Tavistock Publications.

CHAPTER 4

A MADNESS IN HER METHODOLOGIES: AN 'ETHICALLY REFLEXIVE' ENQUIRY THROUGH WRITING AND ART

> *Do the sentences describe something or are they doing something?...You reach a border from which what seemed to be certain appears in its precariousness or in its history, without necessarily disappearing or collapsing.*
>
> (Derrida, 1995a, pp. 117–8)

Abstract: Chapter 4 orients the reader to this book's unusual approach to practitioner research through engaging with questions of poststructural research methodology, especially with the writing methodologies that have emerged from the work of a number of contemporary poststructural feminists. In this chapter I also engage with the discursive character of the visual and the contemporary 'aesthetic turn' in art therapy, in relation to the project of shaping a narrative and poststructural approach to art therapy.

In my work, different genres of writing are engaged as a methodology for imagining therapy beyond the conventions of positivist clinical writing and the individual 'case study'. I am not so much concerned to establish new forms of validity as to upset the apple cart—or perhaps the medication trolley would be a closer analogy—of increasing contemporary demands for both therapy and research to operate within the domain of Evidence Based Practice (Gilroy, 2006). In particular, I aim to denaturalise the taken-for-granted status of the individual 'case study' within the art therapy literature. At the same time, I do not wish to reconstitute the humanist subject by replacing scientific certainties with an assurance of 'authentic human experience', whether that be my experience or that of others. In the face of contemporary discourses—on the one hand of positivism, 'evidence based psychological practice' and risk management (Rose, 2005) and on the other hand of the authentic, self-responsible, self-knowing and self-actualising individual, I am interested in moving beyond the divide of the differing certainties of objective science and subjective experience. I am interested in how *un*certainty may become an ethical resource (Butler, 2004, 2005), within the reflexive and intersubjective spaces of a poststructurally oriented therapeutic and research practice.

My research takes up a poststructural iteration of 'ethical reflexivity' (Davies, 2006a) in response to a dilemma beautifully articulated by Constance Ellwood:

> There is an ongoing tension between, on the one hand, [the] need to name one's own discursive construction and its effects on the research, and, on the other hand, an acknowledgement of the impossibility of a modernist, transparently self-knowing subject capable of such naming. (Ellwood, 2006, p. 69)

From a poststructural perspective, 'ethical reflexivity' is a methodological concept in need of re-vision. A modernist conceptualisation of ethical reflexivity (Gerwitz and Cribb, 2006) suggests that researchers, while obliged to become aware of their social and ethical values, neither can nor should quarantine them. Rather, an ongoing questioning of and response to the ethical implications of social research should be intrinsic to any 'truly' reflexive research methodology. However, conceptualisations of 'reflexivity' and 'ethics'—and thus of 'ethical reflexivity'—from within such a modernist framework for qualitative research assume that the researcher is a rational and moral subject, engaged in a conscious dialectic with his or her research subjects and data, and thus continually progressing the validity of research.

The reflexive subject of humanist theory is problematised by Davies (2006b, 2006c), who takes up the Butlerian insight that the "full knowledge of self that is implicated in humanist ideals of ethical practice must…be put aside in favour of an awareness of the emergent process of mutual transformation" (Davies, 2006b, p. 436). Ellwood similarly seeks to go beyond humanist notions of the self-reflexive researcher by

> enact[ing] instead an 'ethical reflexivity', which, drawing on Butler (2004), values the notion of remaining open and vulnerable, as a researcher, to what is not, or cannot, be fully known or controlled. (Ellwood, 2006, p. 68)

The (im)possibility of poststructural research

The methodologies of my book hover, uncomfortably at times, between a Foucauldian discourse analysis/genealogical approach and a deconstructive approach. According to a genealogical perspective, a researcher cannot effectively critique the centring of the self in Western thought and practice from within theories of subjectivity and practices of subjective writing (see Rose, 1998; Scheurich, 1997), because this move inevitably reconstitutes the centring of the subject. From a deconstructive perspective, however, it is not sufficient to elaborate a critique of the modern subject. The very possibility of a decisive critical agency, the authority of the researcher to practice genealogy or any other form of critique, must itself come under erasure.

In attempting to *enact* this dilemma in my book, I am hopefully not too far from the spirit of Foucault's ethics of permanent critique, arts of self, and books of experiment/experience. While this is not a conventionally Foucauldian piece of research, I suspect that being 'Foucauldian' is not necessarily the only way to engage with the radical potential of Foucault. I cannot solve through argument, nor dissolve through writing, the tensions within and between poststructuralisms. Neither can I settle the differences between poststructuralisms and other critical approaches. I must opt for an ethic of discomfort, a practice of contradiction, an alarming uncertainty as to when and where 'I' am failing/falling.

She flicks back through her notes. On one page she has scrawled:

> "Tak(ing) testimony seriously enough not to tame its interruptive force into a philosophy of presence and the speaking subject (Derrida 1996)" (in Lather, 2001, p. 215) requites a textual aesthetics that refuses to naturalise the subjects of research and therapy...

She loves such unintended resonances of error, their powers to destabilise that which reason apparently 'requires'. She prefers the practice and potential of 'just writing' to the proceedings and proceeds of writing justifications—would choose any day the poetics of a requiem over the politics of a requirement. And yet she recognises that poetics and politics cannot be separated in this way.

Writing methodologies

'Writing methodologies', once named as such, risk becoming another under examined convention of qualitative research. Against this, the incitement to write, and the refusal of such methodologies to be turned into a set of instructions for how to conduct poststructural research, are potentially transformative. While I do not wish to give writing a status outside of dominant discourse, I do think that what I learn and unlearn by responding to the incitement to write is at least as important as any other attempt I make to 'do' discourse analysis or deconstruction.

Scheurich (1997) suggests that the emergence of transgressive writing methodologies within social science research does not necessarily escape the dominance of the realist paradigm. Noting that some of these methodologies claim to replace one form of 'validity' with another, Scheurich argues that a liberalisation of the discourse of validity does not in itself constitute a paradigm shift. When writing methodologies strategically attempt to appropriate the language of validity, this appropriation is fraught with the likelihood of reconstituting the 'reality' of research. Norman Denzin and Yvonna Lincoln (1998) have similarly argued that experimental writing methodologies largely serve as a form of validation for a renewed social science. Moreover, by laying claim to new forms of validity, experimental writing methodologies tend to draw attention away from the imbrication of such texts with "state power" (Denzin, 1998, p. 315) and governmentality.

In these critics' own terms, one could scarcely declare the 'writing methodologies' of the social sciences to be 'invalid'. Rather, the critique is both cautionary, and an incentive to reach beyond versions and inversions of the discourse of validity, scientific or otherwise. I hope, in the pages that follow, to cautiously take up the critical and creative potentialities of transgressive writing in ways that extend beyond the binary of valid/invalid. Rather than making a claim of validity for my research, I would hope to touch upon the possibilities and limits of the truths of fiction and the fictions of truth, to find an ethical resource in unknowingness and relationality. In such research, however, 'uncertainty' itself can easily be romanticised and given a truth status. My book is necessarily haunted by the ironic dangers of becoming certain about uncertainty.

Having made my reservations about these methodologies and their claims, I will climb aboard a train of thought that takes transgressive writing as its point of departure, rather than as its destination. On this journey, I am grateful for the texts and the contexts, the companionships and the pedagogies, offered me by other poststructural feminist writings and writers. In experimenting with the possibilities for writing (rather than 'writing up') this book, I have looked to the work of these women for inspiration, support and provocation.

Feminist poststructural writers seem particularly adept at subverting binaries in order to express the apparently inexpressible. The methodologies they have invented and explored verge on dismantling the opposition of philosophy and its applications. Their work extends the parameters of what can be taken as knowledge, while undermining discourses of disembodied knowing and/or knowing subjects. Often this writing involves 'a double practice' or 'double gesture' (Lather, 2001; Spivak, 1996) around the (im)possibilities of creating new knowledges. For instance, Elizabeth St Pierre urges that we "imagin[e] writing as a letting go of meaning even as meaning proliferates" (St Pierre, 2005). Patti Lather advocates 'getting lost' (Lather and Smithies, 1997) as well as 'getting smart' (Lather, 1991). Davies, reflecting on the part writing can play "in the possibility of coming to know otherwise, against the grain of dominant discourses" (Davies, 2006c, p. 1), insists upon transgressive writing as disciplined practice as well as upon such writing's potential to undo a certain disciplinarity.

These writings engage with the ethics of representation while refusing to be paralysed by its dangers. They assert the value of autoethnography and memoir, while questioning the tendency of life writing to reconstitute a humanist subject. They insist that our own selves may be taken as the subject and object of research, while refusing to be confined to an autobiographical project by the impossibility of authentic representation. In this tradition, Susanne Gannon (2005, p. 626) "seek[s] writing practices that zigzag between categories, that produce knowledge in the gaps between analysis and creativity, reason and emotion, intellectual and aesthetic, mind and body, academic and everyday, us and them". St Pierre (2005; Richardson and St Pierre, 2005) explains how she resisted the ethnographic imperative to analyse the older women who participated in her long-term research. She

> became wary of the not-so-innocent assumption of interpretivism that the women should be drilled and mined for knowledge (who are they? what do they mean?) and then represented...this did not seem to be the kind of ethical relation these women who had taught me how to be a woman required of me. (St Pierre, 2005, p. 5)

After all, says St Pierre, it is not these women, but subjectivity itself, that is the focus of her research.

Lather similarly refuses to simply 'deliver' the women in her study to the reader. She also refuses the narrow competency of the reflective and reflexive researcher in favour of a necessarily awkward and jagged aesthetics of writing and an ethics of non-mastery. Lather's (2001) postscript to her co-authored ethnography (Lather and Smithies, 1997) suggests, following Derrida, that we might embrace doubled practices of writing, practices that enable us to respond vigorously to the imperative to make the experiences of others visible in their situatedness, specificity and urgency, while refusing to uncritically reconstitute either authorial presence or the authenticity of the subject's voice. Lather (2001) takes up Visweswaran's (1994) suggestion that feminist ethnography, "[g]iven the realisation of the limits of representation and the weight of research as surveillance and normalisation" (in Lather, 2001, p. 203), needs to embrace its 'failure'. Lather further suggests that performing ethnography at the limits of representation necessitates a deconstructive move into writing from

> voice to inscription, from notions of the intrinsic to ideas of the frame. Refusing textual innocence and an untroubled realism, representation is practiced as a way to intervene, even while one's confidence is

> troubled. Here the task becomes to operate from a textual rather than a referential notion of representation… (Lather, 2001, p. 214)

She begins to write. She often writes about herself like this, in the third person, but then, when she writes in the third person (and even when she writes in the first person), it isn't always about herself. She wonders sometimes if she has bitten off more than she can chew—if reason itself might choke on surfeit or be blinded by excessive indulgence in a regressive masticatory habit called writing. Which may be accomplished in the sense that playing or dancing can be 'accomplished', but may never be complicit, achieved, or identical with itself. She closes her eyes, with her face turned to the sun. After-images burn into a blood red screen. She is swaying a little, allowing herself to be led. A madness in her methodology must eschew logical steps, seize her in its death-defying embrace and dance her to another beginning...

(Auto)ethnographies and beyond

Although I engage extensively in this book with practices of memoir and with an immanent critique of therapeutic cultures, I do not consider my writing to be precisely 'autoethnographic'. The first part of that word, 'auto', suggests a reiteration of autonomy, a concept and practice of selfhood that I actively seek to avoid. Moreover, in concert with the immanent critique of contemporary ethnography (see, for instance, Clifford and Marcus, 1986; Denzin and Lincoln, 1998), I dispute the possibility that the structures or even the stories of a culture or a self, including my self, can be charted and re-presented, however subversively, in a non-coercive approximation of the 'real'.

Gannon (2006) offers a poststructural critique and extension of auto-ethnography. Drawing upon Foucault's genealogical exploration of the differing ethical prescriptions that have historically guided and shaped practices of writing the self (Foucault, 1990, 2000a), Gannon makes a distinction between self writing practices that authenticate the self and lived experience, and those that figure subjectivity as discursive, fragile and performative.

In writing about therapy, I have found that it is just as important to examine and historicise the ethical practices of self-constitution within the domain of therapy itself as it is to make distinctions between the differing historical and ethical modes of self-writing. The tendency to reconstitute the domain of the personal as shaped by autobiography is deeply embedded in therapy discourse and in my ethical constitution as a therapist, suggesting that these discursive/ethical themes, at least to some extent, traverse the distinctions between psychically and socially oriented therapies. Against this dominant therapeutic ethics, my poststructural research orientation insists that I draw attention to the discursive constitution of subjectivities and of 'personal agency'. From a Foucauldian perspective, current socialities, discourses and relationships, the fertile everyday messiness of interactions and events, are constitutive of the domain of what it is possible, and impossible, for me to think, imagine, feel, be and do.

Collective biography

Collective biography (Davies *et al.*, 1997; Davies *et al.*, 2002; Davies and Gannon, 2006) extends autoethnographic writing into a collective writing and research practice that interrupts binaries of self and other, questioning the autonomy of authorship and the subject, and yet refusing to reduce the wayward idiosyncrasies of situated and embodied texts to a co-authored sameness. Collective biography complexifies and moves beyond the dilemma of whether to take oneself or others as a research subject, both because it is a collective practice and because it encourages participants to approach the Other in themselves [1]. Developed by Davies and her colleagues from the memory work of Frigga Haug (1992) and associates, collective biography is both an analysis of subjection and an enactment of discursive agency. The practice of collective biography fosters an aesthetics of writing that gestures toward the "mo(ve)ments" (Davies and Gannon, 2006, p. 7) of subjectivity in the making. This mutual and supportive interpellation of writing subjects is productive of vivid, situated and embodied texts and analyses of subjectivity:

> In collective biography we catch ourselves in remembered acts of turning on ourselves, seeing how we take up forms of power and strategies of surveillance. We attend to the ambivalent processes of subjection. We develop and refine our capacity to reflexively turn our gaze on ourselves in remembered moments of turning, of constituting ourselves and being constituted. (Davies and Gannon, 2006, p. 11)

Some of the pieces of writing in this book began their specific lives in collective biography workshops, but the practice of an embodied and intersubjective writing-as-research can be informed by collective biography without necessarily being limited to the particular formal processes of a collective biography workshop. I have therefore drawn on my experience and knowledge of collective biography and other transgressive writing practices to give myself 'poetic licence', within a research context, to experimenting widely with creative ways of writing (inter)subjectivities and socialities.

The necessity and impossibility of co-authorship and collaboration

Taking up Roland Barthes' (1989) suggestion that literature 'already knows' what science 'says' or talks about, Gannon seeks to go beyond the dilemmas of representation in research through the specifics of imagining and writing (an)other. Gannon is concerned with the "politics, the ethics, of imagining a life and giving voice to a character that does not exist" (Gannon, 2005, p. 625); yet these questions are at least equally urgent in relation to imagining a life for and giving voice to living subjects. However collaborative and recursive the process of research, most researchers ultimately tend to fold the stories of research subjects back into a narrative of which the researcher or researchers are the sole or principal authors (Scheurich, 1995; Williams and Linnell, 2006). In my opening chapter, I problematised the assumption that a co-authored therapeutic account could be produced through the decentring of therapeutic privilege and negotiation of shared meaning. Chapter 6 of this book, in which my accounts of narrative and art therapy with Indigenous children 'in care' are written in very close consultation with an Indigenous worker/carer, becomes something of a 'limit experience' (Foucault, 2000b) for my sustained engagement with the necessity and impossibility of therapeutic co-authorship and research collaboration. I am not sure that the subaltern clinical subject (Swartz, 2005) ever speaks, or could ever speak, in the pages of this book. I am not even sure if the clinical subject of therapy speaks in those moments when memoir and clinical writing come together in a re-presentation of my own experiences as a client of therapy. However, I do hope to offer readers of this book an experience/experiment that gestures towards the possibilities of therapy and of writing about therapy, by bringing to life some traces of how I have attempted to listen to the otherness in others and in myself. I attempt to engage in a writing wherein a fragile and contingent 'I', a necessarily contested 'we', an irreducibly mysterious and compelling 'you', are variously formed and performed, through a careful and risky listening and speaking of each with the other.

Dreaming (of) research

Since I seek to engage with therapeutic and writing practices that open radically upon "the irreducible heterogeneity of the other" (Lather, 2001, p. 222), whether this be the otherness of others or of oneself, such practices cannot be totally mapped out in advance or kept on a tight leash of rational control. Consequently, while some of the research/writing in this book is highly intentional, it inevitably exceeds and sometimes contradicts these intentions. At other times, the writing may from its beginnings be radically extrinsic or decentred, while much of the book falls somewhere in between intention and the unknown.

At the far borders of research that is unintended, I have on occasion stumbled somewhat reluctantly into that mysterious form of enquiry that engages me with and in spite of myself, in my other-than-waking hours. Dreams install an(O)ther as the driver of the text, instantiating a form of writing unbound by narrative conventions of time and place. Bringing the potential of dream writing together with the notion of writing as methodology suggests that dreams may be taken as 'data'. While as a writer this possibility excites me, as a therapist I feel some ambivalence. In particular, I have reservations about the classical Freudian approach that dreams are the fulfilment of a secret wish to which they can be reduced; or alternatively the Jungian approach which predicates the analysis of, and receptivity to, dreams upon a theory of a universal collective unconscious and a realm of archetypes. (This universalising tendency is mediated by an insistence on specificity and fragmentation in the post-Jungian analysis of James Hillman, which Stephen K. Levine (in Knill, Levine and Levine, 2005) claims is a postmodern psychology.) Yet, despite my ambivalence, dream writing as a form of research has insinuated itself into this book project through my unintended experience of dreaming of my research and my intentional writing of that dream.

For Cixous (1993), there is a School of Dreams, which she positions between the School of the Dead and the School of 'Roots'. She recommends, as one writer to another, our attendance at and attention to these schools, these three steps in the almost intolerable descent into writing. With her, we descend through an opening, the door of death. Our dreams transport us; we are travelling, unravelling, towards the uncertain births of our inconclusive beginnings. Dreams indenture us to mystery and unknowing, carrying us through regions of the unspeakable and the unthinkable, through endless substitutions and displacements with no fixed point of origin or destination. Dream writing is an art of transport, of going with the dream and allowing its freedom, since interpretation spells death to the dream. The dream cannot reveal an original secret: rather, dreams acquaint us, in fear and in joy, with "*the feeling of the secret*" (Cixous, 1993, p. 85, italics in original).

She is attempting to 'deepen her analysis' of her therapeutic work with children but feels a tremendous resistance to this process. *I don't want to analyse these stories*, she says to herself, after a long day and evening of working on a chapter that engages with a detailed account of therapy with a child. Telling herself that she is analysing a created text, and that the 'real child' is a humanist and Romantic notion, doesn't seem to entirely alleviate her distress.

Strange phrases drift through her as she is falling asleep that night.

> *The stories of the children are not 'my data'...they are children of flesh and word...*

Next morning she wakes half choked by the disturbing tendrils of a dream. Untangling herself and pushing back the covers, she leans over to pick up the pen and the silver dream book from the bedside table, and begins to write.

in their hands

i don't find them until morning
half dreaming
fingers coiled around
a lump of offal in my chest

the flesh children's hands
are butter pale
or chocolate
with pink moons

the word children are
wearing gloves
of grey silk
over the bone

"put that down"
i say to them "it's mine"
and "go and wash those hands
—immediately"

they giggle
and fall about
as i prise their bloody
fingers from my heart

The poetic as research methodology

Poetry, says Derrida, is to "learn by heart" (Derrida, 1995b, p. 291). This is neither the organic heart rendered knowable and analysable by Western science, nor the glitter-pink heart commodified and sentimentalised within the culture of late capitalism, nor the essentialised humanist heart, figured as the source of true emotion. Pumping in an autopoetic rhythm, the heart does not precede the poem; it is embodied through the poem. Engaged in a singular and unrepeatable economy of memory and desire, each poem is exactly that which we long to know 'by heart'. The poem is not signed by, nor the sign of, the author; it is signed by, and a sign of, the Other (Derrida, 1995b).

When I first began to bring together my practice of writing poetry with my practice of therapy by reflecting in poetic form on my clinical work, I saw this as related to an emerging technique in narrative therapy of the therapist recording the words of the people who come to therapy and offering these words back in the intensified form of poetry (Freedman and Combs, 2001; Behan, 2003; Speedy, 2003, 2005). My poetry is also strongly related to the research practice of presenting 'data' from interviews in poetic form (Richardson, 2002). Richardson offers a philosophical and practical discussion of the poetic form as a poststructural research methodology for the presentation of qualitative interviews. She draws on the potential of poetry to render the specificity of the subject's voice without recourse to notions of authenticity. Richardson also contends that "the poetic form is a viable means for seeing beyond social scientific conventions and discursive practices" (Richardson, p. 877), and that it may therefore be a preferred methodology when wishing to unmask truth claims and draw attention to the constitutive character of writing and reading research data.

Through poetic ways of figuring 'experience', ethics and aesthetics can come together in the shaping of therapeutic understanding and its limits. As an unconventional form for the narration of therapy, poetry draws attention to how stories of the work are not 'true representations' but new productions, and to how the aesthetics of writing about therapy are inseparable from the ethics of the work. As a mode of imaging and resonating with the stories of the 'clients' of therapy, such poetry attempts an expansion of accountability to the clinical subject of therapy. I think it can be useful to think of accountability as just that: account-ability, or the ability of certain modes of practice, including writing practice, to offer complex, situated and embodied, yet denaturalised, accounts. This suggestion goes some way towards a reappropriation of the concept of 'accountability', which has been enlisted in therapy practice as a normalising technique of the neoliberal self. (In a related move, Toni Morrison (2000) has refigured responsibility—another favoured technology of the self within neoliberal regimes—as 'response-ability'.)

Yet poetry also attempts to gesture beyond the accountable in everyday experiences toward the mysterious and ineffable. Butler's suggestion (2004,

2005) that a responsibility to the Other emerges from our vulnerabilities and from the limits of our knowing suggests in turn that our ability to respond can exceed our ability to give an account. Thus 'response-ability' exceeds 'account-ability'. In this vein, poetry might be thought of as a practice of apprenticeship and choreography in relation to the Other (Venn, 2002). To write a poem is to apprentice oneself to the semiotic (Kristeva, 1980), to those aural and kinaesthetic dimensions of language that are closest to embodiment and emotion. Apprenticed to rhythm, to assonance, to metaphor, to metonymy, to the illogical logic of the line, 'I' do not decide the poem in advance of its writing. The poem, which is mine and not mine, begins to write/right itself. The poem takes me in its arms, I follow, and together we dance. We sway, we hover, fainting into a syncope (Clément, 1994), stumbling against each others' irreconcilable difference, or moving as one. The words on the page choreograph/record this mov(e)ment (cf. Davies and Gannon, 2006). The words stutter and stammer (Wyatt, 2008); they dance on the page.

In such a process, intentionality is not entirely lost, but it is radically decentred. Poetic and ethical readings and writings of therapeutic practice can illuminate its liminal and irrational dimensions, so that narrative structure need not reconstitute a rational, 'Enlightenment' view of progress and the subject, and aesthetic practice need not foreclose upon the social and political. A 'poethics' of therapeutic practice is an art of making space for uncertainty: for the mysteries of the psyche, the indeterminacy of the social, and the ongoing elaboration of an infinite relation between the two.

Genre and its limits

Poetry is, of course, only one among many literary and dramatic genres of writing. Moreover, prose can be poetic, and poetry at times mimics the most 'prosaic' of voices. Laurel Richardson, while arguably the main advocate for the poetic as poststructural research methodology, does not always privilege poetry—a move that would set up a binary of poetry and prose. Richardson experiments with the particular methodological potentials of different literary genres. For instance, she takes up memoir and auto-ethnography in writing an academic life (Richardson, 1997). Within this text, she writes an ethnographic drama, a form that is generically suited to surfacing, rather than smoothing over, conflict, in response to a hostile reception to a particular aspect of Richardson's research.

Writing of, and with, Cixous, Mereille Calle-Gruber suggests keeping 'genre' as a question, as a site of textual emergence, rather than as an attribute of texts (Cixous and Calle–Gruber, 1997). In this book, I find myself moving between literary, visual and therapeutic genres in an attempt to chart something of the intersubjectivities that constitute and are constituted by therapy and research conducted under the sign of the Other. I extend the notion of the poetic into my prose writing, my art making, and also my therapeutic practice. At times, I have followed narrative therapy practices and the tradition of 'found' poetry by shaping a poem from the words of people who have consulted me as a therapist. As a practicing poet, I have also experimented with writing poetry as a means of embodying my understandings and experiences of the domains of therapy and research. I have made artworks with, for and in response to the subjects of both therapy and research. In this, I follow a tradition of the expressive arts therapies, wherein it is regarded as crucial for a therapist to continue to practice her art form. I attempt to extend this tradition, which is practiced in the multiple spaces of the studio, the exhibition space, the performance and the literary work of poetry or fiction, into the space of research.

Critical visual methodologies

Visual art therapists, of whom I am one, have a history of protesting the dominance of written and spoken text and arguing for the critical and creative potential of the visual and plastic arts. Although most strongly influenced by the conventions of the individual clinical case study, art therapy has developed a minority tradition of art-based research (McNiff, 1998). Within this culture, I position myself, like John Henzell (2004), as an advocate for embracing the poetic and the imaginative across a range of discursive forms including words. In this, I sometimes feel I have more in common with the broad project of the expressive therapies (see chapter 1) than with the specific profession of (visual) art therapy.

By now I imagine it must be apparent to my readers, as it is to myself, that a long and highly charged engagement with writing shapes my biographical narratives and my understandings of myself as a therapist and researcher. My relationship with writing is of such an intimacy and intensity that it can tend to marginalise a consideration of other arts-based research methodologies. In one sense this is not a problem, since I am engaging the art of creative writing alongside more traditional forms of rhetorical exposition, and since, within a broad understanding of the expressive arts therapies, fiction and poetry are therapeutic modalities. It may even be advantageous that I tend to privilege writing, given that a book is predominantly a written text, and that I do not want this text to appear to give transparent access to experience and meaning, or to use narrative coherence to knit together a coherent subject and/or object of research.

In the previous discussion of writing methodologies and through the experimental rhetorical structure of this book, I have drawn attention to how writing constitutes the research 'findings' rather than simply describing them. Similarly, the visual images in this book are not simply illustrative of either the work of which this book gives an account, or of the written text itself. The images are themselves text, themselves constitutive of a kind of reality.

It seems important to think beyond the binary of either reducing visual art to an illustration of a verbal or written narrative, or of romanticising art as a unique and universal means of access to that which is (assumed to be) beyond words. Gilroy (2003, 2008) has begun to explore the relevance for art therapy of visual culture and critical visual methodologies (Rose, 2001). These contemporary fields support a more critical and reflexive practice of research into the arts by locating art in relation to considerations of culture, discourse, embodiment and the Other. Emerging visual research methodologies challenge the autonomy of both art and the subject. The visceral and material character of the visual arts as methodology is a powerful reminder to approach my work as "the work of art" which, in the words of Marsha Meskimmon, is also "the work of embodiment, of bringing us to our senses..." (Meskimmon, 2003, p. 5).

A critical visual approach also reminds us that visual imagery is constructed, through various practices, technologies and knowledges, at the sites of the production of the image, the image itself, and its audiencing (Rose, 2001). The construction of images within the context of arts-based research, as well as of art therapy, needs to be considered in relation to these sites.

My art therapy academic colleagues and I are engaged in an ongoing collaborative project of researching art therapy pedagogies through a contemporary art practice that embraces digital media, installation, performance, found objects, painting, drawing, mixed media and creative writing (e.g. Linnell, Westwood, Perry and Pretorius, 2005, 2007). Responding to research that empirically and theoretically explores the importance of experiential art making in introducing art therapy to a general audience (Dudley, Gilroy and Skaife, 1998), in the training of art therapists (Waller, 1993) and in art therapists' ongoing clinical supervision (Brown, Myerowitz-Katz and Ryde, 2003), we have turned from the conventions of clinical writing to an aesthetic process that questions the division between 'doing art', 'doing therapy' and 'doing research'.

Unlike the work my colleagues and I produce for these collaborative exhibitions, much of the artwork included in this book was made in a therapeutic context as part of art therapy sessions. The artwork included in chapter 5 was made in a community based clinical setting that gave access to a limited array of fine arts materials and to an electronic whiteboard, within a carpeted space with armchairs and coffee tables that privileged conversation, and was often confined to a little more than the convention of the therapeutic hour. In some contrast to this, the artwork included in chapter 6 was made in a studio environment—the same backyard art studio where I made some of the work I have included in chapter 7—in a more elastic space of time that stretched over approximately two hours from the conclusion of the school day into late afternoon. These differences have strongly informed the differing ways that art production is taken up by both the children and myself. I documented the artwork using either an SLR or 5.5 mega pixel digital camera, often rapidly photographing a piece before the artist took it home. For chapter 5, I scanned photocopies of electronic whiteboard printouts directly into the computer. I worked with computer editing programs to prepare photographs for inclusion in this e-book: making occasional and conservative changes to brightness and contrast to adjust for original lighting conditions, cropping to exclude background areas around the artworks and compensating for some odd photographic angles.

My artworks in chapter 7 were variously made: as rapid 'art responses' after facilitating a studio-based art therapy session, sometimes using the materials left over from the session; as art responses during art therapy experiential workshops; as apparently unrelated works that have retrospectively taken on significance for me in the context of writing about my work; and as intentional forms of research for this book project. These works were made as part of an interplay of my relations with others and (my)selves, rather than intended for 'exhibition'. I have included them in this book knowing them to be both precious entry points and aesthetically flawed.

Having thought carefully about whether or not to intersperse the images throughout the written text, I have chosen instead to produce three 'photo-essays' or predominantly visual texts that punctuate the last three chapters. I hope that this allows the artworks to resonate with each other within and across chapters, with the written text and with readers/viewers, as in a virtual gallery, without the works being reduced to illustrations of therapy stories or eclipsed by clinical modes of interpretation.

All of this underscores the well-established point that no pure reproduction of art is possible. At all stages of production I am constructing both the artworks and a narrative of the artworks, whether or not the 'originals' are made by me. This process of production continues in multiple readings and audiencings, as does the production of the wider (visual, written and imagined) text.

A 'telling' obligation

Derrida (1987) writes an extended meditation upon Cézanne's statement that "I owe you the truth in painting and I will tell it to you" (Cézanne to Emile Bernard, October 23, 1905, in Derrida, 1987, p. 2). According to Derrida, Cézanne's promise is a performative that promises another performative. Cézanne's promise thus bears an infinite and deferred relation to the truth it promises. The 'truth' is that I am bound to tell or perform the truth. Painting thus becomes an infinite response to a debt to the Other, a debt that the promise of painting is always bringing into being.

For all that artwork has strong and shifting meanings in the narratives of therapy, I cannot tell you the definitive truth of such artwork, and neither, indeed, could the person who made it. This does not negate my attempts to paint for you an approximation of the specificities and multiplicities of an artwork, to dramatise for you the contexts and processes of its creation, and to narrate for you some of the stories of its meanings, its audiencing, and its effects. From a poststructural ethical positioning, the contingency of truth heightens, rather than relieves, my responsibility to try to 'tell the truth' as truthfully as I can, entering me into an indefinite and passionate obligation.

I am aware that in addressing textual methodologies under separate headings of writing and the visual, I risk reinforcing a binary that already marks the theorisation of art therapy. In attempting to conceptualise how I might bring the visual and written together while respecting their differences, I have found it useful to turn once more to Foucault. While Foucault's work makes it possible to question the binary of visual and written language, he does not suggest that these different discursive practices are interchangeable or that translation between them is entirely possible. Foucault writes of the difficulty of writing about the visual, advocating for the specific and different discursive character of writing and painting. Foucault, like Derrida, writes of painting, rather than of visual art in general, because each visual art, and perhaps each genre of writing, is also different to other genres. Thus, when I photograph an artwork, that enters the work into yet another discourse, the discourse of photography, and the (im)possibility of photorealism.

Foucault suggests that it is necessary, when writing of painting, to eschew too literal an interpretation of what (or whom) a painting is 'about', in order that the artwork "may, little by little, release its illuminations" (Foucault, 1994, p. 10):

> The relation of language to painting is an infinite relation. It is not that words are inadequate, or that, when confronted by the visible, they prove insuperably inadequate. Neither can be reduced to the other's terms: it is in vain that we say what we see; what we see never resides

> in what we say. And it is in vain that we attempt to show…what we are saying…
>
> [I]f one wishes to keep the relation of language to vision open, if one wishes to treat their incompatibility as a starting point for speech instead of an obstacle to be avoided, so as to stay as close as possible to both, then one must erase those proper names and preserve the infinity of the task. (Foucault, 1994, pp. 9–10) [2]

The straw bale house

She and the other women meet with Andrea Gilroy (2003) for two days of art making, discussion and diarising around their research experiences. They stay in a straw bale house in the Blue Mountains. Formal presentations of their research plans are juxtaposed with leisurely walks, and, in the evening, they share a delicious dinner followed by long soaks and theoretical conversations in a hot tub in the garden.

Andy mentions to her in conversation by the fireside that, as children, many of Andy's colleagues in the art therapy world had wanted to be archaeologists. As a child, Sheridan too, for a time, had wanted to be an archaeologist.

The women are asked if, in the days following the workshop, they could each write something about their research and about the workshop that complements their visual explorations. She wonders how she might attempt to catch the butterfly of her experience in a net of words, without damaging its wings.

archaeologist

setting out from the house of straw and mud she plans to walk all the way to the end of the road but just over the hill is an ugly ceremonial concrete bridge across a muddy creek on a vacant block she can't work out if she's trespassing but she crosses the bridge anyway a narrow track circles up through bush to where a house might have been razed to the ground but the gums aren't scorched and there isn't enough *rubble for a recent fire or a demolition the ground is scattered with half buried broken wood masonry porcelain tin and glass and she can't work out what happened here are they going to build (these new upright markers must be surveyors' pegs) have they carted the old house away she kneels in wet earth on a steep slope held together with tangled roots and digs with her hands for the bones of old china*

two glass bottles some shards of white porcelain almost all the pieces of a small chinese plate the worn heel of an old boot a curving piece of petrified wood carried back in her shirt tales (she relishes this slip of the pen) to the straw bale house her trouser knees wet and dirty grit under her nails she finds a cardboard box for her specimens the dirt encrusted porcelain and the bottles containing miniature hanging gardens of mud and fern she cannot bear to wash away

next morning she gets up early someone else is already rustling and scratching away like a bower bird in the courtyard she creeps downstairs to the kitchen washes each piece in hot soapy water scrubbing the earth from the web of fine cracks washing the sharp fragments back to white and blue she tips the little bottled gardens out into the weeping flowerbed soaks the dirt from the tall bottle uses her fingertip to clean the round one with its gleaming misfit of a lid

hot-tubbing

i have made a case of words
to hold these wordless things
fragile
of doubtful provenance
and irrational worth

dreams cracked
in the firing
desire erupting
along faultlines

so tonight i offer you
a rare viewing
the contours of fifty years
and shards rinsed clean
in a skytub of girlish laughter

She knows now that she will not give up any of this. She will not give up the lightness of wordplay or the leaden weight of words; or the viscosity and viscerality of paint; or the slow yielding of a body of clay; or the quickening and slowing of conversation; or the still, reflective spaciousness of one silence, the stiff awkwardness of a different silence, and the unbearably loud scream of yet another.

She will not refrain from changing the lens, adjusting the focus, or returning the gaze. She will not give up the dance of stepping forward, stepping back, joining with, playing with, sitting with; or the art of listening intently, passionately, reluctantly, in outrage, in pleasure, in pain. She will not give up her patience with suffering or her "impatience for liberty" (Foucault, 2000c, p. 319); nor will she relinquish the rustle of paper and words, the scratching of crayons and heads, the drumming of fingers and hearts.

She will inhabit this space that fills with anger and joy, with love and with fear. She will laugh with someone at absurdity or in happiness, and she will almost drown, like Alice, in a pool of her own/another's tears. Touching and being touched, with a word, an image, a momentary glance, she and the other will swim together toward the shore, toward the unsure.

In this chapter I have sketched out my relationship with those feminist poststructural methodologies, and with writing and arts-based research methods, that inform a close enquiry into my ethics, practices, relationships and subjectivity as a therapist. Chapters 5 and 6 are a direct exploration of working on the borders of art psychotherapy and narrative therapy with two different families. In the first of these chapters I find my ethical subjection as a therapist to be challenged by working with a family whose stories and values resonate with some of my own narratives, within and beyond the domain of therapy.

P.S.

These early chapters are not a prelude to the 'real drama'. These words are not the torches of the usherettes of theory, guiding her to a more 'en-lightened' form of practice. There is no proscenium other than, perhaps, the permeable frame of her enquiry; no curtain to be raised other than the virtual cover of this book, bound, yet unbound, to unknown and undetermined destinations. The work is in progress. The 'play' has already begun.

---

[1] Participants prepare for a collective biography workshop through reading extracts of relevant texts and workshop notes prepared by the workshop convenor. The workshop involves recollecting and writing the earliest memories for each participant provoked by cues associated with a workshop theme. Each participant then reads out her writing to the group, who reflect back on the immediacy and embodied character of this writing, noting points where the writer has veered into reification or explanation. Writings are reworked by their makers in the light of these reflections.

[2] The reference to 'proper names' relates to the limited usefulness of identifying the representational 'content' of a work: in this instance, the names and histories of the subjects who sat for Velasquez's painting, *Las Meninas*.

REFERENCES

Barthes, R. (1989). *The rustle of language.* New York: Hill & Wang.

Behan, C. (2003). *'Rescued speech poems': Co-authoring poems in narrative therapy.* Retrieved May, 2004, from www.narrativeapproaches.com.

Brown, C., Meyerowitz-Katz, J. & Ryde, J. (2003).Thinking with image making in supervision. *Inscape*, 8(2), 71–78.

Butler, J. (2004). *Precarious life: the powers of mourning and violence.* New York and London: Routledge.

— (2005). *Giving an account of oneself.* New York: Fordham University Press.

Cixous, H. (1993). *Three steps on the ladder of writing.* New York: Columbia University Press.

Cixous, H., & Calle-Gruber, M. (1997). *Rootprints: memory and life writing.* London & New York: Routledge. (Original work published 1994).

Clément, C. (1994). *Syncope: the philosophy of rapture.* Minneapolis: University of Minnesota Press.

Clifford, J. & Marcus, E. (Eds.). (1986). *Writing culture: the poetics and politics of ethnography.* Berkeley and Los Angeles: University of California Press.

Derrida, J. (1987). *The truth in painting.* Chicago: Chicago University Press. (Original work published 1978).

— (1995a). Unsealing ('the old new language'). In E. Weber (Ed.), *Points... Interviews, 1974–1994* (pp. 115–131). California: Stanford University Press.

— (1995b). 'Che cos'e la poesia?' (What is poetry?). In Weber (Ed.), *Points...Interviews, 1974–1994* (pp. 288–399). California: Stanford University Press.

Davies, B. (2006a). Collective biography as ethically reflexive practice. In B. Davies & S. Gannon (Eds.), *Doing collective biography* (pp. 182–189). Maidenhead, Berkshire: McGraw Hill/Open University Press.

— (2006b). Subjectification: the relevance of Butler's analysis for education. *British Journal of Sociology of Education*, 27(4), 425–438.

— (2006c, May). *Writing transgressively: towards mo(ve)ment and voice.* Paper presented at Second International Congress of Qualitative Inquiry, University of Illinois.

Davies, B., Dormer, S., Honan, E., McAllister, N., O'Reilly, R., Rocco, S., & Walker, A. (1997). Ruptures in the skin of silence: a collective biography. *Hecate—A Women's Studies Interdisciplinary Journal,* 23(1), 62–79.

Davies, B., Flemmen, A., Gannon, S., Laws, C., & Watson, B. (2002). Working on the ground. A collective biography of feminine subjectivities: mapping the traces of power and knowledge. *Social Semiotics*, 12(3) 291–313.

Davies, B. & Gannon, S. (2006). *Doing collective biography.* Maidenhead, Berkshire: McGraw Hill/Open University Press.

Denzin, N. (1998). The art and politics of interpretation. In N. Denzin & Y. Lincoln (Eds.), *Collecting and interpreting qualitative materials* (pp. 313–344). Thousand Oaks, London & New Delhi: Sage.

Denzin, N., & Lincoln, Y. (Eds.). (1998). *Collecting and interpreting qualitative materials.* Thousand Oaks, London & New Delhi: Sage.

Dudley, J., Gilroy, A., & Skaife, S. (1998). Learning from experience in introductory art therapy groups. In S. Skaife & V. Huet (Eds.), *Art psychotherapy groups: between pictures and words* (pp. 181–203). London & New York: Routledge.

Ellwood, C. (2006). Coming out and coming undone: Sexualities and reflexivities in language education research. *Journal of Language, Identity and Education,* 5(1), 67–84.

Foucault, M. (1990). *The history of sexuality, Volume 3: The care of the self.* London: Penguin Books. (Original work published 1984).

— (1994). *The order of things: An archaeology of the human sciences.* New York: Vintage Books. (Original work published 1966).

— (2000a) Self writing. In P. Rabinow (Ed.), *Essential works of Foucault 1954–1984, Volume 1, Michel Foucault: Ethics, subjectivity and truth* (pp. 207–222). London: Penguin Books.

— (2000b). An interview with Michel Foucault. In J. Faubion (Ed.), *Essential works of Foucault 1954—1984, Volume 3, Michel Foucault: Power* (pp. 239–297). London: Penguin Books. (Original interview conducted 1980).

— (2000c). What is Enlightenment? In P. Rabinow (Ed.), *Essential works of Foucault 1954–1984, Volume 1, Michel Foucault: Ethics, subjectivity and truth* (pp. 303–319). London: Penguin Books. (Original work published 1984).

Freedman, J., & Combs, G. (2001, February). *Bringing forth the poetry in 'little sacraments of daily existence'.* Paper presented at the 2001 International Narrative Therapy and Community Work Conference, Adelaide, Australia.

Gannon, S. (2005). 'The Tumbler': writing an/Other in fiction and performance ethnography. *Qualitative Inquiry,* 11(4), 622–627.

— (2006). The (im)possibilities of writing the self-writing: French poststructural theory and autoethnography. *Cultural studies >> Critical Methodologies,* 6 (4), 474–495.

Gerwitz, S., & Cribb, A. (2006). What to do about values in social research: the case for ethical reflexivity in the sociology of education. *British Journal of Sociology of Education,* 27(2), 141–155.

Gilroy, A. (2003, November). Presentations on art therapy research methodologies to art therapy postgraduate research students at Residential art therapy research workshop, The Straw Bale House, Leura.

— (2006). *Art Therapy, Research & Evidence Based Practice.* London: Sage Publishers.

— (2008). Taking a long look at art. *International journal of art and design,* 27(3).

Haug, F. (1992). *Beyond female masochism: Memory-work and politics.* London & New York: Verso.

Henzell, J. (2004, November). *Looking beyond words: the creative process of art therapy in Australia and New Zealand.* Keynote address at 15th Annual Australian Art Therapy Conference, Brisbane.

Knill, P., Levine, E. G., & Levine, S. K. (2005). *Principles and Practice of Expressive Arts Therapy: towards a therapeutic aesthetics.* London & Philadelphia: Jessica Kingsley.

Kristeva, J. (1980). *Desire in Language: A Semiotic Approach to Literature and Art.* (T. Gora, Trans.). New York: Columbia University Press.

Lather, P. (1991). *Getting Smart. Feminist Research and Pedagogy With/in the Postmodern.* New York and London: Routledge.

— (2001). Postbook: working the ruins of feminist ethnography. *Signs*, 1(Autumn), 199–227.

Lather, P., & Smithies, C. (1997). *Troubling the angels: women living with HIV/AIDS.* Boulder, Colorado: Westview/Harper Collins.

Linnell, S., Perry, S., Pretorius, J., & Westwood, J. (2005, November). *The work of art is the work of embodiment.* Collaborative installation, video and performance at Australian and New Zealand Art Therapy Association Conference, Hobart.

— (2007, September). *Where knowing and not knowing touch: contemporary art as a mode of research, subjective transformation and social engagement.* Collaborative installation, video and performance at 'At the Vanishing Point' Contemporary Art Gallery, Newtown.

McNiff, S. (1998). *Art-based research.* London & Philadelphia: Jessica Kingsley.

Meskimmon, M. (2003). *Women making art: History, subjectivity, aesthetics.* London & New York: Routledge.

Morrison, T. (2000, April). *How can values be taught in the university?* Centre for Human Values, Princeton University. Retrieved June, 2006, from http://www.umich.edu/~mqr/morrison.html

Richardson, L. (1997). *Fields of play: constructing an academic life.* New Brunswick: Rutgers University Press.

— (2002). The poetic representation of interviews. In J. Gubrium & J. Holstein (Eds.), *Handbook of interview research: context and method* (pp. 877–891). USA: Sage Publications.

Richardson, L., & St Pierre (2005). Writing as a method of inquiry. In N.Denzin & Y. Lincoln (Eds.) *The handbook of qualitative research* (3rd ed.) (pp. 959–978). Thousand Oaks, CA: Sage.

Rose, G. (2001). *Visual methodologies: an introduction to the interpretation of visual materials.* London: Sage.

Rose, N. (1998). *Inventing ourselves: Psychology, Power and personhood.* Cambridge University Press. (Original work published 1996).

— (2005). In search of certainty: risk management in a biological age. *Journal of public mental health,* 4(3), 14–23.

Scheurich, J. (1995). A postmodernist critique of research interviewing. *International Journal of Qualitative Studies in Education*, 8(3), 239–252.

— (1997). *Research method in the postmodern.* London, Falmer Press.

Speedy, J. (2003, July). *Using 'poetic' documents in narrative therapy.* Paper presented at the International Narrative Therapy and Community Work Conference, Liverpool, England.

— (2005). Using poetic documents: An exploration of poststructuralist ideas and poetic practices in narrative therapy. *British Journal of Guidance and Counselling,* 33(3) 283–298.

Spivak, G. (1996). More on power/knowledge. In D. Landry & G. MacLean (Eds.), *The Spivak reader: selected works of Spivak* (pp. 287–308). New York & London: Routledge. (Original work 1992).

St Pierre, E. A. (1997). Circling the text: nomadic writing practices. *Qualitative Inquiry,* 3(4), 403–417.

— (2005, April). *Accountability in representation in the 'democracy to come'.* Address to the 2005 Annual Meeting of the American Educational Research Association, Montreal.

Swartz, S. (2005). Can the clinical subject speak? Some thoughts on subaltern psychology. *Theory and psychology,* 15(4), 505–525.

Venn, C. (2002). Refiguring subjectivity after modernity. In V. Walkerdine (Ed.), *Challenging subjects: critical psychology for a new millennium* (pp. 51–71). Houndsmills, U.K.: Palgrave.

Waller, D. (1993). *Group interactive art therapy: Its use in training and treatment.* London: Routledge.

Williams, C., and Linnell, S. (2006). When the doctors consulted the narrative therapist...an experiment in questioning dominant stories of PhD pedagogy. *The International Journal of Critical Psychology,* 18, 56–80.

Wyatt, J. (2008). No longer loss: autoethnographic stammering. *Qualitative Inquiry,* 14(6), 955–996.

CHAPTER 5

CLOSE TO HOME: THE 'POETHICS' OF THERAPY WITH A YOUNG GIRL AND HER FAMILY

The work we do is a work of love...To understand the other, it is necessary to go into their language, to make the journey through the other's imaginary...

This movement is like a voyage...

(Cixous, 1988, p. 146)

Abstract: Both this chapter and the following chapter ground the theoretical and creative explorations of the first part of the book in the specifics of clinical practice. This chapter gives an extended account, through poetry, story, memoir, visual images and discursive analysis, of arts-based and narrative therapeutic work with a particular child and her family whose lives were affected by domestic violence and the abuse of alcohol and other drugs. The chapter describes in detail how I became an apprentice to the ways this family responded to their difficulties, and involves ethical reflection on my therapeutic engagement and process with a family whose stories resonated closely at times with aspects of the biographies of myself and my family. I begin with a poem that tells how I first met the young girl whose story is at the heart of this chapter.

Of groovy grans, brave bananas, and much, much more

(for Leticia, her grandmother and their family) [1]

Remember that first day.
You thought that I might be a witch
or something.
You were wondering.

"Would this counsellor woman be the type
that acted nice while Groovy Gran was there
then turned out really mean when she was gone?
The sort that doesn't let kids play
but makes them stand in corners."

Then you saw a smiling face.
You thought, "Mmmn. Not too bad..."

You drew what troubled you.
Alcohol had Mummy in its grip:
a monster with two thousand legs.
When Mummy wriggled free from one leg's grip

Sheridan Linnell

the monster tried to catch her with another.

Banana Man was a good helper.
He wore a superbanana cloak.
He got his name because bananas are healthy
and taste really good.

Although Two Thousand-Legged-Man was very strong
Banana was braver.
Banana fought with Two Thousand Legged Man
and sometimes won.

Gran thought you were just as brave as Banana.
using your detective skills to find the bottle
and pouring Mummy's whisky down the sink
even though you knew
you'd be in trouble.

Gran said it was like being on a roller coaster.
You drew the roller coaster so I could see.
You couldn't stop or climb off,
you both went up and down with Mummy and the drinking
until you felt "really, really sick".
Gran said she hoped counselling would help you both work out
how to get off the roller coaster.
You said "I'd like Banana Man to win!"

You said that it surprised you when I asked you things
you'd never really told to anyone,
surprised you to find out that it felt good
to "let your feelings go out towards
someone you could really trust".

But how did you work out whether you could trust me?
"When you meet people you can work out straight away,
either you can trust them or you can't trust them."

I thought this an amazing skill and wondered
if you'd help me understand it.
You said "it's about getting a feeling...
Trusting is a safe feeling.
Not trusting is horrible
and icky down your spine".

I want to know more, so you explain:
"You know how people scrape their fingers down a chalkboard?
Do you find that annoying?"
I say, "Yes, more than annoying

it makes me go all brrrrwrrrrrrr"
and you say, "yeah that's right it makes you go
wohaowerrrowerohohohohobrrrrrrr.
Well, that's the feeling".

In the room where we meet there is a map.
Women and children sail the painted seas
past hungry sharks and jagged rocks. Past pirate ships
and mermen singing beautiful and dangerous songs
the women guide their children and their boats
to treasured islands.

One day you asked who made this map, and who could travel there.
And so I told you how some children and their mothers,
escaping from the violence that had tried to steal their lives,
had mapped their journeys, left them here for others,
so they too might find their way through heavy seas
'round obstacles that try to scuttle ships and capsize dreams.

You asked about the island of mending and healing broken hearts,
and wished aloud that you could go there with your mother.
You wondered if your heart would ever heal
and told me surgery might be the only answer.

At the heart hospital they would cut out your heart
because it had been broken far too many times.
Your new plastic heart would be unbreakable
in order that you wouldn't feel such dreadful pain.

The day your mother came to meet with us
you asked her many questions.
"Why did you stay with that man
who made me sleep alone in the cold caravan?"
(You knew at once he wasn't to be trusted.)
"Didn't you know that I was lonely, hungry, frightened?"

You and Mummy hugged and cried and told each other
many unknown and unspoken things.
How the man had sent you to the van
so that you could not hear Mum's screams.
How she was fearful for your lives
but planned and carried out a brave escape.

Together you recalled past houses, dogs and friends,
the favourite places, games and trips you'd shared,
pizza and movies, watching reruns of 'Columbo'
together in the shaded room
on summer afternoons.

How Mum spent her pregnancy
dreaming up a beautiful girl's name for you,
stories of you as a baby, how every time you cried
Mum's own eyes filled with tears.

How she had never wanted you to suffer.
Her great sorrow that her drinking came between you,
made your lives unsafe.
She told how much she loved you,
how she wanted you to know this and remember.
And this time no promises were made because Mum knew:
broken promises can break your heart.

When Mum started drinking again
and went away, you were very sad.
You even wondered if you were to blame.

But then your old friend Banana came!
Instead of fighting Two Thousand Legged Man
and getting really tired
he came to help you off the roller coaster.

This time, Banana used his strength and bravery
to tell you Mummy's drinking
was not, and had never been, your fault.

You told me what Banana Man had told you.
"I know you are as clever as Columbo
but maybe you don't have to work so hard
as a 'detective' anymore.
After all, you are a brave daughter
and have done all that any daughter could."

It was then we all wondered:
Had the time come
for The Great Detective Inspector Leticia
to retire from full-time duty?

Detective Inspector Leticia's Retirement Party

Early one evening, a devoted group of family, friends and associates of Detective Inspector Leticia gathered together in the meeting room of a community based organisation in a small Australian town. This gathering had been convened in order to honour the Inspector's many years of dedicated and skilful service. D.I. Leticia, who had prepared her speech with great thoughtfulness, asked me to read it out on her behalf, because she knew her voice went wobbly at moments of public emotion. In the speech, the Inspector announced her intention to retire from full time detective duty. It would no longer be D.I. Leticia's full time job to look out for the presence of alcohol in her Mummy's life and to do battle with the sneaky and powerful Two Thousand Legged Man. However, Leticia reserved the right in her retirement to undertake detective duties from time to time on a casual basis, especially if she was with Mummy for a visit and was worried that Mummy might be in Two Thousand Legged Man's grip. Leticia's old friend Banana Man concurred that this provision for an occasional resumption of duties was a realistic and compassionate honouring of the great detective's ethics and practices of care, in relation to others in general and her mother in particular.

In her retirement, Leticia intended to focus on having fun with current friends and meeting new ones, making her home with Gran, Paul and Neil, school work, spending time with her chosen father, and spending time with Mummy, when Mummy was around and alcohol and drugs were not holding too much sway in her life. The coordinator of the community based organisation presented Leticia with a special Certificate of Commendation. Glasses were filled with juice and raised in her honour, followed by a round of hearty congratulations. D.I. Leticia cut the chocolate cake provided by her grandmother, and made a silent wish.

Sheridan has recently begun to work as a part-time family therapist in a community based child protection centre, a place where she has previously provided some training and clinical supervision. This shift, from a 'private' to a 'public' practice, and from being one of the people responsible for supporting other workers to be effective in their work to being one of these workers herself, is inviting her to feel somewhat vulnerable and on display. It feels as if she has been 'faking it' and is about to be caught out after all these years.

This afternoon she is attending an 'introduction meeting' with a new family. The word 'assessment' has been dropped in this organisation in favour of something hopefully more reciprocal. Nevertheless, she is aware of the limits of collaboration and co-authorship, especially in a child protection context. She wonders if the word 'introduction' has a flavour of 'induction', and if so, what, as much as who, is being in(tro)duced.

At the introduction meeting, the family will be invited to tell Sheridan and her colleague about whatever is troubling them. She will offer art materials and perhaps suggest possibilities for the family to depict their feelings and thoughts about their situation in a visual way. The two co-therapists will look and listen [2], alert for stories of injustice, including possible histories of unhelpful and pathologising professional interventions. They will think about current 'risks' [3] to children and young people and of the possibility of the abuse of gender-power relations. Perhaps the therapists will suggest at some point that one of them spends time in another room listening to the children, or to one particular child or young person.

Quite often family members will hold different stories about what has brought them to the centre, and it may not be easy to speak about these with other and especially more 'authoritative' family members in the room. Sometimes the woman/mother in the family might be offered a separate conversation, if her story is being somehow marginalised or if she seems reluctant or afraid to speak. Here the ethics and practices of child protection and a feminist politic significantly mediate the idea that the family leads the session. The 'family' is after all both 'real' and 'constructed', and ideas that a family has an organic will, an unconscious and/or a functionality separate from that of its members are viewed in this organisation as theoretical constructions.

The therapists have cultivated a consultative style and an ethics of collaboration. They will ask lots of questions about how this family is experiencing this meeting, what could make it work better for them. They will engage in many reflexive gestures, checking out the appropriateness of their questions and their choices of language. They will deftly pick up the delicate threads of personal and familial narratives, weaving understandings of the connections of these into the grand narratives of culture. They will invite the family to join them in unravelling tangles of frustration, disappointment, sorrow, anguish. In this, the therapists will not be purely instrumental. They are touched, moved by what they hear.

The therapists will wish to become attuned to the particular hopes, aspirations, ethics and preferred ways of being and relating of the people who comprise this family. They will want to understand how the people in this family have kept loving and caring for each other, maintained hope in the face of their difficulties, or whatever other themes arise. The therapists will be interested in specific, apparently small and incidental details—an event, even a thought, that might contradict the family's dominant narratives. The therapists will slow down the process of conversation, searching out unattended moments often unexpectedly suffused with feeling, that might be plotted into an alternative account. This painstaking process interrupts totalising accounts that tend to position the family's problems as a stable, unitary history without fluctuations and exceptions, and challenges individualising accounts that tend to locate the family's difficulties in the psychology of family members.

By the end of this meeting, the family may carry a more overt appreciation, even a centring, of their own and each other's relational strengths and emotional and ethical resources, and this will hopefully be of assistance in taking responsibility, where necessary, for breaches of their preferred ways of parenting, without either minimising their responsibilities or succumbing to a totalisation of their identities. (This issue of responsibility is crucial because, while the organisation does not provide counselling for adult perpetrators of sexual abuse, it does counsel parents, often women living with domestic violence, whose children have suffered or are considered at risk of abuse and neglect, sometimes from these women themselves.)

Towards the end of this meeting, the therapists will ask what each family member would like to happen next, and also let them know about a variety of options inside and outside of the organisation. At this point, the family will almost certainly request an ongoing service. This is what they have come here for, either of their own volition or because someone, possibly a doctor, a teacher, or in certain instances the Department of Community Services (DOCS), has told them it is necessary. Moreover, they have just been listened to, an experience that is more rare than one might think. The 'team' will then meet to decide whether, when and how to offer such a service, given that there is only the equivalent of two and a half full-time counsellors to serve a widespread regional community.

The diverse and compelling stories of these potential 'clients' are inevitably folded back into the organisation's guiding narrative of its capacities, limits, 'mission', values and priorities. Power circulates *back to the team, who, for all their consultative strategies, will still have to decide who and what to 'prioritise'.*

Was 'assessment' such an inaccurate description after all? she wonders.

And yet this word, 'assessment', while it acknowledges the hierarchy of people and values that seek to 'determine' a situation and make a rational decision about the just distribution of a limited resource, does not capture the emotional intensities that over determine such an encounter, the wayward lines that flow across the grid of assessment criteria in excess of rationalities. Thus, a counsellor will sometimes argue vehemently against the team and indeed contrary to her own avowed priorities, advocating for 'her' people to be 'seen'. (This is in part what has prompted the institution of two therapists conducting an introductory meeting together, but then sometimes at the subsequent team meeting the voices of the two will join together in spirited opposition to the reason(s) of the rest.) The counsellor will not understand how her colleagues cannot see, as she sees, the face of someone whose need calls upon an urgent necessity to respond [4]. *Why can't they hear, as she surely hears, the call of this Other? The one(s) to whom, for an hour that opens upon lifetimes, the therapist has just listened, listening as though this one or ones were the most important people in the world, as, in that moment, they are* [5].

When I first met Leticia, she was not yet nine years old. Leticia came to the first appointment with her grandmother, who wanted Leticia to have the opportunity to talk with someone outside the family about how some recent changes in her life were affecting her, and also to talk about some of the difficulties of her earlier life. At this first meeting, Leticia was smiling, bouncy, restless and appeared apprehensive for reasons that her words only revealed many months later. While it is not unusual for children to feel nervous about 'seeing a counsellor', I came to understand that Leticia was particularly well-trained to be alert for danger, especially from adults who had been promoted by other adults as helpful or 'nice'. For much of her life, Leticia had lived either with her mother, or with her grandmother, her grandmother's partner and their two sons. Sometimes Leticia's mother, Emma, had asked her mother (Leticia's grandmother) to look after Leticia because Emma was attempting to 'detox'. At other times Emma's relation with alcohol and other drugs, and with other people, including several of Emma's partners who used such drugs, had made it unsafe for Leticia to be with her. When Leticia lived with Emma, their lives were often unsettled, and sometimes Emma's dependency on drugs and the lifestyle that revolved around accessing drugs had been dangerous for them both.

I remember being impressed, in this first meeting, with how this extended family had managed to work things out over the years in the face of enormous worry, trauma and chaos. It seemed to me that questions of 'child protection' were complex in this family, and that they had met this complexity with intelligence, courage and compassion. There was a sense that Emma brought Leticia to her grandmother because Emma did not want to put Leticia at risk, and there was also a sense that at times Emma was so much in the grip of a drug-dependent lifestyle and all its attendant disruption and risk that she found herself unable to prioritise her relationship with Leticia. Consequently, Leticia had come to live more and more frequently with her grandmother, her step-grandfather Timothy, and their two teenaged sons (who, to Leticia's amusement, were her uncles). Eventually, everyone had come to a tentative agreement that it would be preferable for Leticia to make her home with them for the foreseeable future. Leticia and her mother could still spend time together at least when Emma wasn't too much affected by drugs, because at these times she would often go away and others would be uncertain of her whereabouts. However, Leticia could have a consistent home, go regularly to the same school, make long-term friends, and in general have an experience of a stable environment where people could make and follow through with an ongoing commitment to care for her.

Leticia's grandmother was an articulate, deep-voiced and remarkably composed woman of around my own age from a European immigrant family. The grandmother's heritage was important to her, but it is also, in the service of confidentiality, important not to mention her country and culture of origin. Her family struggled with racism and disadvantage, as families from backgrounds other than English-speaking generally do upon coming to Australia. However, it was not until much later that she told me of how her experience of cultural disadvantage, the effects of gender, and a very particular family story had together conspired to make her feel unworthy and plagued with maternal guilt. Leticia's grandmother is known in this narrative, by her choice and in affection for the similar (but disguised) name bestowed upon her by Leticia, as Groovy Gran. And indeed she was 'groovy', not in an obvious or superficial way, but in her quietly radical attitudes, her superb intellect, mature wisdom, great-heartedness, honesty and indefatigable sense of humour.

After the initial meeting, the counselling team considered Groovy Gran's request that someone provide counselling for her granddaughter, with involvement from other family members where that seemed helpful. I had the time and a strong inclination to keep meeting with this family, and it was decided that I would do so. The work was well within the compass of a single therapist, although in accordance with narrative therapy practice I asked the family if we could call upon my co-worker and the service's coordinator, Deanne Dale, who had participated in the initial family meeting, at times when it seemed useful to bring in someone as an external 'witness' to the work.

As she writes of their work together, calling this woman 'Groovy Gran' feels awkward. It is how Sheridan would speak of Leticia's grand-mother to Leticia, or how she would address the grandmother in Leticia's hearing when speaking of a matter that concerned Leticia, as in "Well, Groovy Gran, it sounds like Leticia has being doing a lot of thinking about such and such since we last met...what do you think?". But this is not how they addressed each other woman to woman, a relation that necessarily occurred on a 'first name' basis. For all that they acknowledged that, in the context of their meetings, one was the therapist and the other the grandmother to this child, they did attempt to recognise each other beyond these identity categories. In fleeting acknowledgement of the powers of contingency and connection, they sensed how each was only a whisper away from being in the other's place. They honoured their connections and their irreducible differences. They could not 'truly' know each other, any more than any 'one' can ever know the other. Yet Sheridan does not think they knew each other any the less, at least in the more subtle reaches of recognition and its limits, because of the constraints placed on social familiarities by the ethics of a professional relation. Indeed, these limits are, for her, both a condition of a particular form of knowledge and connection, and a reminder of the ethics of unknowability.

A major legacy for Leticia, one that she shared in many ways with her grandmother, of living with a mother in the grip of alcohol and other drug dependency, was Leticia's vigilance and sense of responsibility toward her mother. As our meetings progressed, Leticia's descriptions of the lengths to which she would sometimes go to find out whether or not her mother was beginning to drink again, and some of the actions she had taken to attempt to keep her mother and the drinking apart, reminded me irresistibly of the work of a detective. I told Leticia about my thoughts and while she hadn't thought of things this way before, she seemed interested in the idea. Leticia's reference point for detective work was *Columbo*—she and her Mum had sometimes spent time watching daytime reruns of the series together, and this memory seemed to have given Leticia an affection for the shambolic, humorous and insightful (anti)hero detective in his trademark raincoat. So we began to use a metaphor of detection as way to appreciate the detailed work that Leticia had undertaken in her attempts to keep her mother and the drinking apart (and thus her mother and herself together).

As time went on, I came to an appreciation of the complexity of the relations between Leticia and her mother and the legacies of this in Leticia's life. In attempting to conceptualise this complexity, I have taken up metaphors through which Venn (2002) illuminates the becoming of a subject as a relational and embodied process (see chapter 3). The metaphor of 'apprenticeship' to the Other invokes longevity, repetition and the graduated acquisition of skills, within a socially 'indentured' relation of power, loyalty and indebtedness. The metaphor of 'choreography' invokes the trace of an intimate dance of self and Other: steps and 'moves' that are learned in response to the (m)Other. The dance of anticipating and responding to the rhythm, timing, coming and going and so forth of an(Other) becomes embodied and enfolded as 'self', then played out in social relations that in turn deepen the enfolding of self and enfoldment in the social. It seems to me that Leticia had learnt her 'detective' skills through just such a complex apprenticeship and choreography (Venn, 2002): she had come to regard and embody her self as subject both to an ethics of care and hope, inspired by the intimate and companionable dimensions of her relationship with her mother, and to the watchfulness necessitated by her mother's abuse of alcohol and other drugs. Thus Leticia had come to understand and to enact her self as obliged to care for others, and to understand/feel her own wellbeing and that of her mother as dependent on Leticia's alertness to the presence of alcohol in her mother's life. She had even come to consider and to enact herself as morally responsible for her mother's relation to alcohol and drugs.

If power is conceptualised as "a mode of action upon the actions of others" (Foucault, 2000a, p. 341), then perhaps Leticia's unravelling and refusal of, and eventual retirement from, the dominance of these detective duties could be understood as forms of resistance to certain disciplinary and normalising strategies of modern power. Such a refusal is not a negation of the skills and ethics constituted in relation to this modern power. The skills and ethics learned and practised by Leticia in relation to living with a carer in the grip of an alcohol and other drug dominated lifestyle are 'situated' knowledges (Haraway, 1991), but Leticia's situation had changed since she came to live with her grandmother. Some of these skills and ethics were of service to Leticia in these changed circumstances, and others were not. For instance, stringent practices of surveillance of self and others, often attendant to the lifestyles of family members of people struggling with alcohol and other drugs, were filling Leticia's life with impossible responsibilities and leading her into self-recriminations. These were full-time duties from which she became willing to retire in favour of a more relaxed and playful existence.

On the other hand, Leticia had learnt to read her embodied responses to others in a very skilled and useful way, and she had much to offer others when it came to an understanding of whom to trust. She also had an ethics of care towards others that was a valued and ongoing commitment in her life. The process of narrative and art-based therapy has in part been an unhinging of self-limiting and self-blaming practices of surveillance from preferred practices of observation and care. At the same time, a refusal to 'trade' in that to which one has been apprenticed may nevertheless continue to be haunted by the ghostly counter steps of an early choreography.

Leticia's apprenticeship to the lifestyle and wisdom of Groovy Gran provided an alternative to her previous life of surveillance, one which created the possibility for Leticia to go 'off-duty' in favour of play, regular attendance at school, a stable home, consistent carers, predictable bedtimes, regular nourishing meals, safety from verbal abuse and many other taken-for-granted entitlements according to the modern historical construct of the rights/rites and roots/routes of childhood. In a sense this was a 'normalisation' of Leticia's childhood, one that created new possibilities and capacities but also initially limited some of the pleasures as well as the pains of her previous life. Some of our work together, particularly when both Leticia and Groovy Gran came along to sessions, was around this contradiction. Groovy Gran's lively responses to Leticia's sense of humour, her patience with the 'ups and downs' of Leticia 'settling in' to the household, together with their mutual and non-normative appreciation of life's eccentricities, mediated the difficulties of becoming accustomed to more customary ways of 'doing' one's girlhood.

Working within the context of a child protection service and being an heir to the interactive traditions of family and narrative therapies, I did not simply 'sit with what came up' for Leticia. I was actively curious, and I engaged in a process of enquiry. In this respect, my meetings with Leticia and her family 'look' more like narrative therapy than they do like art psychotherapy, but our connection is informed by the sometimes contradictory possibilities of both. Notions of 'transference' are marginal in family therapy, suspect in narrative therapy, and complicated or diffused by practices of working with a person in the context of their family/significant others. Nevertheless, at least one thread of my relations with both Leticia and Groovy Gran is spun from the psychodynamic tradition of transference, in that I tentatively regarded my feelings, imaginings, lateral thinkings and associations in relation to the stories, artworks, silences, movements and stillnesses that inhabited the space of therapy as relevant to the emergent shape of our work together.

Moreover, our engagement with visual art and the imaginative and metaphorical dimensions of story emphasised excessive, lateral, and subtle qualities and resonances that were not reducible to clear outcomes or entirely captured within alternate storylines. Playing together with images and words, we found a space of imagination and connection where (im)possibilities could be played out. Folding these (im)possibilities back into the conventions of life, thereby creating instances of subjective and relational change, left a non-narrativisable remainder—a feeling, perhaps, of having been transported, of returning from somewhere indescribable.

She had set up a space for 'art therapy' with a drop sheet, paints, crayons, papers, card, glue, magazines and modelling clays, but from their very first meeting, Leticia enacted her preference for drawing her responses on the large electronic whiteboard. Leticia worked on the board with coloured markers in a quick, quirky and free-flowing cartoon style, inventing monsters and superheroes, personifying abstractions, animating inanimate objects and writing dialogue in bubbles. Leticia and Sheridan would talk about the image, then Leticia would print out her work, clean the board and start another drawing. At the end of the session Sheridan would make two sets of A4 photocopies, one for Leticia (because the initial printouts would fade) and another for the records of the session.

At first, Sheridan asked herself the question her students are always asking her—*is this Art Therapy?*—as though art/therapy is not (re)invented with/in each gesture, each moment.

Figure 1: *Worrying and dreaming*, Leticia

Figure 2: *The roller coaster*, Leticia

Figure 3: *Two Thousand Legged Man gloating*, Leticia
Leticia printed this image from the whiteboard before circling and crossing it out with a marker.

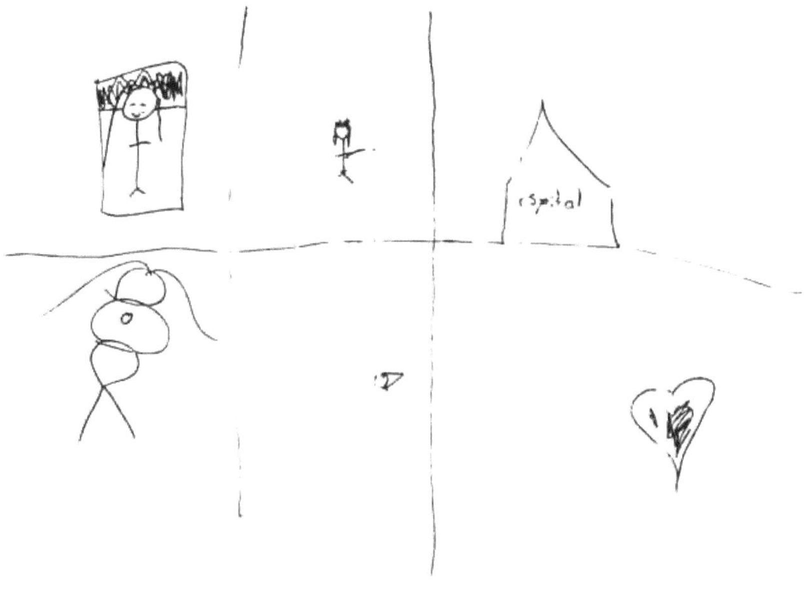

Figure 4: *At the heart hospital*, Leticia

Figure 5: *Banana Man—winner number 1*, Leticia

Figure 6: *Banana Man tells Leticia she is not to blame*, Leticia

Figure 7: *D.I. Leticia's invitations to her retirement party*, Leticia

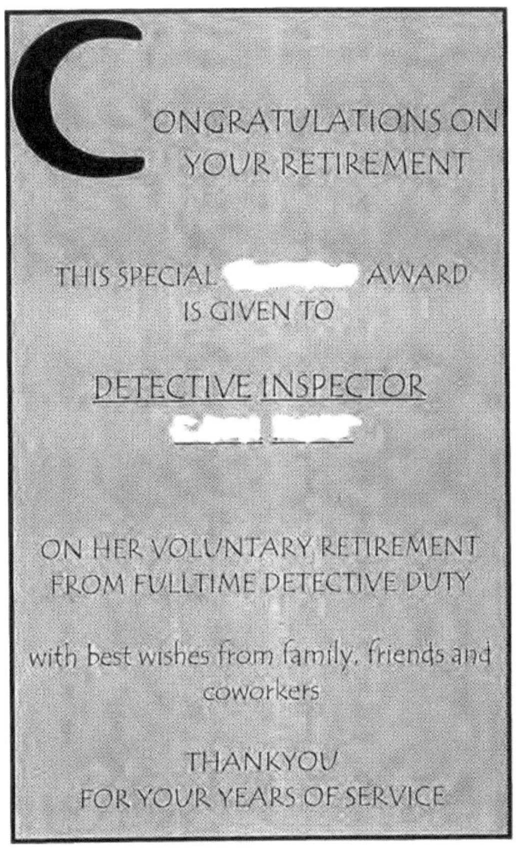

Figure 8: *Certificate of commendation*, design and layout by Deanne Dale

During our meetings together, Leticia brought her concerns vividly into focus, 'drawing' on popular cultures and the works of her imagination (see figs. 1–6, pp. 132–135.) The externalised and fictionalised identities and narratives of Two Thousand Legged Man, the roller coaster, Banana Man and Detective Leticia were active participants in the therapy. This had the effect of exoticising the everyday (White, 2004), thereby rendering what had previously been accepted as 'normal, natural and true' open to the 'work of thought'. Thought, for Foucault, is "freedom in relation to what one does, the motion by which one detaches oneself from it, establishes it as an object, and reflects on it as a problem" (2000b, p. 117).

Whereas commonplace 'expert' descriptions such as 'insecurely attached' and 'the parentified child' would negate the skills and commitments of Leticia's life, the description of Leticia as a Detective Inspector allowed for an appreciation and honouring of these skills and commitments. The figure of Two Thousand Legged Man was met with recognition by all those affected by his grip on Leticia's mother Emma, including Emma herself. The personification made it possible to talk about these effects in a non-blaming way. The roller coaster enabled Leticia, Groovy Gran, myself and other family members to take positions that were less subject to the ups and downs of the alcohol and drug dominated lifestyle. Banana Man was a great ally and a very responsive 'outsider witness' to the changes in Leticia's life.

Leticia and Emma became apprenticed, via the map and its attendant stories, to the lives of other women and children who had attended the community based service where this work took place. Through an engagement with the stories of these other women and children, Leticia and Emma were able to acknowledge the effects of domestic violence in their own lives and relationships. The recognition that they had lived with the experience and legacy of domestic violence also provided a basis for an understanding of the family's difficulties that enabled them to separate from dominant practices of intergenerational mother blaming. Leticia had a clear stance about how stepfathers should and shouldn't act. She was prepared to make a recommendation on this: "Stepfathers shouldn't beat their [stepchildren's] mothers up when they're only really, really little. Or ever, really". This acknowledgement of the effects of domestic violence opened a space for the remembrance and renewal of the connectedness between Emma and Leticia.

At the time that she came to meet with Leticia and myself, Leticia's mother was a participant in a residential rehabilitation program. Emma was not usually permitted to engage in any therapy outside of this program, but on this one occasion the coordinator of the program approved Emma's participation in a joint therapy session with her daughter. In this meeting, Emma expressed her sorrow for the ongoing effects of an alcohol and drug-related lifestyle, particularly on her relationship to Leticia, and took steps towards naming her responsibility as a carer. This seemed to help free Leticia from a misplaced sense of responsibility. Within weeks of this meeting Emma had left the rehabilitation program with someone she had met in the rehabilitation centre and resumed an alcohol and drug dominated lifestyle. At first this eventuality invited Leticia back into responsibility but, in the longer term, the effects of the conversation between Leticia, her mother and I endured in Leticia's increased sense of being loved by, and decreased sense of being responsible for, her mother.

Dis-closures and dis-solutions

As a therapist, I have learned a great deal from Leticia and her story, particularly in relation to my responsibilities and obligations when working with people who are gripped by the influences of alcohol and other drugs and with the families of these people. Leticia and I are in very different positions in relation to privilege and dominance, and I am not suggesting that, as an adult and a therapist, I have the same obligations and responsibilities as a child, especially a child who is positioned as my 'client'. However, there are huge invitations for therapists working in the areas of alcohol and other drugs to engage in surveillance of their clients, particularly within systems of governance that individualise the management of clinical risk (Rose, 1996, 2005). Leticia's retirement raised questions about how I too might make finer and more useful distinctions around complex issues of responsibility, watchfulness and care. Moreover, my apprenticeship to the ethics of care within this family had effects well beyond the professional.

Groovy Gran, along with several generations of Western mothers of the modern age including myself, had undergone training in the ethics of sole maternal responsibility. In the face of her daughter's struggles, this training had consequences of guilt and self-blame. In common with Leticia, Groovy Gran repeatedly asked herself if something she had done had resulted in the dominance of alcohol and other drugs in the life of her daughter. She also held an enduring hope that Emma might escape the influence of alcohol and other drugs.

For many years, I too had struggled with the spectres of maternal guilt in relation to the life difficulties of my own daughter. I found that meeting with this family assisted me to resist the twin, paralysing dictates of modern motherhood, which simultaneously insisted that I was responsible for all of my daughter's difficulties in life, and that if I reached out to her in her adulthood I would compound my guilt by failing to allow her to 'stand on her own two feet'. During this period, I took some very strong action in support of my daughter and grandchildren [6]. Without revealing too much of my daughter's story, I was able to let Groovy Gran know that some of my life narrative had parallelled hers.

When I asked my daughter's permission to speak of our family's struggles with Leticia's family, my daughter said that if her story could help anyone else to not go through what she had been through, she would willingly share it. I was nevertheless very selective in what I told Groovy Gran. I was perhaps influenced by the dominant ethic of therapeutic abstinence, and I was also cognisant that anonymity would not be possible for my daughter and myself in our small community. In this, I was less brave than my daughter. I feared the double judgement that can be inflicted on a therapist who not only lives a less than exemplary life, but has the indiscretion to talk of it in any but her own therapy. I also did not want to position those who came to consult me as a therapist as keepers of my personal and familial secrets. I had a strong sense of the ethics and practices of discretion and care in this family, and that these would be extended to me without me needing to ask, but I decided that it was only appropriate to tell them things that I was prepared to have publicly known.

Ironically, within the small community where I live and work, I am much more disclosing of myself as a poet than as a therapist. What might be regarded as excess in a therapist is often viewed as honesty and 'authenticity' in a poet—even when these identities converge within the same embodied individual, and when the audiences for these different genres of confession overlap. With the publication of a small book of my poetry (Linnell, 2001), much of it fictional but some of it in the lyric tradition, and its subsequent launch at a nearby regional writers' centre, many of the events and themes of my personal life, as well as my ethical and political convictions, had already become accessible to others in our local community. To enter my own stories into a therapeutic relation is, however, very different to entering them into the lives of those who choose to read a poem or attend a poetry reading. Despite the influence of feminist and narrative (re)constructions of therapeutic disclosure (see Wright, Linnell and Dale, 2001), it remains, for me, a potent but fraught event that can either open radically upon the possibility of connection with and understanding from an Other, or foreclose upon the possibility of connection and understanding that comes from maintaining a symbolic position as the Other.

At any rate, having considered all of this, I felt moved to tell Groovy Gran that I had found her stand in support of her daughter and granddaughter to be an effective source of inspiration in my current life and relationships. Since one of the powerful effects for me of meeting Groovy Gran was to dissolve the edges of some of my own excessive tendencies to blame myself, I wondered if this 'taking back' of how I had been 'moved' to action in my own life (White, 1997) might also help to facilitate some dissolution of self-blame for Groovy Gran. Actually, although she avowed comfort in a certain solidarity between us, Groovy Gran told me that the immediate effect of my disclosure was, not a reduction of self-blame, but rather a normalisation of maternal habits of self-blame. Such a realisation of the commonality and cultural constitution of our personal ways of being is a necessary but insufficient condition for the transformation of deeply held and embodied feelings and convictions.

To appropriate another of Venn's formulations, the politics of change is more potent when in concert with the poetics of transfiguration (Venn, 2000). Foucault similarly speaks of writing books that function as an experience for both writer and reader, books through which particular transformative experiences become possible (Foucault, 2000c). Thus it was only much later, when Groovy Gran read the draft of a journal paper based on our work together (Linnell, 2004), that a hoped-for dissolution began its work.

For all my attempts at theorisation, even to the extent of writing this book, subjective transformation is ultimately something that is unaccountable except in its specificity. It was not listening to my 'simple' disclosure of resonance that most powerfully produced difference, in this instance: rather, it was another and different discursive layer of retelling, through writing, reading and thinking. When she read the paper that is the predecessor of this chapter, Groovy Gran, in a move that was to become powerfully transformative, says she began to understand precisely how the narrative of self-blame related to personal stories of her childhood and adolescence, as well as to the grand narratives of culture that train girls to look after others, hold women responsible for maintaining relationships, and blame mothers for the problems that beset their children. It seems to me she had located, not just the meta-narrative of subjugation that joins her stories with mine, but the 'fold' itself, the precise place that in her particular life had delineated a limiting 'actuality'. She had found the place where histories and stories folded inward, creating her subjectivity as an internalised space of blame. And as 'she' unfolded, following the trajectory of the fold and bending it ever so slightly into a different line of flight, Groovy Gran could escape into other territories of life. She could contemplate the Deleuzian question "How might one live?" (May, 2005; Winslade, 2009). She decided that she would, and that she could, go to university in order to embark on a study of poststructural philosophy. And so it was that one of the grooviest and grandest of women began to make a profoundly different sense of her tendency to blame herself, and to renegotiate her sense of worthiness and possibility within actual and imagined worlds.

A question of ethics: what shall we do with the drunken sailor?

Toward the conclusion of our sessions, Groovy Gran and Leticia, who no longer felt the need to meet with me on a regular basis, organised a time for Leticia and I to talk about something that had happened at school that Leticia had found deeply troubling. Her class had been learning a new song, the old Anglo Saxon sea shanty *What shall we do with a drunken sailor?*. The song's traditional answers to this question include punishments that range from humiliation through imprisonment and torture to a painful death. They include being locked up, hosed down, whipped, put in the longboat with the plug pulled out so that the boat sinks, and 'keel-hauled' or dragged by ropes behind the ship, a practice that frequently resulted in drowning.

What Shall We Do with a Drunken Sailor?

What shall we do with a drunken sailor,
What shall we do with a drunken sailor,
What shall we do with a drunken sailor,
Earl-aye in the morning?

Chorus:
Way hay and up she rises
Patent blocks o' diff'rent sizes,
Way hay and up she rises
Earl-aye in the morning.

1. Sling him in the long boat till he's sober.
2. Keep him there and make him bale 'er.
3. Pull out the plug and wet him all over.
4. Take him and shake him, try an' wake him.
5. Trice him up in a runnin' bowline.
6. Give him a taste of the bosun's rope-end.
7. Give him a dose of salt and water.
8. Stick on his back a mustard plaster.
9. Shave his belly with a rusty razor.
10. Send him up the crow's nest till he falls down.
11. Tie him to the taffrail when she's yardarm under.
12. Put him in the scuppers with a hose-pipe on him.
13. Soak him in oil till he sprouts flippers.
14. Put him in the guard room till he's sober.
15. Put him in bed with the captain's daughter*.
16. Take the Baby and call it Bo'sun.
17. Turn him over and drive him windward.
18. Put him in the scuffs until the horse bites on him.
19. Heave him by the leg and with a rung console him.
20. That's what we'll do with the drunken sailor.

* a relative of the cat-o-nine-tails

Presumably the class did not learn the entire litany of consequences for drunkenness at sea listed in traditional variations of the song. However, I have included them here to underline the sheer brutality of what in contemporary times has come to be regarded as a quaint and amusing ditty, easily taught to school children. I am not usually an advocate of sanitising or watering down traditional children's stories, and find that children often relish the uncensored violence of fairy tales and the mordant themes of nursery rhymes: in the English tradition we sing babies to sleep to the rhythms of falling cradles, and teach toddlers to dance to the rhythms of falling heads. Moreover, many a detested head has fallen, metaphorically speaking, in the make-belief territories of therapy. Perhaps this song is in a particular discursive category because it records and reinforces the brutal disciplinary hierarchy of a sailor's life. At any rate, the words resonated with an aspect of Leticia's life and relationships, inciting in her both distress and a desire for justice and compassion, and making her experiences, beliefs and feelings available for a further therapeutic conversation.

During the session, Leticia rewrote the song in accordance with her own ethics and aesthetics of existence. She decided to call her version the *kind* version of the Drunken Sailor.

The *Kind* Version of the Drunken Sailor

What shall we do with the drunken sailor (x3)
Early in the morning?
Put him in a rehab till he's sober (x3)
Early in the morning.

Chorus:
Hey ho and up she rises (x3)
Early in the morning.

1. Visit him in rehab when he's sober.
2. We are happy now he's sober. &c.

The earlier versions of this song give explicit accounts of public punishment reminiscent of Foucault's (1991) account of sovereign power in the opening of *Discipline and punish*. According to Foucault, although sovereign power did not disappear, the dominance of this form of power was superseded by the emergence of disciplinary power in institutions such as prisons, hospitals and schools. Leticia's version of the song rejects the emblematic violence of sovereign power and also the involuntary containment and regulation that marked the emergence of the disciplinary power of the prison. The drunken sailor in Leticia's song is to be rehabilitated. For Leticia this is a heartfelt wish based on the narrative of her experience. At the same time, it is interesting to note that 'rehabilitation' is a process which necessitates engagement with a hermeneutics of self in which the subject must recognise themselves as an addict in order to be re-formed as a sober and normal member of society. The sailor will be brought back to social normality through technologies of surveillance and self-regulation, by connection with others, and perhaps by the realisation that not only his own wellbeing, but also the happiness of those to whom he is connected, depends on his sobriety. Yet while this transformation is often strongly desired by those surrounding the drunken sailor, the sailor's own desire for sobriety may not be easily sustained. In this reading, love and care are not separate from the operations of power. Similarly, even the most collaborative and decentred of therapies can be a means for 'the conduct of conduct' (Foucault, 2000c; Rose, 2000a, 2000b).

I found Leticia's rewriting of possibilities for the drunken sailor particularly poignant in light of how the metaphor of women and children sailing to safety had been significant for Leticia and Emma. With this song, Leticia could simultaneously displace her fears for her mother and broaden her concerns into a position on how society might best respond to people who are struggling with alcohol and other drug related problems. Leticia's song draws attention to the multi-storied character of this work and to the indeterminate character of stories, including the meta-narratives of therapy, which I believe do not need to be reduced to a search for repressed desires, authentic feelings and true meaning. Smooth and unitary accounts of the 'progress' of therapy do not do justice to the contradictions and complexities of 'living narratives'. Attention to the multi-storied character of lives served as a reminder that Leticia might possibly be vulnerable to a resumption of full-time 'detective duties' with their accompanying burden of responsibility and self-blame [7]. During my meetings with Leticia, I was closely attuned to possible invitations to self-blame. For instance, when Emma said that when baby Leticia had cried it had brought tears to Emma's own eyes, I checked out the meaning of this for both of them in terms of that ambiguous territory between responsibility and care. When Leticia told me about looking after some rescued tadpoles (see below), I felt concerned that she might blame herself if some of them died. I therefore enquired as to whether she had considered this possibility, and whether she knew that some tadpoles might not survive even in their usual habitat.

When Leticia's mother had a 'relapse' only weeks after a joint meeting with Leticia and myself that Emma had found particularly confronting, I found it hard to resist blaming myself for this turn of events. On the basis of this, together with my knowledge of Leticia's training in responsibility for others, I could enquire if Leticia was also feeling responsible for the 'relapse'. We could then link this current situation with past histories of Leticia blaming herself and attempting to take responsibility for the drinking, and we could also call upon the support and wisdom of Groovy Gran, who knew a lot about the ravages of self-blame and the difficulty and necessity of refusing its invitations. We could also call on Banana Man, whose struggle against alcohol in the embodied form of the Two Thousand Legged Man was by now legendary.

Therapy is a matter of complexities and contradictions, and its end is never, in my experience, 'conclusive'. Thus Leticia continued to hold ongoing hopes for the rehabilitation of those (most notably, her mother) in the grip of alcohol and drug dependency, and to intimate that the happiness of 'others' (and hence, of herself) might rest upon the success of such rehabilitation. These hopes co-existed alongside her decision to retire from full-time detective duty and her claim that assisting tadpoles to grow into frogs had brought happiness into her heart.

Since she first used the word 'happy' in conversation with Leticia, a wave, indeed a veritable tsunami of 'happiness' has swept over Sheridan's known cultural world. An onslaught of self-help books, courses, research, even institutes of 'happiness studies', has threatened to drown out the singularity of happy moments. Some critics have strategically taken up 'happiness' in order to challenge the economic rationalist agenda, but she is worried by the current outbreak of happiness. She wonders, is this the new ethical substance? She wants to refuse this joyless glut of happiness, along with its implicit pathology for those who 'fail' to achieve the requisite state, but she suspects a media stereotype is ready to ambush her with the accusation that she is turning into a 'grumpy old woman'. Nevertheless, she will not board the pleasure-boat, which reduces the play of *jouissance* to a huge one-liner. She will continue to insist in the specificity of pleasures. Then she catches herself, laughing. What a passionately humanistic gesture this 'refusal' is! Perhaps her exchange with Leticia about happiness was already a discursive droplet that with myriad other droplets are forming the vast *savoir* of the 'happiness' about to immerse us all. But she can still navigate an alternative course of sorts, not in a futile struggle against the prevailing winds, but tacking with and across them, as small sailing boats do.

A matter of heart

When Leticia and I met to review our work together, an aspect of the therapy that Leticia nominated as of particular significance was hearing about the journeys of women and children escaping from domestic violence, and subsequently making the drawing of her heart being surgically removed and replaced with plastic. I was disturbed at the violence of this metaphor and by Leticia wanting a plastic heart. I was very moved to witness such a profound expression of pain. As the following transcript shows, I was also susceptible to some essentialist and humanist notions that locate the heart as the natural seat of human feeling.

S. Do you still think that would be the best thing—to have a plastic [heart]?
L. Yes and no.
S. What's the 'yes' bit?
L. That it wouldn't feel so much pain.
(Anticipating my next question)
And the 'no' bit is I'd rather have my real heart—Hearty, I call him.
S. And what can Hearty feel, as well as pain?
L. Umm...happiness!
S. What makes Hearty happy?
L. Lots of blood! Pumping!
S. Lots of fresh blood pumping in...
L. Not hurting.
S. So how has your heart been lately...hurting...not hurting?
L. I'll ask Hearty!...it's been hurting a bit...

[L. consults Hearty by peering into her school jumper.]

S. Do you mind me asking what Hearty said when you asked?
L. He hurt a little bit, but he felt happy most of the time because he's doing something good for Leticia's tadpoles!
S. Oh your tadpoles! I meant to ask, how are they?
L. They're good.

During one of our meetings, Leticia had told me how she and her best friend had found some frogspawn in a shallow pool of water cut off from the 'mainstream'. Caring about all creatures, however marginalised, and knowing frogs in particular to be a vulnerable and endangered species, Leticia and her friend had run home for jars. They had set most of the spawn free upstream, and also taken a small sample home with them to see what happened. In the ensuing week, the tadpoles had hatched. Leticia and her friend were now looking after the tadpoles until they grew up into frogs and could be safely returned to the waterways. Leticia had taken great care to name each of her six tadpoles—Lucy, Ascha, Sasha, Putzi, Mitzi and Chrissy—only it was very difficult to tell who was who! As the following dialogue suggests, I was interested in how this practice of caring for tadpoles might link with Leticia's sense of herself as an ethical subject.

S. What do you think it says about you that you've rescued these tadpoles?

(As the answer shows, this was an inappropriate way to ask this question!)

L. It hasn't said anything.

S. What do you think someone else would say if they heard a story about a little girl who rescued some tadpoles and took them home and gave them all names and looked after them?

L. They'd put it in the newspaper and then I'd be famous! "Leticia the Frog Rescuer!"

S. What else would it say in the newspaper article?

L. A girl named Leticia, aged nine, saved three million tadpoles that turned into frogs in the stream at the back of her village!

S. Yay! So what sort of special things does someone need to be a Frog Rescuer?

L. A heart. And they like frogs!

I leapt on this statement with rather too much enthusiasm, assuming that Leticia was indicating a need or desire for a 'real' rather than a plastic heart. My essentialist assumptions were quickly 'set straight' by Leticia's response:

L. If the [plastic] heart was a good heart, if it didn't think bad things, then it would probably say "Rescue, rescue!" But my brain would certainly say "Rescue, rescue!"

Here it no longer matters whether Leticia's heart is plastic or real. What 'matters' is not so much the 'authenticity', as the capacities of the heart. Leticia supports neither a hierarchised or inverted binary of cognition and emotionality; rather, she offers a thoughtful and heartfelt expression, a situated and embodied ethics of thinking and feeling that can (in)form ethical action. Her statement can be understood as both an intentional ethics and as a choreographed response. Binary divisions between the natural and the cultural, between thought and feeling, are disorganised by the suggestion of a fabricated heart that thinks, and an organic brain that urges a compassionate response.

A poethics of practice

Throughout this chapter, as in my book as a whole, I have drawn attention to the mutual constitution of aesthetics and ethics in therapeutic and research practice. I have done this as an extension of my theoretical engagements with poststructural theory, through an ethics of account-ability and its limits, in relation to my practice as a narrative therapist and art psychotherapist. This chapter involves a practical engagement with poetry, story telling, art making and song, yet while I believe that art can work to enhance therapy, I do not believe that it is always necessary to draw a picture, write a poem or sing a song in order to take up what might be thought of as a 'poethics' [8] of therapeutic practice.

If, as Rose suggests, the most interesting way to conceptualise therapy is as "a shaping of how human beings enact their freedom" (2000a, p. 3), then therapists and those who consult with them are engaged in the work of freedom (Foucault, 2000d). While we are inevitably implicated in (re)constituting the individualising and totalising discourse of the 'freedom' to find ourselves, we can also 'refuse what we are'. Stories, poems, artworks and conversations in which bananas fly and talk, women and children sail across painted seas in search of treasured islands, and small girls with plastic hearts help their therapists to become other-than-they-were, are experimental texts that reach towards (im)possible futures. Such work can open a space, however fleetingly, beyond modernity.

She remembers a moment when she is sharing a story of her meetings with this family (thanks to Leticia's and her grandmother's generosity in allowing her to speak and write about their work together) with a group of art therapy trainees, as part of an introduction to narrative approaches. She is attempting to explain her thinking about how the ethics and practices of people who come to therapy are often eclipsed by pathologising accounts of 'disorder' and 'damage'—for instance, how Leticia's concern for her mother would be folded into, and invalidated by, the narrative of the parentified child. Sheridan is saying it does not have to be one or the other. Leticia's care and concern could be thought to arise out of both fear and love—that it can be storied as both the legacy of trauma and a commitment to an ethical position. Strangely, in the company of these other art psycho-therapy practitioners, a submerged psychodynamic reading of Leticia's story of rescuing the frogs comes to the fore. Catching the eye of one of her students who has a strong interest in the intersection of poststructuralism, narrative and psychoanalysis, she finds herself saying:

> The psychodynamic therapist in me finds herself wondering if the tadpole story can also be taken as a metaphor of Leticia's life. I think it important to hold such notions very lightly, not as a truth, yet nevertheless allowing them to inform or form the emotional sensitivity of one's response. To me this is what is meant by 'counter transference'.

She reflects to herself on this meta-story, which she has previously touched on but given very little discursive space. Such an 'interpretation' is, in general, disallowed by the ethics of narrative therapy. She knows the interpretation itself to be a 'speculative fiction' (Butler, 2001), created within and by the grand meta-narrative of psychoanalysis. Moreover, this psychoanalytic meta-narrative is reproduced and brought into focus within the inevitably disciplinary and ethicalising environment of the art therapy training course, wherein lecturing staff such as herself become ethically obliged to 'profess' the truths that the Others of therapy are obliged to 'confess', whether in image or in word.

Yet how could she, of all people, foreclose on a possibility simply because it is a fiction? Perhaps a gentle spirit of enquiry will help her toward a sense of what, in this fiction, is helpful in extending a range of intersubjective and subjective possibilities, and what narrows the field. So, she allows herself to play with the different metaphorical and metonymic dimensions of the story, metaphor and metonymy being, after all, the lifeblood of poetry and fictional narrative.

She thinks of how Leticia herself was also somewhat 'cut off from the mainstream' and endangered, until taken home and cared for. She considers the fears that have sometimes circulated around Leticia, fears of how the past might have affected her, fears that not all endangered children 'survive' the experience. Some of the fears that have at times been articulated to Sheridan by other family members (although not to Leticia), as to whether Leticia may have been affected by trauma in ways that will only be revealed as she grows older, might have indirectly permeated Leticia's sense of herself and her world. She thinks too of Leticia's sense of wanting to extend to others what has been extended to her in terms of help to survive. She wonders if the therapy itself might be glancingly referenced in this amphibian metaphor of birth, development, risk, survival, loss and transformation. She wonders too what Leticia might have wondered about her. Through the counselling centre's recent process of consulting a number of children, including Leticia, about what advice they would like to give to other therapists working with children, Leticia's attention has been drawn to the fact that she is not the only child who comes here meet with to Sheridan. Of course Leticia has known this all along, but perhaps it has been foregrounded that she is not the only tadpole in this particular pond? Might she fear that tadpoles/children all 'look the same' to a busy therapist?

Sheridan does not know, and cannot know, if the wild proliferations of this metaphor have any *raison d'etre* beyond her own imagination. She is probably taking it too far. (She remembers a joke she has made in the past—that psychotherapists all seem to suffer from one of the main diagnostic criteria for schizophrenia—'ideas of reference', or notions that unrelated phenomena have something to do with them.) Accepting that this is her story, a metaphorical reading made possible by a psychoanalytically informed account of the subject and relationship, and that the relation of her reading to Leticia's story is uncertain and indeterminate, what are the implications? Since all such responses are both subjectively and theoretically informed, isn't it more a question of what a particular reading opens up, than of validity? Are her imaginings, in this instance, in the service of the person she is meeting with, or do they just privilege a mystified version of therapeutic expertise?

A meta-reading of the frog story might serve to sensitise her, in a specific rather than in a general way, towards the sometimes excruciating imbalance of therapy. She knows that as a therapist she becomes a unique person in the life of her 'client'. Each client is also a unique and special person for her, but it is nevertheless her profession to conduct this particular kind of relationship with several persons, in a circumscribed manner, and for a limited duration. If thinking about the metaphorical possibilities of tadpoles and frogs alerts her to the possibility that a child who has experienced much abandonment and confusion, and whose needs have at times been radically marginalised by other concerns, might fear further abandonment or marginalisation, is that so very reprehensible? Must she always eschew such speculative philosophising, or is it more a matter of considering its discursive effects?

She cannot overemphasise here, to herself and to her students, the importance of a lightness of touch—a wondering, an inconclusiveness, a refusal to either dismiss her associations and imaginings or to give them an authoritative status. Sometimes it becomes possible to give a tentative and speculative voice to her thoughts and feelings within the therapy as she has able to do, in this therapeutic context, in relation to themes of self-blame and surveillance. At other times this route appears insensitive and even dominating. It would not be helpful if she concluded, for instance, on the basis of such considerations, that she must set up a boundaried and exclusive therapeutic relation with Leticia, a frame in which regression and strong transference would be the healing modalities, when so much of their work together has been the work of facilitating and enhancing the meaning of a wider set of relations in Leticia's life. The process that led up to Leticia's decision to 'retire' from her full-time detective duties has emerged out of careful and intricate narrative and arts-based work over many months, informed by the family's stories and sustained by loved ones and companions, in particular Leticia's grandmother.

The process has also been (in)formed by Sheridan's consideration of how her own feelings might be tentative 'clues' to what others might be feeling, or perhaps more accurately to a present/absent subtext of discursively disallowed and/or psychically disavowed thoughts and emotions. Her responses, associations and imaginings are significant (un)knowings that warrant further 'investigation'. Perhaps she, as much as Leticia, wishes to reserve the right to be a part-time detective? Less obviously, her (un)knowings (in)form a delicate underwater dance of therapy 'under erasure', therapy in which the trace of the Other—of Other times, events, fictions, relations, memories, forgettings, imaginings—is always already deferring the possibility of 'presence', always dissolving the threat and promise of the same in the uncharted waters of difference.

Then Sheridan remembers how that particular consultation—the one during which she'd asked Leticia what in their conversations had been important for her, and Leticia had talked about her heart and her frogs—actually concluded. Having cooperated patiently for most of the session with this therapist agenda of 'review', Leticia had found the opportunity to get to the important issue of her week.

> Sheridan, can I ask *you* a question now? I've been wondering what I should call Timothy. He doesn't want me to call him Grandpa, but I want to give him a special name, like I did for Groovy Gran, because he is special too. So I've been thinking,

> should I call him Timmy Whimmy, or should I call him Tim Tam? Which do you think he would like best?

Sheridan had tried to imagine Timothy, a serious and sensitive man whose ongoing support of both Groovy Gran and Leticia has been backgrounded in an account of events which nevertheless depend on his commitment, answering to either of these appellations. Sheridan had wondered if she was being asked (for) something here in excess of the spoken words, but she could not on this occasion call up the ghost of an (im)possible question, let alone compose a response. Stumped, she had tentatively offered, "have you thought of asking *him* what he'd like to be called?"

At that moment Leticia had looked, to Sheridan at least, a little younger and smaller, her hair hanging forward around her face, crestfallen. "But then he'll just say 'Timothy'," Leticia had protested.

Sheridan knew this at once to be true. And in this moment, she also knew how all the characters in this story including herself depended, each upon the other, for recognition and interpellation. How radically they depended, each upon the other, for becoming Tim Tam, becoming Groovy, becoming part-time retired Detective, becoming Poststructural Philosopher, becoming Banana, becoming Sailor, becoming Frog, becoming Tadpole; becoming the writer of this story, becoming otherwise than what and whom they had previously taken themselves to be.

In this chapter, I have considered the ethical and intersubjective implications of therapy with a child and her family whose stories sometimes resonate with my stories. I have taken up poetry, story telling, autoethnography and discourse analysis as modes of enquiry into the detail of this therapeutic work, in order to move beyond the clinical convention of the individual case study and its hierarchies of the normal and the pathological. In the chapter that follows, the crisis of representation deepens and the ethical call of the Other becomes stronger. I enter into the 'telling' obligation to give an account of collaborative therapeutic work I have undertaken with Indigenous children 'in care'.

---

[1] All names including nicknames of persons in this story, other than the names of therapists, frogs and imaginary beings, have been changed for reasons of confidentiality. The young woman at the 'heart' of this story chose the name Leticia for herself.
cont.

[2] Foucault (2005) describes how listening, as a Classical ascetic practice, makes 'truth' one's own and one's self the subject of this truth. Is therapeutic listening for a 'truth' (even if the truth in question is that of the discursive construction of truth) thus a practice that subjectifies the listener/therapist, creating an ethics?

[3] See Rose (2005) for a Foucauldian analysis of the discourse of risk-management.

[4] See Butler (2004) for an analysis, following Levinas, of the ethical encounter with the face of the Other.

[5] See Linnell, Bansel, Ellwood and Gannon (2008) for a collective response, in art and writing, around the ethics and aesthetics of speaking and listening.

[6] I would like to acknowledge that my actions also rested on the support of my partner, Anita.

[7] I became particularly attuned to the production of self-blame and over-responsibility when working in an agency that focussed on the effects of childhood sexual abuse (Linnell and Cora, 1993), some of which can be generalised to other situations of childhood abuse and neglect.

[8] The neologism 'poethics' came to my mind during an orientation to outsider witness responses that was part of an intensive workshop with Michael White at the Dulwich Centre, Adelaide, in September, 2003.

References

Butler, J. (2001). Giving an Account of Oneself. *Diacritics*, 31(4), 22–40.

— (2004). *Precarious life: the powers of mourning and violence.* New York and London: Routledge.

Cixous, H. & members of the Centre d'Etudes Feminines. (1988). Conversations. In S. Sellers (Ed.), *Writing differences: readings from the seminar of Hélène Cixous*, (pp. 141–154). Milton Keynes: Open University Press. (Original interview recorded 1986).

Foucault, M. (1991). *Discipline and punish: the birth of the prison.* London: Penguin. (Original work published 1975).

— (2000a). The subject and power. In J. Faubion (Ed.), *Essential works of Foucault 1954–1984, Volume 3, Michel Foucault: Power* (pp. 326–348). London: Penguin Books. (Original interview published 1982).

— (2000b). Polemics, politics and problematizations. In P. Rabinow (Ed.), *Essential works of Foucault 1954–1984, Volume 1, Michel Foucault: Ethics, subjectivity and truth* (pp. 111–120). London: Penguin Books. (Interview conducted 1984).

— (2000c). Michel Foucault: an interview with Stephen Riggins. In P. Rabinow (Ed.), *Essential works of Foucault 1954–1984, Volume 1, Michel Foucault: Ethics, subjectivity and truth* (pp. 121–133). London: Penguin Books. (Interview conducted 1982).

— (2000d). The ethics of the concern of the self as a practice of freedom. In P. Rabinow (Ed.), *Essential works of Foucault 1954–1984, Volume 1, Michel Foucault: Ethics, subjectivity and truth* (pp. 281–301). London: Penguin Books. (Interview conducted 1984).

— (2005). *The hermeneutics of the subject: Lectures at the College de France 1981–1982.* (G. Burchell, Trans.). New York: Palgrave Macmillan.

Haraway, D. (1991). *Simians, cyborgs and women: the reinvention of nature.* London: Free Association Books.

Linnell, S. (2001). *Cutting room.* Wollongong: Five Islands Press.

— (2004). Towards a 'poethics' of therapeutic practice: extending the relationship of ethics and aesthetics in narrative therapies through a consideration of the late work of Michel Foucault. *The International Journal of Narrative Therapy and Community Work,* 4, 42–54.

Linnell, S., & Cora, D. (1993). *Discoveries: a group resource guide for women who were sexually abused in childhood.* Sydney: Dympna House.

Linnell, S., Bansel, P., Ellwood, C., & Gannon, S. (2008). Precarious listening. *Qualitative Inquiry,* 14(2), 285–306.

May, T. (2005). *Gilles Deleuze.* Cambridge, U.K.: Cambridge University Press.

Rose, N. (1996). Governing risky individuals: the role of psychiatry in new regimes of control. *Psychiatry, Psychology and Law,* 5(2), 177–195.

— (2000). Power and subjectivity: critical history and psychology. *Academy for the study of psychoanalytic arts.* Retrieved March, 2003, from http://www.academyanalyticarts.org/rose1.html

— (2000). Power in therapy: Techne and ethos. *Academy for the study of psychoanalytic arts.* Retrieved March, 2003, from http://www.academy analyticarts.org/rose2.html

— (2005). In search of certainty: risk management in a biological age. *Journal of public mental health,* 4(3), 14–23.

Venn, C. (2000). *Occidentalism, modernity and subjectivity.* London: Sage.

— (2002). Refiguring subjectivity after modernity. In V. Walkerdine (Ed.), *Challenging subjects: critical psychology for a new millennium* (pp. 51–71). Houndsmills, U.K.: Palgrave.

White, M. (1997). *Narratives of therapist's lives.* Adelaide: Dulwich Centre Publications.

— (2004). Working with people who are suffering the consequences of multiple trauma: a narrative perspective. *The International Journal of Narrative Therapy and Community Work,* 2004(1), 45–76.

Winslade, J. (2009). Tracing lines of flight: implications of the work of Gilles Deleuze for narrative practice. *Family Process,* 48(3), 332–346.

Wright, J., Linnell, S., & Dale, D. (2001). 'Spokeswomen': shared counselling as a context giving privilege to the power and intimacy of women's conversations.' In *Working with the stories of women's lives* (pp. 97–108). Adelaide: Dulwich Centre Publications.

FIGURES AND ARTWORKS

CHAPTER 6

BECOMING OTHER-WISE: A STORY OF A COLLABORATIVE AND NARRATIVE APPROACH TO ART THERAPY WITH TWO INDIGENOUS KIDS 'IN CARE'

WITH A COMMENTARY BY, AND IN CONSULTATION WITH, GALIINDURRA [1]

> *The line of analysis of subjective transformation that I have been elaborating, while it makes visible notions of historicity, debt, ethical responsibility—especially in the sense of responsibility for the Other and of historical responsibility—has introduced an additional element. That element is the standpoint indicated by aesthetics, that is to say, the forms and the experience which express the (un)representable or unaccountable or sublime aspects of beingness which the problematic of subjectivity must recognise in order to encompass the complexity of the process of the constitution and reconstitution of subjectivity. The implied inadequacy of one-dimensional approaches alone in addressing this complexity, for instance the reliance on the cognitive viewpoint in psychology or on an unreconstituted, egocentric psychoanalytic discourse, is revealed when one has to deal with cases that refer to people traumatised by a violence which strikes at the core of ontological security, for instance, concerning victims of ethnic cleansing, or working through the legacy of the Aboriginal 'stolen children', or that of the disappeared and tortured, or involving consequences of modern forms of slavery in many industries and practices globally. In other words, the urge to rethink the theorisation of subjectivity is driven by the recognition that there are widespread problems today, affecting individuals and whole communities that exhaust the resources of 'orthodox' theorisations of subjectivity.*
>
> (Venn, 2002, p. 65)

Abstract: This chapter engages with the question of working with 'the Other', and especially with those who are Othered by colonialism, through an account of therapeutic work with two Indigenous Australian children who have been removed from their families of origin. As a non-Indigenous art therapist working in collaboration with an Indigenous community worker and carer, I consider this experience in the context of past histories and present-day effects and practices of colonisation, in particular the legacies of Australia's Stolen Generation. The chapter is framed by a commentary from the Indigenous worker and carer, since collaboration and consultation are just as central to the methodology of writing this account as to the therapeutic work itself. Within this frame, I offer a series of tellings and retellings, and engage with how visual art can gesture toward the unspeakable. I take up poetry as an alternative form of enquiry to the genre of the case study, in order to shape a poetics as well as a politics of therapeutic practice. I consider how this work, and writing about this work, has brought my dominant professional identity and practice into question and engaged me in becoming Other-wise. I begin with the words of Galiindurra, followed by a poem I wrote for the family.

Sheridan Linnell

Galiindurra:

You know, Sheridan, we're working with third generation removed people.

You look at the little faces of the little ones, say, in my care, and you think,"Oh God, her grandmother was in an institution, and she didn't get to parent her children, and now the third generation of these kids are in care".

Little Maree said something to me the other day. She said, "How come all my mum's kids end up in care?" And I said, "Why do you think?" And she said, "I think it's because of the drugs".

I mean, what do you say to an eight year old? Can you say, "It's transgenerational grief and separation?"

There isn't one person in that family who hasn't been affected, who isn't grieving. Yeah, it makes you sad.

Joining the dots

(for Galiindurra and the girls) [2]

'This child will be in therapy for the rest of her life.'
'Separation anxiety.' 'Uncontained anger.'
'Manipulation and lies.'
'She's ADHD and oppositional.'
'Her mother is disordered.'
'Her foster mother needs to provide more boundaries.'
'This child is insecurely attached.'
'She has no empathy.'
'She's damaged and you'll have to contain her.'
'Keep her in the room.'
'Keep it to an hour.'
Keep her in a box.
We'll provide the labels.

my Ashley can be a shy one
she needs to get to know you
she did wreck the doctor's room
she was scared
she hates white rooms and hospital gowns
she's terrified of sirens
she tried to run home from school

so they locked her in a room
she screamed and screamed
they called that 'seeking attention'
told me not to give in to her 'manipulation'
that's not the Koori way
we love honour and cherish our children
she worries when I leave her
but slowly she's understanding that I always come back

when she came to me she was tiny
she sat all day in a corner and didn't speak
she'd been starved and hurt and abused
now she loves to run and play and shout and grow tall
making up for lost time

i've had too much of therapists and their assessments
people telling me what to do when it's not my culture
but people I trust say I can trust you
so maybe we could meet in the park near the lake
we can talk and she and her sister can play [3]

so we meet in the park and we talk
Ashley and Maree are laughing and running back and forth
between Mum and the edge of the water
past the big white geese who have colonised the lake
the sisters are careful and courageous
they are strong and radiant and happy

i learn that Ashley needs time and open spaces
she is also a netball star with her name in the local paper
we meet in the park, then at home, then at school,
we catch the school bus together until she brings herself
to my home-based studio with its bright paints and pastels
we eat our after-school snacks in the kitchen
sharing our love of olives and ripe tomatoes
we have competitions to see
who is the quietest drinker of tea
and Ashley usually wins

my cattle dog in the backyard
is excited by all the new developments in Ashley's life
when Ashley rings the doorbell
Moonam Chomper bounces and woofs with joy

she even adds her paw prints
to Ashley's big paintings drying on the grass
if she could she'd tell us how she can see
Ashley out-tricking lies and making friends
practicing kindness and bravery
she'd tell us her sense of who Ashley can be
in sisterhood and community

some days just Ashley comes and other days she brings
Maree
because some days as Mum says the sisters are inseparable
we paint and glue and write stories on the 'puter'
afterwards we walk back round to Mum's work
for a cuppa and a chat and to show her what we've made

the sisters are Koories and live in a Koori family
they have the same mum and different mums
they live together with one mum and dad and other sisters
and brothers
near to grandparents aunties uncles and cousins
and visit their birth mums dads and families
at home or in hospital or prison
Ashley's birth Mum has another baby
taken from her and put in a white home
a white expert says the baby must 'attach' to her new
white carer
Ashley cries and rages and cuddles the photograph they send
she tells stories of accidents and deaths by hanging
she paints a butterfly with heart-shaped wings
for the sister she is not allowed to see

phone calls letters meetings and reports
to challenge this latest violation
we talk of the stolen generations
of legacies of loss and separation

it's still happening today
now the minister wants to adopt out kids in care
adoption doesn't exist in our culture
they are using their attachment theories and their diagnoses
to steal another generation
and no-one's looking out for the white kids either

i'm appalled that my mob has done this yet again
i won't let it happen in my own back yard
yet Western art and therapy can be forms of colonisation
so one day Mum teaches me how to paint
how to map our relationships to family, culture and place
how to make dots with the other end of the brush [4]
how to choose colours and patterns
to give meaning to connection and feeling
as a witness to separation and loss
as reconnecting and remembering
she gives me permission to paint with her kids
as ceremony, culture and healing [5]

When I first read this poem aloud to Galiindurra in the garden at the Aboriginal community organisation where she works, we cried together. Galiindurra asked me to read it again to Sandra, another Indigenous community worker, and then Galiindurra took it home to share with her family. Galiindurra has since read the poem to other Indigenous families as part of her work with the stolen generations. Galiindurra and I have presented together at conferences. When she was not able to accompany me to Mexico to present our work at the International Conference of Narrative Therapy, I presented a formal paper on a different topic. However, with Galiindurra's blessing and some negotiation with the conference convenors, I read the poem and showed photographs of the girls' artwork to a small, informal gathering of international narrative therapists and community workers, Indigenous and non-Indigenous attending the conference, who agreed to meet as a listening group [6] early one morning between breakfast and the daily plenary. This meeting was particularly important because Ashley and Maree were expecting to hear back from the conference about what other counsellors thought of their stories and their artwork. These conference participants then sent their responses back for Galiindurra and her family. On these and similar occasions it seems our accounts of this collaborative work have resonated with the experiences of Indigenous and non-Indigenous people in Australia and elsewhere. Tears and stories have flowed and continue to flow, embraces and emails have continued to be exchanged.

This chapter is a further iteration or re-telling of these stories (Linnell, 2009), in which I investigate what has flowed in my own life from an involvement with this work, and from writing about the work. At the same time, my stories are inevitably intertwined with the stories of others, in particular with the stories of Galiindurra's mob, as well as with broader social and cultural narratives.

Considerations of power, representation and subjectivity

The above poem tells a story of my engagement, as a non-Indigenous practitioner of art and narrative therapies, with finding ways to meet with and learn from a particular Indigenous Australian child, her sister, and her mother/carer. It focuses on the implications of this work for my sense of my self, my practices, my relationships, and for my (intentional and implicit) ways of being-in-the-world. The poem could therefore be considered as a means of enquiry (Richardson, 2002) [7] into the effects of this work for my subjectivity.

I believe, with Waldegrave, Tamesese, Tuhaka and Campbell (2003), that Indigenous people are best positioned to work with their own. Since such a person was not available within our local community, I have worked in close collaboration with Galiindurra, whose words frame this chapter, in her dual role as an Indigenous community worker and as a carer and other mother to Indigenous children 'in care'. Had Galiindurra not herself been multiply positioned as a worker and carer, and such a central person working in her own community, I believe it would have been vital for another Aboriginal community worker to be a close partner and consultant in the work. To have attempted this work without extensive collaboration and consultation would have perpetuated major aspects of the colonisation that I am seeking to resist. Good intentions, as Ashley's story so powerfully illustrates, are not by themselves enough to minimise the neo-colonial reproduction of dominant power/knowledge.

I do not think it is possible for me, as a non-Indigenous person, to entirely avoid the ways in which I am caught up with the histories and current practices of colonising power, since even my positioning as part of the 'helping professions' is in part a citation of past and current abuses conducted in the name of welfare. As a white practitioner of narrative and art therapy working with Indigenous children who have been removed from their families of origin, I am involved in both reproducing and challenging dominant discourse. I hope that in performing 'therapy' with the guidance of and in concert with Indigenous workers, I/we may not simply re-cite, but also discursively re-shape, in small and specific ways, the possible relations between Indigenous and non-Indigenous people working together to address and redress the legacies of colonisation.

Given the fraught and ongoing histories of European colonisation, I am particularly concerned to problematise 'representation' in this poem and in the chapter as a whole. I have worked with Galiindurra as my consultant and companion, not only for the 'therapy' of which this chapter gives a partial account, but in the writing of the account itself. The decision to write in consultation with and response to Galiindurra, not as a fabricated 'we' that invisibilises power and difference, but in a manner that keeps our voices distinct, is influenced by these concerns of 'representation' and also by the practice of definitional ceremony (Meyerhoff, 1992, 1986), as it has been taken up and developed within narrative therapies (White 1995, 2000). Within the metaphor of definitional ceremony, I am an audience for the stories of Galiindurra, Ashley and Maree. Galiindurra becomes an audience (and you as the reader as well as various others are a further audience) for a poetic and discursive account of how the stories of Galiindurra and the girls, and their wider families and cultures, have 'moved' me—to emotion, to action, to subjective and social change. In attempting to chart and to reflect upon this movement, I am influenced by narrative therapy's ethics of acknowledging and 'taking back', to those who consult with us, an account of how they have influenced and enriched our lives (see White, 1997; also previous chapter).

Practices of telling, retelling and audiencing in narrative therapy engage the indeterminacy and productivity of narratives together with the transformational possibilities of how we are always already connected with others. A beautifully reflexive and recursive interplay of stories intensifies connections between and widens possibilities for all of the participants. The positions of storyteller and witness become interchangeable as meaning and emotion amplify and resonate in widening circles, yet there is always an accountability back to the persons whose story is, for this time, at the centre of the circle. In this sense, this poem and chapter are 'retellings' that rest on and are framed by stories that have been told to me by Galiindurra and the girls, and are therefore accountable back to them. Although I am focussing on my own story in an attempt not to 'represent' the stories of marginalised Others in defining or capturing ways, at the same time I must acknowledge that 'my' story (like all stories) is interrelated with and conditioned by countless other stories, and is specifically a response to these stories told by Galiindurra and the girls. This attempted 'double act' highlights some of the complexities and tensions that circulate around this work.

While I want to acknowledge the complexities of writing about this work, my aim in this chapter is not so much to find 'clarity' within this complexity as to perform an ethics of therapeutic relationship and writing within a neo-colonial context. Just as poststructural subjectivities are not simply achieved but are 'worked' in relation and resistance to the continual reconstitution of the Western modern subject, so 'postcolonialism' is an ongoing work in relation and resistance to the reconstitution of (neo)colonial discourse. I would like to disrupt for a moment the disembodied, universalising and colonising character of both dominant therapy and the dominant cultures of research and academic writing. I hope to make a few ripples in the smooth, mirror surface of these invisible powers through tellings and retellings of a small and openly subjective story, one of many that might be told, about what it has been like for myself as a non-Indigenous therapist working with and in response to an Indigenous family.

At the same time that the metaphor and practices of tellings and retellings encompass much of the richness and complexity of this work, I am also interested, in this chapter as well as in my book as a whole, in the discursive limits of narrativity, and in whether art, poetry, and the embodied mo(ve)ments of therapeutic relations gesture beyond these limits. I am committed to this work as the work of (inter)subjectivity, and thus the work commits me to becoming-Other-wise.

A walk through the poem

In the opening stanza of this poem, I have created a brief drama of colonising and pathologising 'voices' from a range of diagnoses and predictions, most of which came my way before I met Ashley herself.

The various professionals who provided these labels were not, as I understand it, lacking in good intentions, or in the skills of their professions, and indeed several of them expressed empathy and a sense of responsibility in relation to the historical and current situation of Aboriginal and Torres Strait Islander Australians. These professionals were doing their jobs. What this 'doing' actually 'did' was, on the one hand, to provide a supposed basis in 'evidence' to obtain access to assistance for Ashley, but at the same time these labels produced a pathological and impoverishing description of her, indicting her past and present life and making gloomy predictions for her future.

This version of Ashley and her life relies on Western psychological theories that assume that autonomous selfhood and the nuclear family structure are universally normal and healthy, rather than that they are the rather odd and largely unworkable product of a particular moment in European history. These theories are also implicitly mother-blaming (see Burt 1997). Through the lens of these theories, Ashley is assumed to have difficulties in forming 'attachments' (Bowlby, 1965; Ainsworth, 1985) because of the alleged inadequacy of her first experience of mothering. Moreover Galiindurra, as Ashley's current carer, is subjected to perceptions of having 'failed' to implement the practices of another dominant twentieth century psychological discourse, that of 'behaviour' and its management (Rose, 2000).

In contrast with such assessments and prognoses, Galiindurra herself offers a very different telling of Ashley's actions, a very different account of the possible meanings of these actions, and consequently a very different notion of who Ashley is and can be. Rather than attachment disordered, Ashley is sometimes shy. Rather than being generally 'out of control', Ashley wrecks the doctor's office because of specific fears that are a legacy of past medical abuses. Rather than being attention deficit and hyperactivity disordered, Ashley is expanding her capacities to give voice and to move, to play and to grow. She is making up for lost time, for a past life of severe difficulty and deprivation, and for the legacies of the loss and dispossession inflicted on generations of her birth family including her mother and grandparents.

Remembering some of the words spoken to me by Galiindurra (who asked to be known as Mum in the poem) during our initial meetings, I have shaped these words into lines of poetry. I initially wrote down these lines to give back to Galiindurra herself, in appreciation of the intellectual rigour, political skill and great-heartedness of her words/work. The words/work of carers are often marginalised within the hierarchy of relations set up in the professional discourse of 'care' and I think it is crucial, if a description of 'therapy' with Ashley and Maree is not to reproduce a relation of dominance, to acknowledge and honour their carer's alternative practices of care. I also want to invite readers of this chapter to feel something of what is being extended to me here as a non-Indigenous person, on what social bases this tentative trust and hope is being extended, and to what accountabilities I am committed in response.

Galiindurra's words place both Ashley's difficulties and the responses of Western psychologies within a socio-political context that acknowledges the continuing effects of colonisation. Galiindurra expresses her understanding of the cultural and ethical practices of caring for children that are kept in circulation within Aboriginal cultures, practices that are marginalised by and often counter to the discourses and discursive practices of 'behaviour management' and 'child management'. I am a member of the psychologically related disciplines that perpetuate these ideas, but on the say-so of other local community workers with whom Galiindurra has existing relationships of trust, she nevertheless decided to 'give me a go'. This was a very limited 'choice', given that Galiindurra as a foster carer was subject to various official and 'expert' opinions and to associated demands for Ashley to 'see someone'.

Galiindurra:
As an Aboriginal person, when they said to me, you know, "We'll get this kid into therapy" I thought, "Oh, God, I'm going to be judged again, I won't be doing something right".

I had these fears, and I have to be honest, I did have fears. The fact is, Ashley has been dreadfully affected, and this makes for one of the most difficult situations anyone has ever had to work with. So it was: "Oh Lordy, here we go again! This kid can't go to school unless she goes to therapy"...And then we met and there was this instant 'I like her'. And that doesn't happen very often. I usually have this wall around me for protection. And you've supported me not just in the therapy sessions but by coming to meetings and being the voice they'll listen to.

I have wondered whether, in writing this chapter, I am once more being "the voice they'll listen to". Is such speech and writing irreducibly paternalistic, a further act of colonisation, even though Galiindurra and I both understand such acts as 'strategic' and, furthermore, we each understand that the other understands this? There is something deeply uncomfortable in advocating for someone who is such a consummate advocate herself, but whom the system in this instance marginalises as insufficiently 'objective'. I take a position for Galiindurra's perspective as the best possible 'assessment' of these children's needs, and for Galiindurra's care as the best possible therapy for these kids. I hope that this to some extent mediates the reproduction of colonising power inherent in the discourses of therapy and child protection.

Ashley and her foster sister Maree, together with their other siblings 'in care', are part of a current stolen generation. Contemporary government policy has been implemented, in this instance, by placing Ashley and Maree with an Aboriginal family who are dedicated to maintaining their connections with their families of origin and cultures. Galiindurra in particular works hard to mediate the effects of wardship, and the girls are to all accounts safer, happier and more in touch with their cultural heritage than they were in their families of origin where, sadly, due to the severe ongoing and intergenerational effects of colonisation and dispossession, they could not be physically and emotionally sustained. Ultimately though, decisions about the welfare of these Aboriginal children rests with a Eurocentric government that until 2008 had not apologised for the violent decimation of Indigenous cultures. Any Australian government is heir to the systematic practice of taking Aboriginal and Torres Strait Islander children away from their homes and communities, and is also implicated in 'stealing' a current generation of these children (Link-up NSW and Wilson, 1997). This is also the system that has contracted me to meet with Ashley.

Galiindurra:

When we have more than a third of our kids in care, you know, there are all sorts of questions that need to be asked. Actually that figure's gone up since the Bringing Them Home Report [8] *and it's rising every year. Now you'd think when people are well educated and well informed the rate would be going down, that would be your hope, but that hasn't been the case.*

The story of my meetings with Ashley is a story of being continually challenged to go with the practices that fit for Ashley and her family, sometimes in opposition to what others have recommended. There was a strong professional view, for instance, that Ashley needed 'containment' [9], one of the taken-for-granted assumptions that have leached from psycho-analysis into more general understandings of therapy, and that she should therefore be 'seen' within the boundaries of a therapy room. In refusing this recommendation and meeting with Ashley outside of the assumed containment of the therapy room, I was following the guidance of Ashley's carer. I did not want to reproduce the tactics of governance and control by which colonisation of Aboriginal people continues into the present day. I did not want to be implicated in furthering the production of this child's identity as a problem through trafficking in pathologising categories, and still less did I wish to encourage Ashley's carers and herself to embrace such categories as modes of existence. This more insidious form of governance (Foucault, 2000a), which Foucault calls normalising power, is one which we are routinely subjected to/participate in within contemporary Western cultures, and it has arguably been one of our most dangerous exports in the name of processes of so-called civilisation.

Moreover, the recommendation to keep Ashley within the room is to my mind an overly literal version of 'containment', which in psychodynamic understanding refers, not to an enclosed physical space, but rather to a therapist's ability to be intellectually and emotionally sensitive to, and to provide a consistent and reliable space of understanding and support for, a person's emotional and psychic experience, particularly for very distressing feelings and experiences. From the perspective of a non-normative and culturally sensitive psychodynamics, I might therefore consider a lakeside meeting to be a 'containing' response to this particular child and family, for all that lakeside meetings do not fit within the codified practices of normative psychotherapy. However, even this more metaphysical and inclusive understanding of 'containment' meets its limits in this work, since it behoves me to regard my position as that of an 'apprentice' to the custodial wisdom of this family rather than as that of an 'experienced other' (Bion, in Leclerc, 2006) responding to an unconscious need.

While the individual psychotherapy approach advocated by the referring psychiatrist and paediatrician seemed culturally and situationally inappropriate, family therapy (conventionally understood) seemed almost equally inappropriate, since this family clearly was the best therapy that Ashley had ever had. On Galiindurra's recommendation, I decided to start meeting with Ashley within the context of close communication and frequent 'catch-ups' with Galiindurra, and see what happened from there. As the poem suggests, I met Ashley very much on her own terms, in places and ways for which, with Galiindurra's support, Ashley expressed a preference. Her desires and capacities to visit and work with me in my art therapy studio developed from a platform of careful consultation and relationship building. This included a period of collecting her from the school, initially by car, then travelling with her on the school bus. In time, Ashley was able to catch the bus herself. At first I met her at the bus stop; then she began to walk from the bus stop on the corner of my street to my studio. We would talk about the steps Ashley had undertaken and enquire into the effects of these steps on her current life, her sense of herself and her abilities. This graduated process had an affinity with and was broadly informed by cognitive behavioural notions such as desensitisation, as well as by narrative therapy. However, these therapy ideas took second place to Galiindurra's suggestions and to a process of experimentation, and were certainly never formalised into a 'treatment plan'.

As Galiindurra explained to me, there were some days when Ashley was "just not separable from her sister". Maree, a slightly older foster sibling, kept a lookout for Ashley at school, shared a room with her at home, and would let Galiindurra know whenever things were getting a bit out of hand. So it developed that the sisters would sometimes come together to paint and draw in my studio after school on Wednesday afternoons. Maree became very fond of these visits, and Galiindurra was of the opinion that Maree herself could benefit from joining the art therapy, since Maree's own family of origin story was also marked with distress, loss and confusion. After each session we would walk round the corner to meet Galiindurra for a cup of tea at her place of work, she would catch me up on some of the developments in their lives, and the girls and I would catch her up on what we'd been doing that afternoon. The sight of me running along the streets in the wake of two girls and a dog, wet paintings flapping in the breeze, has occasioned much good-humoured laughter from some of the other Indigenous community workers at Galiindurra's workplace.

Additionally, I have had an invaluable therapeutic assistant, albeit a very hairy and lively one, in the form of my blue cattle dog, Moonam Chomper [10]. In the tradition of narrative therapy, Moonam Chomper became an outsider witness (White, 1995, 2000) to preferred developments in Ashley's life and relationships, and to her sense of her self and her capacities. The importance to Ashley of Moonam Chomper's regular participation in our meetings only really became apparent when Galiindurra and I met with Ashley to ask her whether it would be OK for me to include this poem, her artwork and some stories of her coming to see me in my studio, in my writings about art therapy and narrative therapy. When I asked Ashley what name she would like to be known by in these writings, she at first nominated to be called Moonam. Galiindurra and I nodded towards each other at this, both noticing just how important a four-legged friend can be. We agreed that Moonam would be very honoured to share her name with Ashley, but that it could be a bit confusing to have two Moonams in the poem. Ashley could see the difficulty this might create for other people, so she elected to be known instead by the name of her best two-legged friend.

Therapy, like art, is as much invention as it is citation. While some of what constituted 'therapy' in this situation is encompassed by theorisations and descriptions of the arts therapies and narrative therapies, other aspects of this particular therapy would not necessarily make an appearance in the textbooks. The following list reiterates and expands upon the poem to give a flavour of the sort of things that Ashley, Maree and I found to be 'therapeutic' during and around our meetings:

- hand-printing
- making houses from cardboard boxes for sisters to live in together
- writing stories about girls and geese
- dot painting
- making cards and writing letters for mums and dads
- making presents for baby sisters
- painting as an expression of being sorry [11]
- making up songs and singing them, for instance the one that goes "there was a little girl who loved to play in the garden, in the garden"
- working out who sat in the front of my car last time around
- laughing at jokes
- falling over in the grass
- being the artist's assistant
- playing noughts and crosses and losing
- cuppas and chats
- looking for netball results in the local paper
- throwing the Frisbee for Moonam Chomper
- talking to Moonam and guessing what she would say to us if she spoke English or we spoke Dog
- surprising Mum with what we've made
- asking questions when that's OK, but not too many
- writing and responding to this poem

I have attempted, in this poem, to find words for a multiplicity of family and community relations around Ashley and Maree. In retrospect, I suspect that I have not made sufficiently visible the work that Galiindurra constantly does in order to keep the children connected with their birth mothers and families of origin, given how profoundly disadvantaged both girls' birth families have been by legacies of loss, dispossession and racial violence, how they continue to be subjected to racialised injustices, and how this context of disadvantage is rarely foregrounded as such by white support services. Galiindurra herself says she understands her ongoing capacity to provide for these children as made possible and sustainable within a broader familial circle.

Galiindurra:
I have great support. I have a whole family who have taken these kids on. Everyone just loves them to pieces, which is really lovely. I have the support of my mum and dad next door and my daughter and her fiancé, and all of my big kids. I have your support, Sheridan, which has been a mountain of support.

Sadly, given the legacies of past colonial practices of 'removal', this poem also tells a story of the present-day removal of an Aboriginal child into a white family. This is supposed to be illegal but, as Galiindurra says,

There's a whole school of people who believe in the Act [12] *and then others who say, "Bugger it, I've got a nice little white placement for that kid and that's where it's going".*

During the time of my meetings with Ashley, her baby sister was taken from her mother at the hospital where the child was born and placed in care with a non-Indigenous family. Ashley and her brother were forbidden to see their new sibling, a decision based on advice from a psychological expert on 'attachment'. The local Department of Community Services (DOCS) worker and manager were outraged at this decision, taken by another area of the department. Thus a theory of attachment was invoked to support tearing a family and culture apart. Through a serious of assumptions about the need to mimic primary maternal care, 'attachment' to a new carer was deemed to be in conflict with this Indigenous child's 'attachment' with her birth mother, her siblings, her family and her culture. In the poem I remember Ashley, who has been so anguished and angry, at this redoubled loss, that she has cried and raged and broken things and brought her carers almost to their wits' end. I remember how she sits thoughtfully at the bench in the art therapy studio and slowly and carefully creates a painting to send to the baby sister she has never seen.

After more than two years of protest, a slow process of negotiating access, and some specific and immediate as well as longer term concerns for the wellbeing of the child within her foster placement, Ashley's little sister eventually came to live with Galiindurra, Ashley, Ashley's younger brother and the rest of Galiindurra's family.

At such times, what is inadequately called therapy must become part of a platform for collective political action, if anything 'therapeutic' is to happen at all. We—because, for all that I am a non-Indigenous person imbricated with neocolonial privilege, I believe that a 'we' of Indigenous and non-Indigenous people acting together can and must be constituted in response to such an outrage—'we' are moved to action by these injustices. These actions can flow in more directions than one. It moves me deeply that, in the midst of an ongoing cultural genocide, Galiindurra has room for compassion for the effect of government policies and practices on white kids in care, as well as on Indigenous kids and families.

Galiindurra:
Now the minister wants to adopt out kids after two years in care. We have no concept of adoption in our culture. That was the main thrust of our parliamentary submission on the Permanency Placement Bill [13], *but we were also concerned that no one seemed to be looking out for the white kids.*

The idea of adopting out kids in care, of whom over a third are Indigenous, a statistic vastly out of proportion with the numbers of Indigenous people living in Australia, was vaunted years ago, at the time that Ashley's sister was first taken away. Ashley's sister came home, but a revamped version of the permanency placement legislation was soon back on the agenda.

Galiindurra emails her a copy of the proposed legislation about the new bill, with a suggestion that if she and like-minded people feel concerned about this latest bill, they could email their concerns to her so that she can pass them on to the office of the Minister for Community Services. Sheridan drops what she was doing—or does she? Perhaps this is another way of taking up what she is doing—and dashes off a reply. The legislation is being tabled in Parliament today, so she has no time to polish or to reconsider her words, but she tries to keep her language fairly formal so that Galiindurra can cut and paste from the email into an unsubmissive 'submission'. Sheridan scans what she has written, hesitates, adds her formal qualifications, and presses 'reply'.

> Dear Galiindurra,
>
> Yes, this proposed legislation does concern me greatly, on the following grounds:

1. The high incidence of Indigenous children in care is a situation which is itself a legacy of past colonial practices, including the removal of such children from their families, and has been exacerbated by the failure of our governments and institutions to redress these injustices. Some 'postcolonial' policies and practices have unfortunately perpetuated removal and separation, and the suggested legislation would do just this. Adoption (in my understanding) is not traditionally practiced by Indigenous peoples, who have other more family and community based systems and practices for the care and support of children. It behoves our government and society to legislate and to act in ways that support and learn from, rather than undermine, these cultural practices. 'Care' should be provided in a way that is as consistent as possible with these cultural practices.

2. Within the legislation, which is in itself inappropriate for Indigenous children, the measures suggested for Aboriginal and Torres Strait Islander children are grossly inadequate. The suggested legislation is retrograde in that it does not include the same safeguards as the Child Care and Protection Act. The Act specifies that an Aboriginal or Torres Strait Islander child in long term care must be placed with (respectively) an Aboriginal or Torres Strait Islander family, by preference their own extended family, or if that is not possible then by preference within their community, as well as having continuing regular contact and connections with their family and culture, all of which it is government's ongoing responsibility to ensure. Even if such safeguards were implemented, it is unclear if and how an adoptive family would be monitored and supported to put them into practice.

To put it bluntly, the legislation facilitates the modern day removal of Indigenous children from their families, cultures and identities. The devastating effects of such policies are by now well documented.

3. The legislation is also deeply flawed in terms of the 'best interests' of all children in care.

The language of "investment" in these children's futures is misleading when in fact the suggested adoption practices actually remove governmental responsibility to invest morally and financially in the well-being and future of these children. In this sense, adoption of children in care fits with an agenda of privatisation, de-regulation and small government, rather than with progressive notions of welfare, community responsibility and human rights.

The proposed legislation is based on an assumption that biological parents with long-term problems are unable to change their capacities to parent, whereas they often lack the support and resources to make these changes. Service cuts are making this situation worse, and adopting out the children of such parents simply papers over the cracks in the system.

Adoption is usually a practice that relies on strict assessment of adoptive families, stricter than that for foster carers, whereas the legislation bypasses these safeguards.

Children who are placed in foster care are usually by definition vulnerable and often continue to need specialist support. The continuing monitoring provided by the appropriate government department can support these children and their long-term carers, and is a means of minimising the possibility of further abuse in care. These safeguards and supports would not apply to an adoptive family.

Care systems already provide a great deal of permanency and security for children in long term stable care. Thus an established stable care relationship does not depend on adoption for its continuity.

The onus is strongly on biological parents whose children have been removed to show their fitness as parents, and the wishes of children are considered paramount in any considerations of restoration. Perhaps this system needs some adjustment to ensure the child's best interests are being met, but a radical change toward adoption is unwarranted.

Adoption is not necessary to ensure connection between children and their long-term carers, since obviously families would only consider adoption if connection already existed.

We need to challenge the idea that children cannot handle multiple relationships and to promote more community acceptance and support of the numerous situations in which children have affiliation to more than one domestic family unit. Children of almost every culture and generation have been raised in a variety of ways, supported by extended family and community. The notion that the nuclear family is the best form of care is not scientific or sustainable.

The history of adoption is troubled by numerous examples of children feeling displaced from their identities and suffering as a consequence, usually because their connection to their family of origin, and in particular to their mother, has been severed. While modern adoption practice modifies this, birth certificates and letters are scarcely an adequate substitute for living contact with the people who brought you into the world.

There are many instances where birth mothers and fathers are unable to provide primary care but, with support, can still maintain a relationship with their children.

In the minority of cases where even supervised contact with a particular parent is physically or emotionally unsafe for the child, child protection provisions should be sufficient to allow for those children not to have to see that parent. Some clarification of the blurred jurisdictions of the various courts would be useful in such instances.

The 'best interests' of children are notoriously difficult to assess. Life situations and developmental theories change, whereas adoption is permanent. Let's put more intellectual, emotional and financial resources into the problem of how so many of our children come to be 'in care', rather than perpetuating social and cultural hierarchies and injustices through 'adopting' this legislation.

Please could you pass on my concerns.

Yours sincerely,
Sheridan Linnell
(AATR)

A message comes back promptly.

Go girl please pass the message on we need all the support we can...can I email this to the minister Galiindurra

Sheridan forwards the email to her 'list'. As an afterthought, she pastes it into this chapter, as well.

She is spreading the word(s).

Learning to paint: the possibilities and limits of 'art therapy'

When she made art in the studio, Ashley worked in a vivid, lateral aesthetic style, incorporating many handprints and vigorous brushmarks (see figs. 1–7 for selected photographs of Ashley's artwork) [14]. For the first few months it was difficult for her to keep the paint and the glue within the artwork, and at times she was immersed elbow deep in paint. I set up a series of buckets of soapy water and towels outside on the grass, to minimise the messiness spreading to her clothes and to other surfaces around the studio. On one occasion when I was not quick enough, she made handprints over a wall. We talked about this and agreed to work with Maree to convert these prints into a permanent mural, on the understanding that in future Ashley would not paint on the walls or desks. Ashley kept her part of this bargain. As time went on she was able to direct her energy more and more into art making, only returning to the earlier generalised mess-making at times of severe distress.

Sometimes Ashley painted in a gestural and semi-figurative style that approximated something like Western expressionism. Often she made cards for her birth mother or for Galiindurra Mum, or other relations. With so many in her extended family, there was usually a birthday imminent. At other times she made Aboriginal flags in numerous sizes out of paint, pastel, pen, pencil, paper, cardboard, felt and clay. During the period of time when she was not allowed to see her baby sister, Ashley worked intensely on the construction of cardboard houses from shoeboxes, often painted in the colours of the Aboriginal flag, furnished them with felt, card and matchsticks. These cardboard houses became something like sets for a play of her life. She inhabited them with a pair of multicoloured pipe cleaner and tissue paper dolls, whom on several occasions she called "the sisters" (fig. 7). At times Ashley would be deeply involved in her own style of work and at other times, especially if something was worrying her, she would compare herself to Maree, attempt to imitate Maree's productions, and then get frustrated when she could not do so. Sometimes Ashley and I would work together, with me in the role of an 'artist's assistant' carefully following her direction, or sometimes we would evolve a more collaborative and 'conversational' style (cf. Eisdell, 2005). I found Ashley's artworks, both her paintings and her 3-D constructions, very aesthetically satisfying, but she herself was often disappointed with her difficulties in achieving neatness and realism, especially when she was comparing herself to Maree. As ever, I was struck by the unforced metaphorical resonance between how people, especially children, 'are' in their artwork and 'are' in the other aspects of their lives.

Meanwhile, Maree was in general a more 'intentional' artist, whose practice I had so far understood to be an expression of her experiences within multiple cultures and her understandings of her Aboriginality as a living category. Maree usually worked in the studio with great enjoyment, in a vibrant and skilled engagement with the traditions and conventions of contemporary Aboriginal painting. She would move confidently between and hybridise Indigenous and Western art forms, as indeed do many urban Indigenous artists. As she worked, she would sometimes explain to me what she was doing, and where her ideas had come from. Her work was much appreciated by other members of her family and community for its skill, joyfulness and incorporation of traditional processes and motifs (see figs. 8, 9, 10, 14 and 15).

Of course there are always limits to intentionality and rationality in artwork, and some of Maree's most compelling works resonate with feeling in excess of her intentions. Her painting 'Boat' (fig. 11), with its odd, emotionally suggestive use of negative space, is somehow echoed in two of my own art responses (see chapter 7, figs. 1 and 2). Maree's watercolour painting of 'Mum' (fig. 12)—which could evoke either/both Galiindurra Mum and Maree's birth mum, although Maree hesitantly said the painting was of Galiindurra—has dribbles of glitter glue, like tears, on a watery face, eyes that appear closed, an open mouth full of silver glitter. Whether the sadness this painting provokes in me arises from the painting, from my relationship with Maree and her stories, from my own stories, or from all of these is a question that remains necessarily open. 'Madness is short, happiness is long' (fig. 13) seems to me to be an extraordinary synthesis of traditional imagery with written text, and of a conscious articulation of thoughtfulness and emotional complexity with an unspeakable, perhaps unthinkable, excess. Maree said little of this painting, but she read the text aloud during our meeting.

One day, while I was with the girls in my studio, I noticed that Maree had abruptly, and with a notable absence of pleasure, begun to work in another style. This latter form of mark making consisted of repeated, laborious attempts to 'correctly' represent figures in a perspectivised landscape according to the traditions and conventions of European realism. This invoked for me a colonial norm of representation, and also led me to reflect on the influence of primary schooling with its production of developmental norms and educational standards about 'how to draw'. Neither of the girls wanted to talk much during this particular meeting, and I was reluctant to persist with questions that might be experienced as intrusive. I found myself feeling something of a weight in relation to Maree's attempt to 'get it right'. Reflecting on this, I wondered if, in its sudden appearance and intensity, this form of art making might be overdetermined with broader emotional and social struggles to 'get it right'. These signs in turn alerted me to a sense that something might be 'wrong'.

In this session Ashley attempted to copy Maree's work, as she often did, expressing some frustration at the difficulty of imitating this exacting task. Ashley's image, in which the figures on the swing are painted out, seems to hold a distorting mirror up to her sister's work (fig. 6).

After the session, I checked out with Galiindurra how she thought things were going for Maree, and Galiindurra responded with stories of some very painful and difficult recent events in Maree's life. This in turn opened a space for conversations with Maree about her troubles and concerns.

Galiindurra:

Something that sticks in my head is what happened with Maree and her beautiful Aboriginal art—bright colours, and suns, and spectacular art that looked like Ken Done eat your heart out!

And the fact that I hadn't yet had the chance to discuss with you the significant things that had just been happening in Maree's life, and you just sort of said to me, "What's happened with Maree lately?" And I said, "Well...!" And I went on to tell you about the traumatic things that had happened between her and her mum. And that she felt quite insecure about her place with me because of things her new granddad who had come into her life, her white granddad, had said to her.

And it all just was portrayed in her art.

From this beautiful free flowing art, her artwork turned into these people on swings with their hair perfect, and she got distressed when it wasn't perfect. And it showed just how she felt in her life.

One minute she's this free spirit and everything's going fine and we're just cruising along, "I can do what I like and it's all acceptable" to the next minute, "Oh my goodness, what if I don't do it right, what if it's not perfect, what if it doesn't fit into the picture I should be painting? Will I still be as loved and honoured and treasured as the child I am?"

Ironically, art therapy, understood on the one hand as a means of imag(in)ing the psychically and/or socially unspeakable, and on the other hand as a practice embedded in dominant Eurocentric assumptions about the 'nature' of aesthetic and intrapsychic phenomena, in this situation both uncovered a potential *and* met a limit. Art therapy (as it is generally understood) allowed for the emergence of traces of distress and uncertainty that were yet to find words. These traces emerged in the discursive field of painting though variations in gesture and style, rather than through the content or direct representation of a 'story'. The Eurocentric aesthetic that was taken up, in this painting, in place of Maree's usual aesthetic, was simultaneously a colonising process *and* a means of symbolically expressing and communicating distress.

An ethical/aesthetic dilemma has attended upon art therapy in this particular context. While I take a position of seeking to disrupt the ongoing colonisation effected by white psychologies and therapies, I also acknowledge that there is no position to take outside of discursive relations of power. I neither wish to perpetuate European art practices as the norm, or to appropriate Indigenous Australian cultural practices (Johnson, 2002). Nor, for that matter, do I wish to insist that Indigenous children who are growing up within a complexity of cultures must practice their art in traditional ways so that I can feel less guilty about the effects of colonisation.

In a subsequent meeting, Galiindurra taught all of us how to paint, in a contemporary and eclectic version of Indigenous cultural practice, our relationships to people, places and other significant aspects of our lives. This move was not about a simple inversion of cultural norms, since this work relies for its effectiveness on the ongoing negotiation of complexity and contradiction, and inversion would only reproduce a necessity to 'get it right'. Rather, Galiindurra's action in teaching me to paint performed a temporary 'dissolution' (White, 2004) of a particular dilemma.

Galiindurra's teaching extended the discursive and aesthetic range of art therapy in this therapeutic context, through an enactment and documentation of the safety, love and connection that had recently been threatened for Maree, a threat that was part of greater Indigenous histories of dispossession and loss. We could then ongoingly include what Galiindurra had taught us in our repertoire of studio approaches, and I was at least partly freed from the doublebind of either marginalising or appropriating the traditions of Indigenous mark making.

Galiindurra:

The thing that's come to me about art therapy is that it's so in tune with our culture, about how important art is to everyone in our culture. And Aboriginal art is so unfailing; you can't do a thing wrong. It doesn't matter what you do, whether you splash a bit of paint in the middle and that's coming from you, and you can call it Mother Earth or whatever you like. And you can't do a thing wrong, put a few dots and that's your masterpiece, you know.

Figure 1: *Hands*, Ashley, Acrylic paints on paper, 30cm x 42cm

Figure 2: *Untitled*, Ashley, Acrylic paints on paper, 42cm x 59cm

Figure 3: *Untitled*, Ashley, Acrylic paints on paper, 42cm x 59cm

Figure 4: *Flag*, Ashley, Acrylic on canvas board, 20cm x 26cm

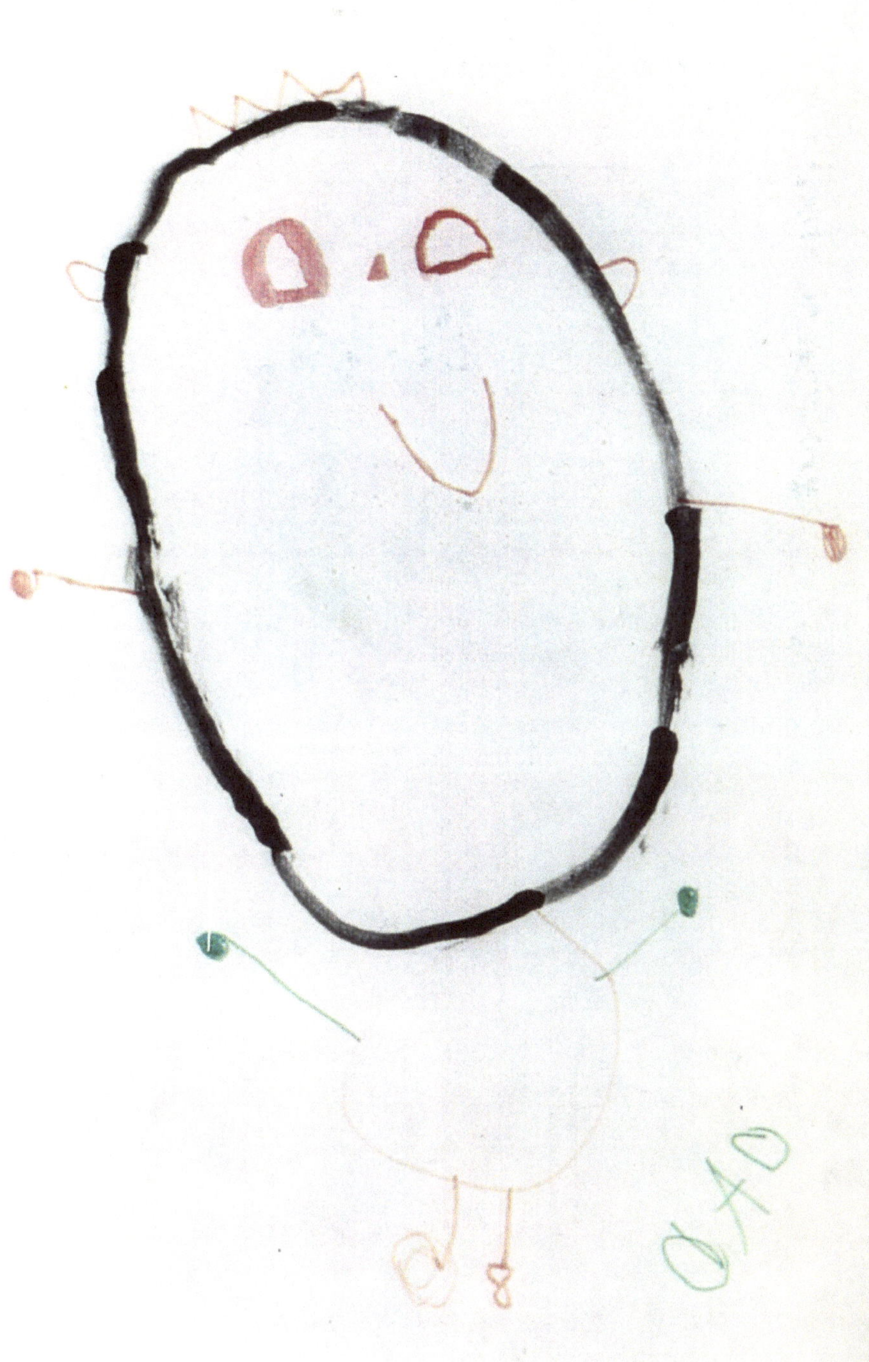

Figure 5: *Dad,* Ashley, Watercolour and coloured marker on paper, 59cm x 42cm

Figure 6: *Swings,* Ashley (response to Maree's painting of children on swings), Acrylic on paper, 30cm x 42cm

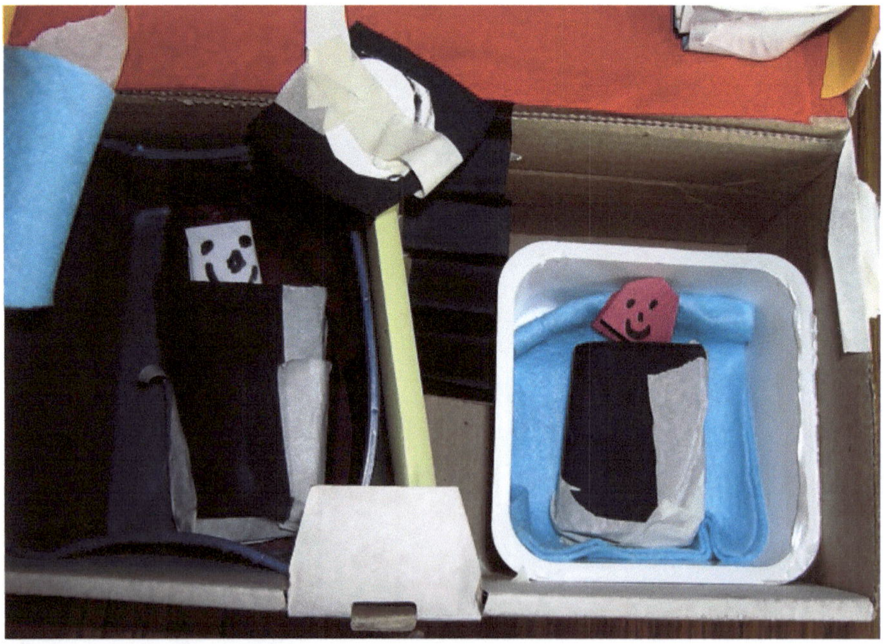

Figure 7: *Sisters*, Ashley, 3D construction, mixed media, 22cm x 35cm x 12cm (approx.)

Figure 8: *Untitled*, Maree , Acrylic on canvas board, 20cm x 26cm

Figure 9: *Landscape,* Maree, Acrylic paints on paper, 59cm x 42cm

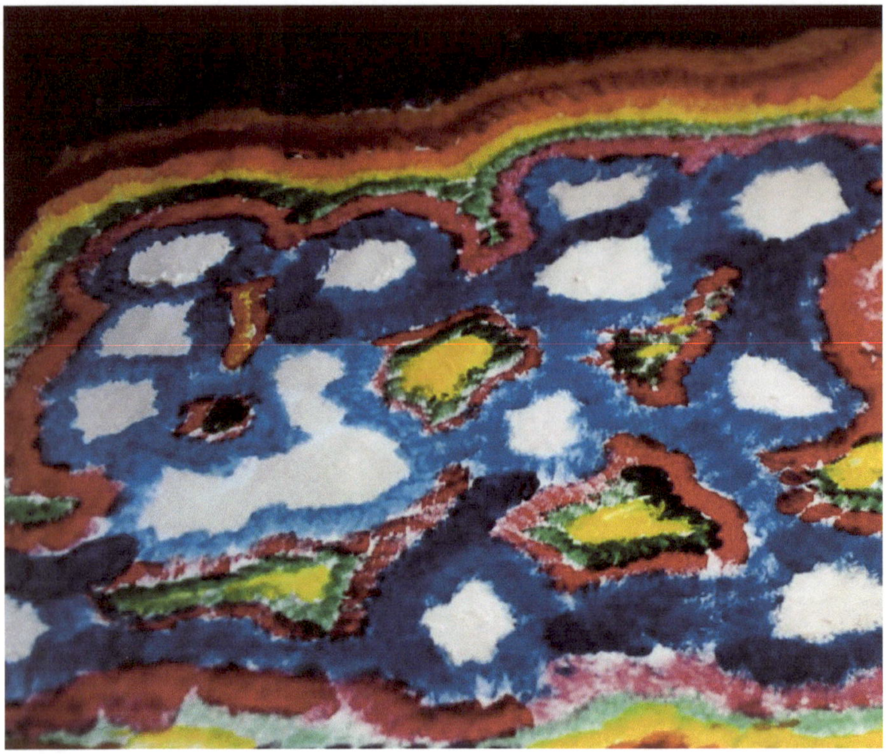

Figure 10: *Untitled* (detail), Maree, Acrylic paints on paper, 59cm x 86cm

Figure 11: *Boat* (cropped), Maree, Acrylic paints on paper, 42cm x 59cm

Figure 12: *Mum,* Maree, Watercolour and glitter-pen on paper, 59cm x 42cm

Figure 13: *Madness is short, happiness is long*, Maree, Pastel and coloured marker on paper, 30cm x 42cm

Figure 14: *Self portrait* (drying on studio table), Maree, Acrylic paints, glue and glitter-glue on paper, 42cm x 59cm

Figure 15: *Me, my place*, Maree, Acrylic paints on paper, 42cm x 59cm

Questioning practices and constituting ethics

This work has engaged me in 'questioning practices' in relation to my conduct and identity as a narrative and art therapist. Rather than assuming that I am an intrinsically 'ethical' person and will therefore behave appropriately, it has been necessary to ask myself what ways of being and relating I could aspire to in this work, and what kinds of ethical practices I could embrace in order to move towards these ways of being and relating. If what I aspire to in this work is a mode of being and relating that minimises the possibility of reproducing the power relations of colonisation, what is called for is far more than a set of guidelines for non-Indigenous therapists working in partnership with Indigenous people. It could be said that the aspect of myself that is the ethical focus—or the ethical substance—of this subjective work is my inscription with Eurocentric modes of being and relating, so habitual, embodied and culturally dominant that it has become invisible.

I had been introduced, long before I began meeting with this particular family, to an understanding that I occupy a position of cultural privilege, that this privilege is systematically produced and reproduced at the expense of others, and that crimes of violence and dispossession have been and continue to be perpetuated by my people against the traditional inhabitants of Australia. Since there is no position available to me 'outside' these relations of power, I have come to understand myself as ethically obliged to be actively anti-racist and anti-colonialist. This includes an obligation to familiarise myself with the stories of the Indigenous people, whom my own people have slaughtered, raped, imprisoned and robbed of their children and land, and an obligation to engage in negotiated practices of apology, restitution and reconciliation.

One summer, she holidays at Myall Lakes. The lakes and beaches are lined with tents, caravans and Kombi vans. As she sits outside her tent beside the lake, she recalls that one of the worst recorded massacres of Indigenous people happened at the similarly named location of Myall Creek (Elder, 1988) [15]. Myall Creek is not actually in the Great Lakes area, and her current campsite is related to the murders only in name. The site of the Myall Creek massacre is actually over five hundred kilometres away, inland and to the northwest.

The name 'Myall' has invited her, as by now it invites many contemporary Australians, to remember an event distant in time and space, yet close to the bone. After the European perpetrators of the Myall Creek massacre were hanged, killings of Indigenous people apparently became, not less brutal or less common, but secretive and unreported

(Elder, 1988). Massacres reputedly happened in the late nineteenth century on the coastline just south of where she is sitting right now, between Myall Lake and Hawkes Nest, at a place called Dark Point [16]. These deaths are part of local lore but went formally unrecorded.

Smells of sun lotion, mosquito coils and barbecued meat float on the warm evening breeze, effacing the more subtle scent of tea tree rising from the impregnated waters. She continues to sit on a folding chair outside her tent, writing in her little book, the sky turning red and darkening, curling with parchment clouds.

> *Each vacation brings more of us.*
> *Unconscious caravans of summer pilgrims*
> *come to bathe in the melaleuca waters*
> *of the lake. At sunset, a whine and sting,*
> *as small atonements puncture our skins.*
> *The sky is a raging document of all*
> *that we disavow.*

Many years ago, she had been one of a group of Indigenous people and non-Indigenous supporters [17] working together to mark the bi-centenary of the invasion and appropriation of Aboriginal lands by the British, an occasion that much of Australia saw as a celebration of nationhood rather than as a call for mourning. In the group's meetings, priority was given to Aboriginal and Torres Strait Islander speakers. Major decisions were made by a consensus of the Aboriginal and Torres Strait Islander members of the group, in the light of discussion by both Indigenous and non-Indigenous members. She remembers having felt, at a bodily level, the strangeness and anxiety of stepping back from the taken-for-granted position of influence that often came her way in other meetings, presumably from being articulate and university educated, although she had always felt her privilege to be mediated, within the terms of a prevalent politics of identity, by gender, sexuality and a working-class background.

The moving complexities of gender, culture and race were not resolved by the group's strategy, which led to some complex and heated debate within the group as to whether, for example, a group of immigrant women (including Black women) had been marginalised in the group by being positioned as part of the category 'non-Indigenous'. Identity politics met its limits in the endless entanglement of narratives and subject positions that make up the indeterminacy of any 'identity'. Yet there was a pragmatic and powerful sense in which a temporary and partial suspension of privilege had shaped her imagination of marginalised realities, and thus shaped in her an ethics of relation to marginalised Others [18].

Difference and connectedness—becoming-other in the work

This therapeutic work has had a profound influence, not only on my practices as a therapist, but also on my sense of my self. I have a sense of 'becoming-other' in this work, perhaps becoming a category of person for whom I have yet to find a name. I am not indigenous to this country, so while I have much to learn from Aboriginal and Torres Strait Islander people, I know it is important to avoid any move that would be an appropriation of another's identity, another theft in a litany of thefts that have so far included land, children, identity and culture, including what Western culture calls 'art'. Our partnership is an attempt to embrace difference rather than efface it, and to acknowledge relations of power rather than to render them invisible.

Working with Galiindurra and the girls has continually offered me opportunities to address my (often subtle) imbrication in the historical and continuing practices and effects of colonisation. Yet at the same time that this work draws attention to my difference and privilege, distinctions between binary or dividing categories such as 'worker' and 'client' and 'professional' and 'personal' are continually coming into question. The dividing categories of worker and client are challenged by my ongoing apprenticeship to Galiindurra, by whom I am guided as to what are appropriate responses to her family and culture. I actively position myself as the junior partner in our collaboration, against systems and practices that seek to render me 'expert'.

In responding to the generosity and trust extended to me by people who historically and currently have many strong reasons to distrust someone of my cultural and professional background, I am called upon to become other than who the dominant narratives of my profession and culture suppose me to be. Not long after I met Galiindurra, she told me of the potential to become an 'aunty' in the life of these girls. This is a possibility that, as I initially understood it, would enter someone into ongoing familial/social relationships and their accompanying obligations. In practice, I have not felt 'pressure' from Galiindurra to 'be there' for the family in ways that were incommensurate with other aspects of my life, although, as the emphasis of my work has moved from therapy toward education and research, I have been concerned with the limits this places on my availability as a therapist, and sometimes, gripped with ambivalence, I 'pressure' myself. I am deeply touched by Galiindurra and her family's inclusiveness, both because I and my family have been embraced in this way, and also because it reminds me how 'I', despite dominant modern constructions of separateness, am composed through my 'relations'.

I am aware that it is problematic to adapt Foucault's 'ethics' (2000b)—surely intended as an analytical tool for understanding how we come to constitute ourselves as particular kinds of subjects—as a moral prescription for an aesthetics or art of self. One of the dangers of such intentional 'ethicalisation' is that of substituting solemnity for seriousness, and of becoming paralysed with self-consciousness. If I consciously shape myself as a subject of anti-racism, as indeed I am committed to do, how can I minimise the likelihood of reproducing the tactics of self-surveillance that typify modern power and prescribe multiple versions of failure (White, 2002)? Will I feel obliged to 'convert' myself and other non-Indigenous therapists through exemplary stories of my shortcomings and partial redemption? Is that what I am doing in this chapter? Wasn't such missionary zeal one mode by which the colonisation of what is now known as Australia took place? How can I take responsibility alongside other non-Indigenous people (particularly those who, like myself, come from a colonising nation) for arguably the most heinous of injustices, the genocide of Indigenous peoples, while at the same time acknowledging the marginalisations of non-dominant gender, class and sexuality, and the effects of these in my life? How can I figure de-humanising injustices as linked to each other, without diminishing them or appropriating/colonising one discourse in terms of another?

An intentional ethics is a necessary but insufficient move toward transformation, especially in relation to expressing and countering how taken-for-granted racisms are embedded and embodied. When, for all my efforts to the contrary, the ghosts of an imperial heritage reappear through the cracks of my own conscious commitment to the politics of anti-racism to haunt the narrative therapist, the art therapist and the poststructural researcher [19], how can I challenge these powerful remains in ways that do not fully reproduce modern forms of confession and judgement (Foucault, 1980)? What would constitute a poetics, as well as a politics, of transformation, in relation to racial identity as an ethical and social substance [20]? How can 'I' become 'Otherwise'? (Venn, 2002).

She attends a workshop on writing methodologies in which she and other members of the Narrative, Discourse and Pedagogy Research

Concentration are excited to have the opportunity to meet with Laurel Richardson. They have each been asked to bring some research material that they want to work with, so she has brought a large self-portrait in charcoal and pastel, and a few paragraphs that she thinks are sounding a bit stiff. She unrolls her picture and begins to read out some words about what her ancestors have done to the Indigenous people of the land.

After the first couple of sentences, she is crying—not just a few discreet/discrete tears, but an uncontrollable flood of grief. She can feel her 'self' unravelling, right here, in front of her colleagues and an overseas guest. She cannot bear to look at Laurel, whose unwavering expression of gentle and respectful concern might precipitate a further deluge. (Even as she is sobbing, she hopes she is not diluting the possibility of critique in what Lather (2001, p. 211) "has come to call the validity of tears".)

When all of the participants have shared their data, they take some time to write that material differently, drawing on the resources of poetry, fiction and memoir. Red-eyed and shaky, she takes a sentence about her own inscription with racism, and follows it down an unexpected rabbit hole of memory.

The unthinkable

For some reason Mum seemed preoccupied that summer with the possibility that I might marry a Black man. "Sheri," she'd muse as she washed and I dried, "I just don't know what I'd do if you brought home a black boyfriend. As for your father, he wouldn't have him in the house." Dad added, trying to be helpful, "On the other hand, you could do worse than marry a Jew. They are a very clean people."

I didn't know why they were so worried. I was yet to bring home any kind of boyfriend.

And after all, we'd moved out of a predominantly Black neighbourhood of London to the fringes of pale, middle class Surrey, then half-way around the world to take up residence in a suburban, white brick veneer house on an A. V. Jennings housing estate, surrounded by other ten-pound-a-passage, white, working class British migrants who'd sailed here in the wake of the White Australia Policy to 'make a better life'. Frankston was scarcely Brixton. Where were all these Black and Coloured boys I wasn't supposed to marry?

I was intrigued to find out that Terry, who was directing the local pantomime in which I played a very clumsy bear, had a younger, adopted Aboriginal brother called Tim. Compared to my parents' attitudes, I thought this progressive. Although I was taking Australian History for my final exams, I had never heard of the Stolen Generation. Tim and I painted some of the set for the play together. He seemed like a nice, quiet, usual kind of boy, except that he was unusually polite. I wanted to know what had happened to his Aboriginal family but thought it would be rude to ask. His skin was the colour of honey. He didn't show even the slightest inclination to ravish me. I suppose I was a bit disappointed, really.

Years later, when I told Mum—thinking that while she would find it difficult she must surely have guessed by now—that my partner of five years was a woman, Mum went deadly pale.

"Oh, Sheridan," she sighed. She only ever called me Sheridan when I had done something bad. "I would have found it easier if you had told me you'd murdered someone. You'd better leave the house before your father gets home."

"But Mum," I protested rather obviously, "murder kills people." My mother went into the bedroom and stayed there for a very long time.

The extension to me of an inclusiveness, generosity and forgiveness, so different from the dominant exclusionary practices of many modern

Western families, engages me in the ethics of a necessary indebtedness to those whom my dominant culture and family of origin have constituted and abjected as Other. How can I respond sufficiently to these obligations? What is an appropriate ethical relation to my (necessary) vulnerability to the good opinion of others, particularly to the opinions of those others who are Othered by dominant culture? Here I find myself echoing and learning from Galiindurra's empathic rendering of the imagined thoughts of Maree. There is no moral or emotional equivalence between the experience of an Indigenous child, with a legacy of removal and dispossession, and the self-doubt of a privileged white adult therapist; yet, at the same time, modern Western power renders us all 'subject'. Hence I find myself asking, or more likely acting on the unarticulated basis of, questions such as 'What if I don't get it right? Will I still be loved and honoured as the person and therapist I aspire to be?'

Galiindurra herself is exquisitely attuned to the pain of non-Indigenous people realising and wishing to find a response to the ongoing effects of colonisation. When I first met her, she periodically gave me publications containing commentaries, poems, histories and life stories written by Aboriginal people, many of whom who had been taken from their families. In this gesture, as in many others, 'gift-giving' and 'education' were seamlessly linked.

The emphasis in this chapter on my own ethical and subjective transformations in relation to the work described is in itself an ethical decision. I wish to counter a dominant and taken-for-granted focus in therapy, and in writings about therapy, on subjective transformations for the 'client'. I also want to avoid as much as possible the danger of reproducing the politics of assimilation through the techniques and assumptions of therapy—for instance, the implication that the participants in this particular therapy were in need of being normalised/transformed according to a Western psychological agenda. Consequently, the trajectory of this chapter tends toward the transformation of the therapist herself—even to the limit of breaking open 'therapy' as a category of work and 'therapist' as mode of existence.

However, this is not simply the story of the 'consciousness raising' of a white therapist. The ethics and aesthetics of writing from a subjective viewpoint are not based in an idea that I 'change' through a rational process in the course of this story. My apprenticeship to Galiindurra's knowledge has been intertwined with the choreography of our developing intimacy, engaging me in a poetics, as well as a politics, of subjective transformation. Nor are these ethics and aesthetics based in the idea that I alone am the subject of change. Firstly, I would not be any kind of therapist at all if those who consult me did not also benefit from the location or creation of significant difference in their lives, their relationships, and/or their sense of who, and for whom, they might be(come). Moreover, if subjectivity is fluid and social, then relationships are mutually conditioning and transformative, dances of contradictions and connections, rather than unidirectional. The girls, as Galiindurra's transcribed words attest, have also experienced changes through this therapeutic relation. Galiindurra, too, is changed through our connection—as, indeed, we all change all of the time in relation to each other—although I believe it is for Galiindurra, rather than for me, to speak (or not) of the specificity and significance of how this relation has affected her.

Such a 'mutuality' of relations and transformations becomes almost impossible to speak of when one of the parties to the 'mutuality' is a descendant and beneficiary of those who invaded the lands of, and committed genocide against, the other party, and when the legacies and ongoing practice of these injustices currently shape many of the realities of and relations between Indigenous and non-Indigenous people [21]. Nevertheless, I believe the suggestion that only 'I' change in the process of this story of therapy would reproduce the othering of racialised Others, through an inverted hierarchy in which these Others must be static in order for me to be transformed. This would not only be theoretically flawed, it would be ethically flawed as well. An acknowledgement of the radical and mutual vulnerability and openness of each to the other has been suggested as a possible basis for a poststructural ethics (Butler, 2004). These ethics do not, in my opinion, exclude a consideration of historical and current practices of domination and the responsibilities that can be taken up, by people who have perpetrated or benefited from such practices, in order to attempt some redress of hurt and injustice. Indeed, these ethics both underline the urgent need for such responsibilities and suggest that these responsibilities can only be taken up in helpful and non-dominating ways by listening and responding to a call from those others whom we have harmed.

A necessary tension, then, plays out in and around this work, and in writing about this work. From a poststructural position, I understand subjectivities as multiple and mutually constituted through power, and so I am interested in a dissolution of binaries, a transformation of fixed categories and a production of more fluid subjectivities, relationships and social and cultural realities. As Venn (2002) has cogently pointed out, this poststructural break with "the idea of a self-sufficient, self-centred subject, doubling as the autonomous, objective agent of history...is in solidarity with the rejection of occidentalism" (pp. 51–52), or of dominant Eurocentric ways of thinking and being. However, while poststructural and postcolonial politics can and frequently do inform each other, the latter may strategically take up a more 'fixed' notion of identities and cultures as a basis for challenging racisms and rehabilitating marginalised and subjugated histories, identities and cultures. As someone engaged with both poststructuralist and anti-racist ethics and practices, it becomes necessary to conceptualise how racialised categories are ongoingly produced and embodied, become dominant, subjugated, centred or marginalised through operations of power. At the same time, such politics demand respect for how subjugated categories—even those categories produced as an effect of dominant colonial power—can themselves become a strategic basis of resistance. An instance of this, highly relevant to this chapter, is how colonial power has sought to erase the multiple histories, cultures, languages and practices of the Indigenous peoples of the continent now known as Australia, and how Indigenous people have reclaimed this multiplicity and diversity at the same time as making a strategically and experientially unified 'Aboriginality' the basis for resisting/responding to the legacies and ongoing practices of colonisation.

The stories told in this chapter could be perhaps be thought, not as exemplary, but as moments in the emerging shape of a post colonial politics and poetics (Venn, 2002), the trajectory of which might move beyond the strategic reversals of identity politics into a critical consideration of the politics of the very notion of identity. This is not to suggest that 'we' should reject consideration of the subjugation of particular persons or cultures as a basis for political action, or that we should turn away from rich accounts of identity and culture as modes of redress and 'self-determination' for individuals and communities. Any such move would be another reversal—one that re-institutes dominant power and seeks to eradicate difference through the tyranny of the same. Rather, it seems necessary to think about and challenge the continuing marginalisation of non-dominant identities and cultures together with making a critique of essentialised and bounded notions of identity and self. Western and modern notions of identity tend to rest on binary oppositions and deadly hierarchies that split the self from the Other, the individual from the social, the doing from the telling, and then exile those who challenge such distinctions from the very notion of the 'human' (Butler, 2004). Through the dissolution rather than the inversion of such binaries, poststructural practice can contribute to effective acts of 'reconciliation'.

Galiindurra:
What would I say to them [to non-Indigenous art therapy students who find themselves working with an Indigenous family]?

I'd say to be non-judgemental. To be honest. And vice versa that the family need to be able to be honest about their fears and expectations and any other issues.

I just think we're always judged. Often, we're told, "You are too outspoken". Or perhaps we are too 'not spoken'—you know.

I would try to say to them, "This is how I am. I can modify my behaviour but I can't parent like a whitefella". I'd say to them, "Chill out, take it easy, because if you feel uptight, you probably are!"

Being told that Ashley had to see you felt like a judgement of my parenting, but it has worked out really well. Ashley has grown, your whole family is part of my connected family, there's a real spiritual connection and the kids feel really honoured and loved.

In the kitchen

> Often the enigma is in the
> other's face, on the page of their face. On their body-
> face. What does this face tell me?
> I'm trying to name that which promises itself, what escapes me
> What speaks mutely to my eyes
> (Cixous, in Sellers, 2004, p. 109, underline in original)

Ashley is about to open the fridge to see if there are any more olives, when she notices a school photograph that Sheridan's youngest grandchild has attached to the fridge door with a magnet. Sheridan usually prepares for these meetings by putting aside the more portable manifestations of her daily living, but she didn't want to remove the photograph, placed there with her granddaughter's own hands.

Ashley touches Louella's pale Irish forehead and pink cheeks, tracing her black curls and the outline of her smile. "Who's that?" Ashley asks, seemingly suspended between a kind of tender curiosity and a hint of bristling pique that some other child has intruded into her space.

"That's my granddaughter, Louella," Sheridan replies.

"How many grandchildren do you have?"

"Two."

"What do they call you?"

"Nana. I said I'd like them to just call me Sheridan, but they wanted to call me Nana. What do you call your grandmothers?"

"Nan and Nanna. And Grandma. Sheridan, could I call you Grandmother?"

Sheridan begins to say carefully, "Ashley, I'm very touched that you would like to call me Grandmother—perhaps you want to have a special name for me, too...?" but, at the sight of Ashley's face, drops the momentary attempt to be a proper psychotherapist and touches the child lightly on the arm.

"You can call me what you wish, my dear."

Ashley nods in satisfaction.

"Let's go to the studio now, Sheridan," she says.

This chapter, and the previous one, have located my enquiry into art psychotherapy and narrative therapy in the intricate and hazardous landscapes of therapeutic practice. Such stories of therapeutic relations challenge the politics of representation, at the same time expanding an imagination of what the ethics, practices and subjects of therapy can be. The 'I' figured in this book has been transformed by practices of therapy and writing. Therapeutic practice has been conceptualised together with post-structural, feminist and postcolonial theory. In the next and concluding chapter, I fold these narratives of my therapeutic engagement with specific others back into an autoethnographic exploration of the possibilities of thinking art therapy and narrative therapy together—possibilities that have now expanded through a detailed attention to the call of the Other, as it is embodied through specific others.

---

[1] Galiindurra is a Wiradjuri woman. She has chosen to be known here by her Wiradjuri name, rather than by her commonly used European name, in honour of her heritage and to ensure confidentiality for the children in her care. Galiindurra means, appropriately, 'peaceful waters'.

cont.

[2] The girls' names have been changed for confidentiality.

[3] The words in this poem in italic script are Galiindurra's words, which I transcribed from notations and recordings of our conversations, and offered back to her in free verse form.

[4] 'Dot-painting' is, of course, only one technique, and by no means a universal one, within the rich and diverse traditions and practices of Australian Indigenous painting.

[5] This poem and my comments are included with permission of the sisters and their carers.

[6] While informal, this meeting was oriented by the metaphor of definitional ceremony (Meyerhoff, 1986; White, 1995, 2000, 2003) and occasioned powerful retellings that brought together responses from Indigenous and non-Indigenous practitioners from countries beyond Australia. These responses and their meanings for Galiindurra and the girls are not included here, because I am concerned with the possible appropriations involved unless the account was clearly co-authored. I would like to acknowledge the thoughtfulness of the participants, and the particular generosity of Indigenous people sharing their own stories of grief in such a context.

[7] See Laurel Richardson (2002) for an account of the poetic as poststructural research methodology. See Chris Behan (2003) and Jane Speedy (2003, 2005, 2008) for accounts of engaging poetry as a form of documentation in narrative therapeutic practice.

[8] The National Inquiry into the Separation of Aboriginal and Torres Strait Islander Children from Their Families was established in May, 1995. The report *Bringing them home* was tabled in Federal Parliament on 26 May, 1997. A detailed guide to the background, process, findings and recommendations of the Inquiry and links to the report itself can be found on the website of the Australian Human Rights and Equal Opportunity Commission at <http://www.hreoc.gov.au/ social_justice/stolen_children/>.

[9] The notion of containment was developed by Wilfred Bion as an extension of the theories of Melanie Klein, and is also related to Winnicott's notion of the holding environment (Britton, 1992).

[10] Moonam Chomper was named Moonam in honour of the first words spoken by my brother's child. When Gemma was a baby she sometimes cried at night, so my brother Andre would carry her out into the garden and point out the brightness of the moon and the stars. This vision of the night sky so amazed and soothed Gemma that her first utterance was "moonam and tars, moonam and tars!" I think I can safely leave the etymology of Chomper to readers' imaginations, especially if you have ever lived with a puppy.

[11] The practice of 'painting to say sorry' emerged as a specific response to a therapeutic meeting with some of the children of this family that took place on National Sorry Day. As I thought befitted the spirit of the occasion, I made a formal apology to Ashley and her siblings—since this was a visit to the family home her brothers were also present—for what white people had inflicted on her people. (This was prior to the Australian government's apology in 2008.) Ashley and her siblings were at first curious about this, and then, it seemed to me, quite solemnly accepting. I began to make a drawing that I hoped would add to this expression of sorrow. Ashley spontaneously joined me in this work, which became, I felt, one small, aesthetic movement in the ongoing process of reconciliation.

[12] The Child Care and Protection Act specifies that Aboriginal and Torres Strait Islander children in long term care must be placed with an Aboriginal or Torres Strait Islander family, by preference their own extended family.

[13] The Permanency Placement Bill was drafted in 2002 by the Minister responsible for Community Services. Had it been passed, the bill would have allowed children removed

cont.

from their biological families to be legally adopted by foster families after two years in care. A similar piece of legislation is currently before the New South Wales state parliament (October, 2006).

[14] Ashley and Maree often chose to take their work home, so some works are photographed in situ and others are not photographically recorded. Both girls have albums with copies of the photographs of their work.

[15] "In early May 1838 a group of about 40 Aboriginal people set up camp on Henry Dangar's Myall Creek station. A posse of blood thirsty stockmen and squatters arrived one day seeking revenge for cattle losses. The Aboriginal people at the property had no involvement in these attacks on stock. Despite this knowledge the men cold bloodedly killed 28 old men, women and children and later another three. Children were decapitated and people hacked to death. A young women (sic) was forced to witness her people being killed and was then repeatedly raped. Governor Gipps ordered an investigation into the massacre with a view to prosecution. There was a great deal of public antagonism towards the government over this decision. In the initial trial the 11 men were found not guilty, in the retrial 7 men were charged with murder and sentenced to be hung. The intended message of this trial and hanging from the government was that Aboriginal people could not be treated in this way. The message that was received was that if you did kill Aboriginal people, don't tell the authorities and cover up any evidence. The result was that nearly all further massacres went unrecorded" (http://www.cat.org.au/forgottenwar/myall.html, accessed September, 2006).

[16] "On the beach between Hawkes Nest and Myall Lakes there's a rocky outcrop with a sad history that few people know about—it's called Dark Point. There are reports that in the late 19th century groups of aboriginal people were herded onto the rocks and pushed off. Very little is known about the massacre, for example, no one knows who committed the crime or how many people died" (http://www.abc.net.au/newcastle/stories/s1172287.html, accessed October, 2006).

[17] This was the Bicentennial Protest Group, who organised a nation-wide march in 1988.

[18] Dominant culture easily becomes invisible and read as universal. David Denborough (1996) gives an autobiographical account of how persons from dominant cultures may become aware of their whiteness and middle-classness through working closely with persons subjugated within these dominant cultures. Yet an equally potent problem arises when "the term *white privilege* is treated as if it were monolithic, ahistoric and unambivalent in experience" (Britzman, 1998, p. 103), since dominance, hatred and racialised hierarchies are also produced by eliding the differences within, and ignoring the limitations of, identity categories.

[19] Batha (2006) asks what might constitute an ethical form of curiosity/ investigation within narrative therapies. She cites Linda Tuhiwai Smith (1999), who wrote that 'the word itself, "research", is probably one of the dirtiest words in the Indigenous world's vocabulary' (p. 1).

[20] Deborah Britzman (1998, p. 103) suggests that "identity is not the sum of a singular and conscious acts, but rather a social relation and a psychical event caught up—even as it catches itself—in the unconscious detours of history, memory, and communities".

[21] Foucault (2003) makes chilling connections between colonisation, racism and genocide. He argues that "Racism develops with colonisation, or in other words, with colonising genocide" (p. 257). Normalising power/biopower must become racist in order to exercise the old sovereign 'right' to kill: to murder people, populations and civilisations, both directly and also through "every form of indirect murder: the fact of exposing someone to death,

cont.

increasing the risk of death for some people, or, quite simply, political death, expulsion, rejection, and so on" (p. 256).

References

Ainsworth, M. (1985). Patterns of infant-mother attachments: antecedents and effects on development. *Bulletin of the New York Academy of Medicine,* 61(9), 771–791.

Barber, V. & Campbell, J. (1997). Living colour in art therapy: visual and verbal narrative of Black and White. In J. Campbell, M. Liebman, F. Brooks, J. Jones, and C. Ward (Eds), *Art therapy, race and culture* (pp. 21–36). London and New York: Jessica Kingsley.

Batha, K. (2006). Ethical curiosity and poststructuralism. *The International Journal of Narrative therapy and Community Work*, 1, 57–64.

Behan, C. (2003). Rescued Speech Poems: Co-authoring Poetry in Narrative Therapy. Retrieved May, 2004, from http://www.narrativeapproaches.com

Bowlby, J. (1960). Separation anxiety. *International Journal of Psychoanalysis.* 41, 89–113.

Britton, R. (1992). Keeping things in mind. In R. Anderson (Ed.), *Clinical lectures on Klein and Bion* (pp. 102–113). London and New York: Tavistock/Routledge.

Britzman, D. (1998). *Lost subjects, contested objects: toward a psychoanalytic enquiry of learning.* Albany: State University of New York Press.

Burt, H. (1997). Women, art therapy and feminist theories of development. In S. Hogan (Ed.), *Feminist approaches to art therapy* (pp 97–114). London and New York: Routledge.

Butler, J. (2004). *Precarious lives: the powers of mourning and violence.* New York and London: Routledge.

Commonwealth of Australia. (1997). Bringing them home: Report of the National Inquiry into the Separation of Aboriginal and Torres Strait Islander Children from Their Families, retrieved December, 2009 from http://www.humanrights.gov.au/social_justice/bth_report/index.html

Denborough, D. (1996). *Beyond the prison: gathering dreams of freedom.* Adelaide: Dulwich Centre Publications.

Eisdell, N. (2005). A conversational model of art therapy. *Psychology and psychotherapy theory, research and practice (U.K.: The British Psychological Society)*, 78, 1–18.

Foucault, M. (1980). *The history of sexuality, Volume 1: an introduction.* New York: Vintage Books. (Original work published 1976).

— (2000a). Governmentality. In J. Faubion (Ed.), *Essential works of Foucault 1954–1984, Volume 3, Michel Foucault: Power* (pp. 201–222). London: Penguin Books. (Original work published 1978).

— (2000b). On the genealogy of ethics: an overview of work in progress. In P. Rabinow (Ed.), *Essential works of Foucault 1954–1984, Volume 1, Michel Foucault: Ethics, subjectivity and truth* (pp. 253–280). London: Penguin Books. (Interview conducted 1983).

— (2003). *'Society must be defended': Lectures at the College de France 1975–1976.* (D. Macey, Trans.). New York: Picador. (Original work published 1997).

Johnston, P. (2002). *Talking you, talking me, talking Aborigine.* Unpublished research paper.

Leclerc, J. (2006). The unconscious as paradox: impact on the epistemological stance of the art psychotherapist. *The arts in psychotherapy,* 33, 130—134.

Link-up NSW & Wilson, T. (1997). *In the best interests of the child? Stolen children: Aboriginal pain/white shame.* Aboriginal history monograph 4. Australia: Paragon.

Myerhoff, B. (1982). Life history amongst the elderly: performance, visibility and remembering. In J. Ruby (Ed.), *A crack in the mirror: reflexive perspectives in anthropology.* Philadelphia: University of Pennsylvania Press.

— (1986). 'Life not death in Venice': its second life. In V. W. Turner & E. M. Bruner (Eds.), *The anthropology of experience* (pp. 261–286). Chicago: University of Illinois Press.

Richardson, L. (2002). The poetic representation of interviews. In J. Gubrium & J. Holstein (Eds.), *Handbook of interview research: context and method* (pp. 877–891). U.S.A: Sage Publications.

Rose, N. (2000). Power in therapy: Techne and ethos. *Academy for the study of psychoanalytic arts.* Retrieved April, 2003, from http://www.academy analyticarts.org/rose2.html

Sellers, S. (Ed.). (2004). *The writing notebooks of Hélène Cixous.* New York: Continuum.

Speedy, J. (2003, July). *Using 'poetic' documents in narrative therapy.* Paper presented at the International Narrative Therapy and Community Work Conference, Liverpool, England.

— (2005). Using poetic documents: An exploration of poststructuralist ideas and poetic practices in narrative therapy. *British Journal of Guidance and Counselling,* 33(3), 283–298.

— (2008). *Narrative inquiry and psychotherapy.* New York: Palgrave Macmillan.

Tuhiwai Smith, L. (1999). *Decolonising methodologies: research and Indigenous peoples*. Dunedin: University of Ontago Press.

Venn, C. (2002). Refiguring subjectivity after modernity. In V. Walkerdine (Ed.), *Challenging subjects: critical psychology for a new millennium.* Houndsmills, U.K.: Palgrave.

Waldegrave, C., Tamesese, K., Tuhaka, F., & Campbell, W. (2003). *Just therapy—a journey: a collection of papers from the Just Therapy Team, New Zealand.* Adelaide: Dulwich Centre Publications.

White, M. (1995) *Re-authoring lives: Interviews and essays*. Adelaide: Dulwich Centre Publications.

— (1997). *Narratives of therapist's lives.* Adelaide: Dulwich Centre Publications.

— (2000). *Reflections on narrative practice*. Adelaide: Dulwich Centre Publications.

— (2002). Addressing personal failure. *The International Journal of Narrative Therapy and Community Work 2002*, 3, 33–76.

— (2004). *Narrative practice and exotic lives: resurrecting diversity in everyday life*. Adelaide: Dulwich Centre Publications.

FIGURES AND ARTWORKS

CHAPTER 7

INCONCLUSIONS: (WHERE WILL IT ALL END?)

> *What is the agency of the one who registers the imprints from the other? This is not the agency of the ego, and neither is it the agency of one who is presumed to know. It is a registering and a transmutation that takes place in a largely, though not fully, preverbal sphere, an autistic relay of loss and desire received from elsewhere, and only and always ambiguously made one's own. Indeed they are never fully made one's own, for the claim of autonomy would involve the losing of the trace, and the trace, the sign of loss, the remnant of loss, is understood as the link, the occasional and nearly impossible connection, between trauma and beauty itself.*
>
> (Butler, 2004a, p. 5)

Abstract: This concluding, but necessarily inconclusive, chapter gestures toward different possibilities for conceptualising and practicing ethical 'arts of existence' in the domains of both therapy and research. The chapter underlines how writing as a form of poststructural research, like psychotherapy, calls for an ethics of uncertainty, unknowability, vulnerability and obligation to the Other. In this chapter I bring together the threads of my various accounts of the therapeutic and the theoretical, of art therapy and narrative therapy, and of research and writing practice—accounts that push against the limits of therapeutic 'identity' and engagement. The chapter weaves together these different threads and also enacts how these threads unravel and escape into many different possibilities or lines of flight.

Figure 1: *The art therapy boat,* Sheridan, Collage and glitter-paint on paper, 30cm x 42cm

Sheridan Linnell

Figure 2: *Wreck*, Sheridan, Oil pastel on paper, 42cm x 59cm

Figure 3: *Omelette*, Sheridan, Acrylic paints on paper, 42cm x 59cm

Figure 4: *Behind the gate*, Sheridan, Black and white photography, photocopying and hand-colouring, 30cm x 24cm

Figure 5: *An archaeological find* (interior of 3D construction), Sheridan (photographed by Clare Dash), Cardboard, tissue paper, collage, oil pastel and found objects, 42cm x 34cm x 22cm

Figure 6: *Dreaming (of) research*, Sheridan, Charcoal and crayon on paper, 56cm x 76cm

Figure 7: *Crooked self-portrait, with dog*, Sheridan, Charcoal and graphite on paper, 86cm x 59cm

Figure 8: *Grand Daddy*, Sheridan, Charcoal on paper, 86cm x 59cm

Figure 9: *Grandmother*, Sheridan, Charcoal on paper, 86cm x 59cm

Figure 10: *S(her)idan silhouette*, Sheridan, Charcoal on paper, 76cm x 56cm

Figure 11: *What happens to all the unspeakable things?*, Sheridan, Charcoal and pastel on paper, large irregular size, 170cm x 120cm (approx.)

She is sitting again in the consulting room at the back of the narrow inner city terrace, recalling the previous session. The white walls of the therapy room had become the hospital bed where her mother laboured, an unmarried mother in the fifties. She had felt the hush, the shame, the prohibition under which she herself had entered this world. She had known she couldn't possibly have remembered this; it was a physiological and developmental impossibility. And yet she re-members herself remembering, composing herself at that imaginary point of origin, pulling the bits and pieces together into a tentative, stammering confession.

She is beginning to find words to tell the other how, following their last meeting, an exquisite and tortuous sadness had seeped into the texture of her week, when out of the blue her therapist says, *This is difficult but I have to stop seeing you. This will be our last session. I'm sorry but this is not something I could have anticipated.* She is shocked of course, stunned into an initial and very awkward silence but, somewhere almost inaccessible, she is not really surprised. A confirmation of something deeply held, though always held at a distance. She becomes solicitous, asks if the therapist is all right—she has noticed the other looking a little pale of late—knowing though that she will get no answer. She asks if this sudden ending applies to everyone the therapist sees or only to her, knowing that it must apply to everyone, and knowing that it applies only to her. The therapist suggests that she sees someone else and tries to give her a list of names. She won't take them. Thinks, recoiling simultaneously from the ugliness of the thought, *Fuck you—don't expect me to say yes just so that you can feel better.* She is feeling huge and distorted, a woman with grossly ballooning arms and legs, a huge distorted belly and head, features stretched into monstrous unrecognisability. She floats toward the ceiling, looking down on the tiny therapist doll who is mouthing something.

She forces herself to hear it. *I wonder if you feel you have been too much for me.* She's back in her chair with a thud, deflated to a dense fiery coil. Patronising bitch. She'd been wondering anyway whether to continue. Where had it gotten her. She hands over the ninety dollars, thinking how next week she'll be able to buy that new book on

Deleuze she hadn't been able to afford. As she walks out she's suddenly very sorry; has she been rude, has she made it harder? She wonders fleetingly if the therapist is sick and going to die. Touches even more fleetingly on something comforting in that possibility. At the door, she leans towards the therapist and hugs her. Immediately she feels embarrassed, knowing she has breached some code even at the moment when such rules surely should have ceased to concern her. She feels how the other receives her embrace with equanimity, just as one who had practised forbearance might receive a blow.

She must have this particular colour. The red that comes in the tiny metal tube has the viscosity and hue of fresh blood. She spills it onto the white paper, into a white porcelain basin, onto white tiles, a white cotton sheet. The clawing inside, the incessant chatter of voices, the rope coiled in her stomach and pulling tight around her throat. She watches one hand take the blade and pull it across the other wrist. At first the line is bloodless like the scar it will leave behind. Then blood wells and spreads, becomes an outpouring. The little metal tube shines like a knife in her hand. At first she bleeds incontinently onto the page, week after week, the flow not so much lessening as finding the contours of a life, her life, running into crevices and gullies and pooling in the bottom of craters. She begins to spread it with the large brush, dragging the red across planes of luminous blues, blending to a purple starved of the oxygen of immediacy but pleasing in its sovereign dignity. Or pushes it into a wet glistening yellow so that a promise of something begins to rise orange at the far edge of the page.

Just behind her there is someone of whom she is barely aware, who slides fresh sheets of paper before her, who keeps the little tube knives full and flowing with lifeblood. And slowly, over months, as the blood is staunched on the page, the words begin to flow out of her and towards this other, in trickles and splashes and outpourings. Sometimes the other seems far from her, inaccessible, and she must try to soothe her hurt through a liberal application of paint. At other times she shrinks in fear or shame from an intrusive presence, retreating into the space of the paper, cupping her hand around the work so the other cannot see. Sometimes they feel so close it is almost unbearable. Their words and their silence flow into an intangible space stretched out between them, a valley, a fold of skin, warm, diffuse, t/here. *No wonder,* she says, almost to herself, *no wonder, no wonder.* She whispers this refrain only to herself and wonders how the other can hear it. *No wonder I have felt, no wonder I have done, no wonder I could not....* Her tears drop clear onto a page thick enough to hold them. It's different from the chemical shock when she dabs her fingers in the red paint and takes them carelessly to her mouth, breaching the fiction. Her tears taste like her own blood, her own body, salty but without the red. Excrescence of her own impossible being. On her tongue.

Looking back, she notices that she has concluded each of the previous two chapters with a vignette, a story of naming and of the unnameable, which shows her in a somewhat bumbling and stuttering mode, trying a bit too hard, missing cues, stuffing it up. Now, in the penultimate moments of this monstrous book, she has exposed herself/anOther as the monstrous subject of therapy, as she who becomes too large for the room, the frame, the page.

Where will it all end...?

Butler (2004b) has claimed that her texts are addressed to those of us who are 'beside ourselves' with rage, grief and passion, and indeed I did write the fictionalised accounts of therapy that open this (in)concluding chapter in a condition of being 'beside myself'. Such writings are counterpoint to the painstakingly negotiated accounts of therapy in the two preceding chapters. They expose the limits of co-authorship through a radical resort to fiction and memoir. There is a kind of unspeakability in such stories, particularly for a therapist committed to undoing the notion of an unconscious, 'abnormal' and/or 'monstrous' subject of therapy (Foucault, 2003).

I am strongly inscribed within a narrative approach to therapy, and have taken myself up more passionately within this approach than any other. Yet I could not write the stories of therapy that begin this chapter within narrative therapy's conventions of co-authorship and frank accountability back to the client. In this sense, the writing of such stories, confabulated from some of my experiences and imaginings as both client and practitioner, may mark a limit in the ethical self-constitution of my self as a narrative therapist [1].

If my current practice as a narrative therapist meets its limits in accordance with what Butler figures as the limits of narrative itself, perhaps a turn, or in my case a return, to the (im)possibility of psychoanalysis becomes a necessary fiction. In such a (re)turn I know of course that it, that I, cannot be the same as I was, but then perhaps I have only lost what I never had (Butler, 2001, 2005).

Yet, while these stories touch upon the limits of narrative coherence, they also engage in a questioning of normative psychoanalysis. The first two stories attempt to picture how psychoanalysis may test subjective and narrative coherence and rationality, and the second of these stories touches upon the terrible vulnerability of the 'patient' to a rupture of the analytic frame. In the third story, art 'matters' (Butler, 1993), and this mattering of art reinstates a sight/site of embodiment, disrupting the Cartesian hierarchy within psychoanalysis that would relegate the making of art to a metaphor of the metaphysical.

Such stories as these can only be produced, I think, at some (dis)juncture of narrativity, a non-normative (or perhaps a differently normative) psychoanalysis (Butler, 2000, 2004a, 2004c; Ettinger, 2004) and a poststructural poetics/aesthetics. This is not to say that such stories are more poetically 'true' than the stories in the last chapters, just as those stories are not more discursively 'true' than these confabulations. All these accounts, however carefully negotiated, are fictions. In the accounts I have offered of therapy with Leticia, Ashley, Maree and their families, I have attempted to respond to others who constitute who I am/becoming and yet who can never be 'captured' by my attempts to tell the stories of our relations. In the accounts that open this chapter, by mingling memories of my experiences of being 'in therapy' with memories and fictions of being an art psychotherapist for others, I have attempted to respond to my self as a subject, and as anOther who constitutes and exceeds my self.

The inclusion, in this book, of both imaginative flights and carefully located co-productions speaks to a necessity to bring all the resources of imagining and writing that I can to the (im)possible task of re-presenting and producing the work of therapy. I aspire towards a practice that honours, questions and exceeds the modes of discourse and the styles of existence that constitute the theories and practices of therapy, and the ethical self-constitution of the professional, pedagogical and clinical subjects of therapy. I work 'narratively' in my persistent questioning of dominant discourses and narratives, my fascination with the rich discursive possibilities of people's lives and relationships, and my attention to those moments at the margins that might otherwise be considered 'below notice'. I dissent from the reconstitution of the humanist subject within versions of discursive therapy that emphasise 'agency' and 'intention', and from the deadening production of templates for narrative practice (Bird, 2004) that limit the potential to invent and research the relations of therapy in the moment.

I attempt to pay attention to, rather than to abject and disavow, those constellations of feelings, thoughts and sensations, often insistent or over-determined, slightly syncopated or 'out of time', that constitute what in analytic terms is called a counter transference. Allowing these constellations to (in)form, and noticing how they are already (in)forming, my therapeutic responses troubles the tendency to construct lives as temporal linearities and selves as narrative coherence. Those who criticise the notion of transference usually do so by disputing its rationality and verifiability, missing the salience of the approximate and risky character of transference for the unfolding of a therapeutic relation. Counter to this, Winnicott celebrates well-timed mistakes as opportunities for therapeutic restitution. Foucault asks, "Should not the whole theory of the subject be reformulated, seeing that knowledge, rather than opening onto the truth of the world, is deeply rooted in the 'errors' of life?" (2000, p. 477).

A more compelling argument holds that the transference is constructed by and reinforces relations of power. I agree with this critique, but I would also suggest that all forms of knowledge construct and re-cite the 'truth' of the subject within relations of power. The problem is rather that the powers of psychoanalytic interpretation tend towards totalisation and domination, re-siting resistance to this power/knowledge as pathology. My response to the dilemma of how I might take up the potential of psychoanalytic notions of transference, while refusing these notions the status of truth and the tactics of dominant power, is admittedly somewhat idiosyncratic. I attempt to take account of my 'counter transference' responses while refusing to 'analyse' another person's 'transference' toward me. I am more reluctant still to categorise that person's ways of being and relating on the basis of such an analysis. I see such categorisation as a compensatory move that restores 'reason' and re-territorialises the psyche by substituting a coherent theoretical and psychological narrative for the 'lost' coherence/incoherence of the subject. My bias is to some extent supported by some contemporary moves in psychoanalytic theory and practice (e.g. Casement, 1990a, 1990b) and by art therapy's tradition of refusing to reductively interpret the client's artwork. But then, what do you call a counter transference that is no longer counter to a transference? I suspect that this orientation makes me always an imperfect therapist, but then therapy is necessarily imperfect, and this is an imperfection I am willing to embrace.

The metaphors and practices of the arts are critical, I believe, to an ongoing opening to the possibilities of difference. Dominant discourse, in its persistence and vulnerability, is made visible and revisable through the critical capacities of art and writing. The difficulties and possibilities of transformation (despite the co-option of that term within the narrative of the neoliberal subject) are continually being constituted through writings and visualities that trouble distinctions between theory and practice, representation and production, research and therapy, self and Other.

A narrative art therapy 'makes illustrious' the narratives of the subjects of therapy. A psychoanalytic art therapy gestures, through semiosis, to a mythical, pre-symbolic realm of connection and loss, triangulating transference through displacement into, and containment through, the making of art. These are compelling fictions of how art 'works' in a therapeutic context, but separately they are not enough. The embodied and visceral processes of the plastic arts do not simply 'materialise' the social and the subjective, or the intrapsychic and the intersubjective, dimensions of 'being'. Art in therapy can interrupt the body/psyche binary, suggesting both a body in excess of its imprisonment within the soul and a soul/psyche in excess of the subject. Art in therapy extends the being of bodies, selves and relations into unexpected becomings. The subjects of art therapy are not only practitioners of an aesthetics of self and of a psychodynamics of relationality. The subjects of art therapy are themselves becoming-artworks; they are inscriptions, installations and performances of the art of becoming Other-wise.

The enactment of a poststructural ethics and aesthetics in this book makes ending it necessarily difficult. To insist on a narrative resolution or conclusiveness to the account(s) given in this document would be to foreclose upon the ethical resources that inhere in unknowability (Butler, 2004c). Rather than attempting in this work to reconcile art psychotherapy and narrative practice, artistic practice and theoretical analysis, therapy and research, I have struggled to allow the tensions and connections between these approaches (and the philosophies and histories that (in)form them) to play themselves out and be shaped through my writing, my art making, my stories of therapeutic practice, my relationships with others, and even through my embodied and psychic sense of who, and for whom, I might be. The task has been that of refusing to choose between or force a resolution of contradictions: of experimenting with what arises and might yet arise from a refusal to foreclose on the radical and transformative possibilities of either/both.

At the limits of narrative coherence, one can perhaps 'enact' or 'write' (but scarcely 'write about') openness to the Other. It is this radical vulnerability that institutes/constitutes the psychic and the social as mutually imbricated, and which also confounds attempts at disembodied, conclusive or 'once-and-for-all' knowledge. Sometimes the exigencies of therapeutic practice (as of any practice) demand that I 'take a position', and I do so with passion and conviction. At the same time, I attempt to resist the tendencies for ethics to solidify into moral prescription, theory to become a normalising means for the judgement of practice, and practice to become exemplary rather than exploratory.

Therapy, like writing, is at best experimentation and performance, earnestly and playfully pursuing the fiction of truth while tolerating and even embracing indeterminacy and uncertainty. And writing, like therapy, is incomplete, faulty, fragile, dangerous, longing to love and to be loved, given over to the other, forever opening on anOther possibility.

What have I done?

The question could belong to the opening of a retrospective or the script of a lovers' quarrel, to the site of a confession or the scene of a crime.

How is the subject of therapy or of research to tell her story? If each life and its interrelations precedes and exceeds the subject, where does the narrative begin? What account can she give of herself to another that is adequate to the beginning of an unknown relation, always already sketched in by the traces of the Other, washed in a faint hope of trust and renewal, and marked by the inevitability of delusion?

How do the questions of, and the questioning of, poststructural philosophies (in)form the stuttering moments of meeting and missing, the dancing and duelling, the forms of silence and the forms of speech, the making and the unravelling, that constitute a moment of therapy or research in all its complexity?

How does what we see relate to what we don't see, what we say relate to what we don't say, what we hear relate to what we don't hear? How are seeing and saying, not seeing and not saying, hearing and not hearing, related each to the other? How is what we think related to the unthinkable, and what we feel related to that which it might be unbearable to feel?

Is discourse conditioned by a constitutive 'outside', or is that notion itself an effect of discourse? Does the soul/psyche imprison the body, or is the psyche a site of resistance (intrapsychic, political and discursive) to the disciplining of bodies and the ethicalisation of subjects? Are those binary choices themselves an effect of the binaries of self and Other, psychic and social? If an ethical resource inheres in uncertainty, what 'method' pertains to the art of uncertainty?

She wonders if she should hold her early induction into the arts of narrative therapy, which is after all *par excellence* a therapy of questions, responsible for her apparently endless production of more and more questioning. Not entirely, she decides, since the questions of narrative therapy, while they have a multiplicity of possible replies, do tend to be answerable, at least. Alongside the posing of questions that invite unexpected replies, her research has invited a different order of questions. These are the questions that open space for enquiry, for connection and for innumerable becomings, precisely because such questions cannot be adequately 'answered' even while they demand ethical and aesthetic responses.

She asks herself what she has made of this book, and what this book has made of her. As she looks back through its/her passages, she notices how its shape both mimics and digresses from the shape of therapy, and both mimics and digresses from the broader contours of her life as therapist, artist, researcher and all the rest. The practice of art is continually teaching her about its capacities, reliable and wayward, for mimesis and transformation, for materialising the weight of 'reality' and opening up (im)possible lines of flight.

If art 'matters', as she believes it must, then perhaps her book of experience, in which ethics and aesthetics are intertwined, does 'make sense'.

She thinks, also, how important theory is for her practice as a therapist —how Foucault's theories in particular have revolutionalised her ways of conceptualising the words and actions of people in therapy. The notions of the positivity of power, of power's capacities to form the subjects and objects of power, and of the ubiquity of resistances to power, have shaped her understandings of the ethics of therapy.

When she began this research, she was in some ways intent upon legitimating a 'Foucauldian' view within art therapy and strengthening that perspective in the theoretical framing and ethical practices of her own therapeutic work. However, she soon realised that this was not a very interesting thing to do. There is no point in researching something for which you already think you have most of the answers. That would be at best frustrating and at worst deadening. She does not want to relegate Foucault to a truth status within her therapy, research and writing, an implicit and assumptive 'basis' that only becomes exposed as discursive practice when it clashes with more dominant 'realities'. Neither does she want to proceed with a Foucauldian 'template' for these practices, disciplining her work according to a new set of norms. She wishes to engage with and against Foucault, as his apprentice and dance partner, but she will not be docile. She will sometimes tread on his toes, and she will dance with many others as well. (Moreover, she suspects he would approve of this, but she refuses to depend on an assumption of approval.)

What has been transformative in the process of writing this book has been the cultivation of a poststructural research ethics of creativity and uncertainty, of a highly articulate incoherence, a wondering and a wandering. She wants to go on practising a writing that can argue passionately and provocatively, while knowing such writing cannot ever get it right. She wants to publicly declare her love for the ineffable and uncertain qualities of both therapy and writing, for its bumblings and stumblings, its stammers and stutters, its failures, even.

She wants to go on writing therapy's disjunctions and contradictions and unexpected trajectories, rather than to shape a narrative of therapy that brings it to order within a 'regime' of proper poststructuralism, or even of properly improper poststructuralisms.

What has she written?

Now that would be 'telling': how this text approximates, and fails to approximate, a fractured and imperfect story of her self and her becomings within and through relations with theories, practices, experiences, fictions, dreams, persons, socialities, cultures, and moments. How it gathers the force of narrative and yet is impossibly, improperly lateral. How it begins with the wide sweep of histories, theories and philosophies and comes to bear upon the particularities and idiosyncrasies of persons, situations and relations. How she/it aspires to mystery and to the moment, to paint the sky and to concentrate an angel on the head of a pin. She hesitates to say that her book is 'a work of art', and then remembers, "...couldn't everyone's life become a work of art? Why should the lamp or the house be an art object, but not our life?" (Foucault, cited in O'Leary, 2002, p. 21).

Her writing is a performance. It enacts the giddy (im)possibilites of deterritorialisation and embodies a longing for home. It performs her relations to others—the apparent contradiction between the necessity to produce her own 'original' research and the inevitability, which she hopes she has played up rather than effaced, that any such work is an ensemble piece, and that she, her self, is also in many ways an ensemble. This book re-cites, inevitably, much of that which it seeks to challenge or undo, in ways of which she can only be partly aware. Thus it embodies, painfully, her own vulnerability and fallibility, since readers will sometimes see what she does not see: not only those subtleties and complexities that more experienced researchers might pick up, but the obvious that is not obvious to her.

Perhaps her book is, in this sense, also a confession and an atonement. It gives balance to therapeutic privilege, since in her writing she is exposed, as those who come to her for therapy are exposed, in ways beyond her knowing. She writes and the writing writes her. Together she and the Other constitute a poethics of practice, between and beyond an aesthetics of the self and an aesthetics of becoming Other-wise, between and beyond passionate and permanent critique and an ethics of uncertainty.

Writing this text has given her pause. Spun from her body, thoughts and emotions, it has unravelled her. It is Other to her. Woven from threads of discourse longer and more enduring than her self, it reminds her of mortality [2].

She slips the memory stick into the pocket of her favourite jacket, wondering, as she has wondered many times before, how all these memories can possibly fit into such a slender wand. She turns off the computer screen and looks around her studio. It is night now, after a morning of providing clinical supervision, an afternoon of art therapy, and an evening of working on her final chapter. The paint has dried on the children's artworks and their images are already sleeping in the wide drawers of the silver cabinet, under the racks of paints and brushes.

In these last months, such days have become less frequent. Most of her time has been dedicated to writing. She has slowly overtaken the long wooden bench, beautifully situated under three north-facing windows, with sheets of white paper in overlapping piles. The expression 'a nest of paper' drifts into her mind, a warm bed for the hatching of words.

She feels oddly maternal. So much paper suggests that she must be going to hatch a massive chick of a book. An eaglet perhaps, but no, it is bigger than that—a pterodactyl, or even a dodo. Should she be concerned? Will her offspring be extinct before it is born? Will the monster devour its maker and destroy what it loves? Will it tear the flesh of its readers or, worse, perch awkwardly on the edge of their desks, nodding at them in sleepy-eyed inanity? Will her creation be earthbound or will it be able to fly?

It is almost time. She tucks the sheets of white paper around all the words and phrases and sentences and paragraphs and chapters and kisses them goodnight. She pulls the curtains, extinguishes the light. A yellow light is shining in the back window of the house as she walks toward home across cool grass.

Where are you this evening? her partner says to her, perhaps a little jealously, as they sit before the fire. Sheridan has just found out that her book—appropriately enough—is to be published as an e-book: a 'virtual book'. It is and will be the moving signifier of many emergent readings. Reaching out, she takes the other's hand in both of her own, feeling the warmth of blood, the smooth fragile skin, bones fine like those of a bird. In her mind she is still tracing a line of flight along the fold that divides art psychotherapy from narrative therapy. This writing has taken her elsewhere. Subtle distinctions have opened onto unimagined horizons; critical tensions have bent the expected lines of enquiry, arcing into territories and creating subjectivities previously unknown. She strokes the rough pads of long fingers, smooth, moon-grey ovals of fingernails, their pale crescents and creamy sharp rinds. A strong narrow wrist and its tender underside, marbled with veins. Deepening lines of head and heart crossing in the crinkled hollow of a palm.

She dreams of paper. Late that night, as she closes her eyes, she can hear a rustling—not the scuttle of bush rats or flutter of mice, or the thundering of possums across the roof, but a rustle of feathers, or silks. The sound becomes stronger and more rhythmic, a beating of wings, or hearts. A trillion milk-white pages, embossed with midnight text, imprinted with the rich hues of drawings and paintings and sculptures caught in a magical projection of reflected light, are stirring and rising from their places. They circle the studio, swooping over the silver cabinet, where the originary artworks stir in turn, safely contained in their orderly folders and trays.

Layers of imaginary, perhaps virtual, worlds, of memories and dreams. Traces of that which cannot be recalled, and of that which was never quite t/here. Marks and gestures, signs and symbols, textures, tonalities; the viscerality of paint and clay; the weight of displaced trauma and the vivid realisations of embodied pain. Fine art papers enfolding sublime presences of absence and loss, an exquisite and ineffable lightness of touching and being touched.

The images are held in the cool metallic frame of the silver cabinet within the sturdy and graceful structure of the rustic timber studio, a place for the encirclement of nightmares and the embodiment of dreams. An indeterminate space and a chamber of echoes—coffin, house and crib, cell of tortures, bush bower and desert camp, a place of refuge, a room of one's own. The site of a meeting place and of a massacre. A charnel house and dance hall, the cellar below the stair/stare. House of worship and a house of disrepute. A temple of wisdom and a ship of fools.

The dark grows brighter. In the theatre of the unthinkable, the images in their bounded and infinite beauty and terror are awakening to a flight of words. Behind her dreaming eyelids, the fonts in all their absurd and vivacious finery are throwing a party. Most of the Handwriting family are here. *Clear-eyed Lucida* dances a two-step with **bold Bradley**. Another Handwriting—*Dakota is her name*—slouches in wearing a cowgirl hat and braces, watched with suspicion by Times New Roman, who stands stiffly to attention by the door. CHALKBOARD holds up a list of the evening's entertainment. American Typewriter, wearing a fedora and smoking a big Havana cigar, is drinking bourbon and rye at the bar and secretly taking notes on everything.

Two pale men are waltzing together as if their bodies are one, all the time arguing vehemently in voluble and difficult French. One of the men appears to be wearing her favourite 'Experience' jacket, which to Sheridan's chagrin fits him better than it will ever fit her, and the other looks entirely comfortable in that shirt she never could quite decide about. As she looks around the room she notices how a dress here, a scarf there, a certain material, pattern or cut, seems strangely familiar. Some of the guests at this celebration seem to have raided her wardrobe, or did she borrow the fabric of her dreams from them?

Outside, where the sounds of the festivities are muted, two women are walking arm in arm, laughing softly and murmuring the passionate endearments of friendship under a tracery of branches, beneath the pen-and-ink wash of a night sky punctuated with the steely points of stars. They murmur of certain passions and of passionate uncertainties, of their love of knowledges and their knowledges of love. One of them begins to sing, and then the other—a light, syncopated duet, a wordless and lilting overlapping of oohs and aahs. They pause, swaying, and in that momentary silence a door swings gently open in their song, and the dreamer passes through...

> Grace occurred at exactly 2.55 P.M., five minutes earlier than expected; the kin and witnesses were deeply moved, while the barber-violinist showed us from a distance the hands of his clock to invite our verification of the absolute accuracy of his predictions...
>
> Then the orchestra lit into a tarantella of thanksgiving to the saint...(de Martino, cited in Cixous and Clément, 1986, pp. 21–22)

> She is cured...but the celebration is over... (Cixous and Clément, 1986, pp. 21–22)

How can she end, when she feels as though she has barely begun?

> [I]t is that last word, I think, that is most important to forestall. (Butler, 1997, p. 126)

---

[1] I did write these stories in a manner that I hope is consistent with the ethical considerations usually followed in narrative therapeutic practice. I have drawn substantially *cont.*

on my memories of having been a 'patient' in psychoanalytic therapy—a situation that I believe produced certain effects of transference—and also more generally upon my work with people who have experienced severe childhood trauma. The stories are fictionalised, but in the very few instances where it became apparent to me that I had drawn details directly from my work as a therapist, I either deleted that detail or negotiated closely with the relevant person as to whether and how I might include this material in the paper.

[2] Davies (2000) plays upon morality/mortality to figure a poststructural ethics of writing.

REFERENCES

Bird, J. (2004). *Talk that sings: therapy in a new linguistic key.* Auckland: Edge Press.

Butler, J. (1993). *Bodies that matter: on the discursive limits of 'sex'.* New York: Routledge.

— (1997). *Psychic life of power: theories in subjection.* California: Stanford University Press.

— (2001). Giving an Account of Oneself. *Diacritics*, 31(4), 22–40.

— (2004a). Bracha's Eurydice. *Theory, Culture and Society*, 21(1), 95–100.

— (2004b). *Undoing gender* (pp. 17–39), New York and London: Routledge.

— (2004c). *Precarious life: the powers of mourning and violence.* New York and London: Routledge.

— (2005). *Giving an account of oneself.* New York: Fordham University Press.

Casement, P. (1990a). *On learning from the patient.* London: Tavistock/Routledge. (Original work published 1985).

— (1990b). *On further learning from the patient.* London: Tavistock/ Routledge.

Cixous, H., & Clément, C. (1986). *The newly born woman.* Minneapolis: University of Minnesota Press.

Davies, B. (2000). *A body of writing.* Walnut Creek, CA: AltaMira Press.

Ettinger, B. L. (2004). Weaving a woman artist within the matrixial encounter-event. *Theory, Culture and Society*, 21(1), 69–93.

Foucault, M. (2000). Life, experience and science. In J. Faubion (Ed.), *Essential works of Foucault 1954–1984, Volume 3, Michel Foucault: Aesthetics, method and epistemology* (pp.466–478). London: Penguin Books. (Original work published 1985).

— (2003). *Abnormal: Lectures at the College de France 1974–1975.* (G. Burchell, Trans.). London & New York: Verso. (Original work published 1999).

O'Leary, T. (2002). *Foucault and the art of ethics.* London & New York: Continuum.

Figures and Artworks

POSTSCRIPT

While this book is not intended as the 'last word' on anything, I hope I have made a useful contribution to how art therapy and narrative therapy can be conceptualised, practised and imagined. Having unsettled the current terms within which these therapies are usually understood, I have attempted to offer some alternatives that do not simply reproduce the current discursive order. As promised at the beginning of this text, I have offered a 'book of experience' rather than a handbook, an enactment of possibilities rather than a prescription for actions.

'I' have been changed through the writing of the book, as well as through the theories, relationships and practices of which the book gives an account. The 'I' in this text has been imagined and transformed: read, as well as written, into being. This text has been constituted differently by each specific, embodied reader. You have been invited to create, as well as to respond to, the text you are reading. And, if you have come with me this far, then perhaps 'you' are already Otherwise.

ACKNOWLEDGEMENTS

I extend many thanks and much appreciation to my mentors, companions and readers: in particular, to my wonderful editor, Bronwyn Davies; Link-up NSW Aboriginal Corporation; Jill Westwood and Andy Gilroy from Goldsmith's College at the University of London; Deanne Dale and Ian Hanslow; Michelle Cherubin; Carolyn Williams; Peter Bansel and the Narrative, Discourse and Pedagogy Research Group at the University of Western Sydney; and the late (and great) Michael White, as well as Cheryl White and David Denborough from the Dulwich Centre. Thanks also to Salma from Bentham Science Publications. To my art therapy students and colleagues at the University of Western Sydney, and to those people who have come to my art therapy studio, thank you for your generosity and for all that you continue to teach me.

Many thanks to Dulwich Centre Publications <www.dulwichcentre.com.au> for allowing me to include a revised and extended version of ideas and practices that I first described in a paper for the International Journal of Narrative Therapy and Community Work, and to the Australian and New Zealand Journal of Art Therapy, the journal of the Australian and New Zealand Art Therapy Association, which published an earlier and much condensed account of my therapeutic work with one of the families whose stories appear in this book.

I am grateful to the University of Western Sydney, especially the School of Social Sciences, for supporting this book project. Thanks to Elena Knox, who did an excellent job of designing, proofing and preparing a camera ready copy of the book, and also to both the School of Social Sciences and the Social Justice, Social Change Research Group within the University of Western Sydney for generously funding Elena's contribution. Finally, no acknowledgements would be complete without offering my heartfelt gratitude to Anita Swanson, Alison Meares and my other family members and friends. Your love, listening, encouragement, support, recognition and tolerance has sustained me over the years of this project.

INDEX

C

D

G

H

I

J

K

W